Media Ownership and Agenda Control

Media Ownership and Agenda Control offers a detailed examination of media ownership amidst the complexities of the information age, from the resurgence of press barons to the new monopoly power wielded by internet giants. Much of the discussion pivots around recent revelations and controversies in the media industry, such as the findings published in 2012 from the Leveson Inquiry, the US Federal Communications Commission's ruling on net neutrality in 2015, Edward Snowden's decision to leak National Security Agency (NSA) documents in 2013 and the legal battles over ancillary copyrights waged in Germany and elsewhere.

Justin Schlosberg traces the obscure and often unnoticed ways in which agendas continue to be shaped by a small number of individual and institutional megaphones, despite the rise of grassroots and participatory platforms, and despite ubiquitous displays of adversarial journalism. Above all, it explores the web of connections and interdependence that binds old and new media gatekeepers, and cements them to the surveillance and warfare state. This ultimately foregrounds the book's call for a radical rethink of ownership regulation, situating the movement for progressive media reform alongside wider struggles against the iniquities and injustices of global capitalism.

This title's re-evaluation of the nature of media ownership and control in a post-digital world will prove to be an invaluable resource for students of Media Studies and Journalism, as well as all those with an interest in the changing dynamics of media power.

Justin Schlosberg is a media lecturer, researcher and activist based at Birkbeck, University of London, and current Chair of the Media Reform Coalition.

Communication and Society

Series Editor: James Curran

This series encompasses the broad field of media and cultural studies. Its main concerns are the media and the public sphere: on whether the media empower or fail to empower popular forces in society; media organisations and public policy; the political and social consequences of media campaigns; and the role of media entertainment, ranging from potboilers and the human-interest story to rock music and TV sport.

For a complete list of titles in this series, please see https://www.routledge.com/series/SE0130

Journalism in Context
Practice and Theory for the Digital Age
Angela Phillips

News and Politics
The Rise of Live and Interpretive Journalism
Stephen Cushion

Gender and Media
Representing, Producing, Consuming
Tonny Krijnen and Sofie Van Bauwel

Misunderstanding the Internet
Second Edition
James Curran, Natalie Fenton, and Des Freedman

Africa's Media Image in the 21st Century
From the 'Heart of Darkness' to 'Africa Rising'
Edited by Melanie Bunce, Suzanne Franks, Chris Paterson

Comparing Political Journalism
Edited by Claes de Vreese, Frank Esser, and David Nicolas Hopmann

Media Ownership and Agenda Control

The hidden limits of the information age

Justin R. Schlosberg

Routledge
Taylor & Francis Group

NEW YORK AND LONDON

First published 2017
by Routledge
711 Third Avenue, New York, NY 10017

and by Routledge
2 Park Square, Milton Park, Abingdon, Oxon OX14 4RN

Routledge is an imprint of the Taylor & Francis Group, an informa business

British Library Cataloguing in Publication Data
A catalogue record for this book is available from the British Library

Library of Congress Cataloging in Publication Data
A catalog record for this book has been requested

ISBN: 978-1-138-77545-9 (hbk)
ISBN: 978-1-138-77546-6 (pbk)
ISBN: 978-1-315-76616-4 (ebk)

Typeset in Times New Roman
by Apex CoVantage, LLC

Printed and bound by CPI Group (UK) Ltd, Croydon, CR0 4YY

For Zephyr

Contents

List of Illustrations

Figures

Table

Acknowledgements

I am hugely indebted to the following people for their feedback and encouragement during the research and writing of this book: James Curran, Stephen Cushion, Natalie Fenton, Des Freedman and Victor Pickard. I am also deeply grateful for the inspiration and support from all of my colleagues at the Department of Film, Media and Cultural Studies at Birkbeck, University of London. It is an immense privilege to have been given the time and space to carry out a project like this, and for that I also owe a big thank you to the publisher, and in particular Niall Kennedy for his relentless patience in the face of my appalling timekeeping.

This book was also informed by the time and insights kindly offered by journalists and editors including Duncan Campbell, Nick Davies, Stephen Engelberg, Ryan Gallagher, Christopher Hird, Ewen MacAskill and Alan Rusbridger. I have nothing but the deepest respect for their shared and impassioned commitment to speaking truth to power.

Finally, I am extremely lucky to have had support and encouragement from my family including my parents, brothers and my partner Chloe, who has borne the brunt of my absence and still managed to offer precious wisdom and insights.

Part I

Heard and Not Seen

Chapter 1

Introduction

With great power comes great invisibility. This was the defining feature of what Stephen Lukes called the 'third dimension of power' (Lukes, 2005 [1974]). In contrast to both coercion and persuasion, here the very exercise of power is obscured not only from those subjected to it, but potentially even those who wield it. It was this obscurity that prompted Lukes to ask:

> Is it not the supreme and most insidious exercise of power to prevent people, to whatever degree, from having grievances by shaping their perceptions, cognitions and preferences in such a way that they accept their role in the existing order of things, either because they can see or imagine no alternative to it, or because they see it as natural and unchangeable, or because they value it as divinely ordained and beneficial?
>
> (2005 [1974], p. 28)

The potential for powerful voices to shape 'perceptions, cognitions and preferences' has always been at the root of media ownership concerns. But historically these concerns tended to invoke a kind of power that is visible and vested in the hands of wealthy proprietors, who used their media assets openly for political leverage. In conventional histories of the British press, the rise of so-called press barons during the first half of the twentieth century epitomised this kind of power. Lord Beaverbrook, regarded by some historians as the first Baron of Fleet Street, told a Royal Commission inquiry in 1947 that he ran the *Daily Express* "merely for the purpose of making propaganda and with no other motive" (Curran and Seaton, 2003, p. 42).

Yet in spite of such bravado, the press barons were neither more hands-on nor propagandist compared to their predecessors and successors. As James Curran and Jean Seaton have shown, in reality:

> They did not break with tradition by using their papers for political propaganda; their distinctive contribution was rather that they downgraded propaganda in favour of entertainment. Nor did they subvert the role of the press as a fourth estate; on the contrary it was they who detached the commercial press from

the political parties and, consequently, from the state. What actually happened is, in some ways, the exact opposite of historical mythology.

(2003, p. 37)

But the conventional history of the British press depicted them as fourth estate deviants—examples of how media proprietors can undermine the values of independent journalism in their pursuit of profit and power. This served to mystify the ways in which propaganda and control were exercised by preceding and subsequent media owners who were less vocal, and less visible.

Today, the complexities of the information age have meant that the political, cultural and ideological influence of those who control major media groups seems ever more uncertain and, according to some, ever less significant. Behind the very concept of an information age lies a belief in the empowering potential of digital communications, fostering new forms of civic accountability. In place of a mass media audience, it has produced an endless 'tail' of fragmented user communities; in place of traditional gatekeepers—those who once exercised editorial control over mass media institutions—we have 'prosumers' and 'produsers', citizen journalists, hacktivists, culture jammers, gatewatchers, the 'networked fourth estate' and, above all, the crowd.

From this perspective, it is easy to see why media ownership appears less of a problem than it once was. If those who control mass media institutions no longer shape or define the agenda—be it the media agenda, public agenda or policy agenda—then there is arguably no longer a need to challenge media ownership, even when it is highly concentrated. The era of the media mogul may not yet be behind us, but the ability of wealthy individuals or vested interests to dominate public conversation seems, on the face of it, a product of the past.

My aim here is not to dismiss this broad narrative as naïve idealism or blind faith. There are many compelling reasons for believing that the implications of media ownership in a post-digital universe are not what they once were. But I do want to challenge this central premise: that the risks of concentrated media power for liberal democracies are dissolving amid an ever expanding horizon of information sources. On the contrary, I want to try and persuade you that rather than dissolving, these risks are rapidly *evolving* and in many ways intensifying, and that the agenda influence of major media brands has not so much waned but become increasingly opaque in a media landscape that is at once converged and fragmented, mass and social, open and closed. In light of these contradictions and complexities, there is a pressing need to think about, question and research media ownership in new ways, and to re-evaluate its implications for democracy and accountability.

Historically, both critical and defensive accounts of media ownership have tended to focus on the relationship between media concentration and diversity of expression (e.g. Kawashima, 2011). This often presumed connection has channelled academic and policy attention to media ownership through the lens of media *plurality*. What matters here above all is that there is a sufficient number of independent producers capable of fostering a marketplace of ideas and producing an informed citizenry. But the relationship between media plurality and diversity of expression is by no means clear-cut. Whereas some studies have indeed demonstrated an inverse correlation—suggesting that less media concentration corresponds to greater diversity—others have found the opposite, suggesting that the more competitive a media market is, the more prone it is to producing homogenised content across the board.[1]

In his seminal work on concentrated media power, Edwin C. Baker (2007) argued that ownership matters partly because concentration is a problem irrespective of its impact on diversity of expression. According to this view, discussions of media ownership that focus exclusively on output diversity tend to miss a crucial point: that the range of sources matters more for democracy than the range of viewpoints. In essence, democracies require multiple independent media as a check against the *threat* of owner-driven bias that can manifest in subtle and often invisible ways; and as the best guarantee that certain types of content will not be suppressed in an otherwise diverse media offer.

It's hard to argue with the view that democracies, by definition, cannot be meaningfully supported by highly concentrated media industries. Indeed, the idea of plurality as a democratic safeguard in this sense is a well-established policy norm in liberal democracies. For decades, lawmakers and regulators have espoused concerns that media concentration places too much power of voice in too few hands, to the detriment of plurality. Yet in spite of the rhetoric, media ownership policy has consistently been captured by the interests of large media conglomerates such that even when legislation has been drafted with clearly stated plurality objectives, it has nonetheless served to fuel the consolidation of media markets within and across sectors (Doyle, 2002; McChesney, 2004; Freedman, 2008).

For many critics, part of the problem is rooted in the way in which the plurality question is defined and addressed by policymakers, especially with its orientation towards a neoliberal market logic that places maximum weight on minimal intervention. Recently, there have been attempts to re-evaluate what plurality means from a radical perspective, as Karl Karppinen put it:

> Old hierarchies of media ownership and control continue to persist, but there are also new forms of domination and concentration that are only beginning to emerge. These create a need to critically reflect on the pluralism made possibly by the new media, its limits, and the nature of the barriers that still persist [. . .] Communicative abundance alone does not render questions about the distribution of communicative power and political voice obsolete, but only reconfigures them in a more complex form.
>
> (2013, p. 110)

In reconfiguring the plurality question, Karppinen shifts our attention towards inequalities of access and—more acutely for the purposes here—*prominence.* This allows us to think beyond just the number of independent voices or outlets present in any given media system; or the diversity of viewpoints that are (in theory at least) accessible or represented; or the contested formulae that are used to measure levels of market concentration. It asks us instead to consider the various conditions in a formally pluralistic media system that can result in some voices being hugely amplified whereas others are left unheard. What seems certain is that against a backdrop of communicative abundance—indeed *saturation* (Compaine, 2005)—there remains a broadly coherent mainstream agenda defined by the limited range of headlines and hits that attract audiences en masse.

This requires us to consider a diversity of viewpoints not across media output as a whole, but within the confines of a mainstream agenda; that is, within the 'head' of the long tail of cultural and information niches characteristic of the digital realm (Anderson, 2009 [2006]). But equally, it requires us to think critically about the tail and the degree to which fragmentation and personalisation can undermine the public sphere and act as a barrier to certain voices and viewpoints reaching a critical mass audience.

This juxtaposition of niche and mainstream accounts for the book's preoccupation with 'the agenda'. Its core themes resonate with and draw on the radical pluralism advanced by Baker, Karppinen and others. But it sharpens the focus on what I believe to be a critical aspect of inequity in the 'distribution of communicative power'. In particular, the book starts from the premise that amplification—the ability to be *heard*—is the major currency of communicative power, and that such power is all the less open to challenge because of its relative obscurity.

In this new reality, the boundaries of the mainstream agenda are neither sharply defined nor static and the potential levers of influence neither transparent nor one-directional. What this calls for is a broadening of media ownership questions beyond the traditional and linear perspective of control typified by the press barons. Since then, most critical work on media ownership has tended to focus on the agenda influence of individuals or corporations behind media outlets. But the direction or origin of agenda influence is not always obvious in relations between media owners, advertisers, political actors or other institutional elites. As a consequence, this approach has fostered a kind of intellectual apartheid, isolating ownership issues as peculiar to the private media in advanced capitalist democracies. A public media organisation may be formally publicly owned, but there are many different ways in which public ownership can be structured, and this can have a profound impact on the organisation's accountability, independence and vulnerability to both state and commercial pressures. At a time when public media are facing an existential threat across Europe and much of the world, it is especially urgent that this kind of scrutiny is brought within the framework of media ownership debates (Cushion, 2012).

Recent developments also point to trends and patterns that transcend the divide between liberal, transitional and authoritarian societies. In the UK, disclosures during the Leveson Inquiry in 2012 revealed the intensely intimate relations between media and political elites and the private exchanges and reassurances offered during key moments of media policymaking (Leveson, 2012). This 'integrated elite structure' is also endemic in Putin's Russia and much of the post-Soviet region, where political patronage of media oligarchs has become a defining feature of the ownership landscape (Vartanova, 2011). In Turkey, the opacity of media ownership and merger activity "has allowed an increasingly close relationship between the political establishment (particularly the ruling party, AKP), the Islamic networks, and media conglomerates" (Tunç, 2015). And in South Africa, a brief flirtation with authoritarian-style censorship under President Zuma has given way to a strategy of making and installing regime friends in key positions of both private and public media institutions (van der Westhuizen, 2013).

I am not suggesting that the problem of media ownership is equivalent across these different geopolitical contexts, or that journalists in Western democracies face anything like the scale of threats, pressures and attacks that are routine in countries like Russia. But I do want to suggest that agenda control is often best secured through alliance between political and media elites rather than conflict, and that this is a feature increasingly common to media systems that span the democratic-authoritarian spectrum.

To reach the heart of the matter then, we need to broaden our conception of media ownership beyond the limits of any given media institution or market. To this end, media ownership is considered here as a node within a wider network of power that integrates state and market forces, within and across borders. Above all, the book starts from an acknowledgement of the varied and complex ways in which political, market and media power tend to act in concert, albeit with imbalances in any direction and intermittent moments of conflict and crisis. Des Freedman articulates media ownership in this sense as a *relational* property that connects "the major social institutions and processes that circulate and embody media power in the world today" (2014, p. 15). It requires us to examine media ownership not just in the context of shareholdings, but as a dynamic and complex set of relationships with other sources of power and influence that make up the 'media-technology-military-industrial complex'.

In many cases, the media's entanglement and centrality within webs of networked power manifest directly in corrupt journalistic practices. This was the case, for instance, in 2012 when the owners of India's Zee News were accused of offering to pull an investigative report centring on one of its major advertisers in return for US$16.4 million worth of committed advertising (Saeed, 2015). In other contexts, as we will see, agenda control is exercised without the presence or need for such overt threats or deals, but is nevertheless contingent on relations of power involving media owners. But in some contexts, those who control media companies may not be directly implicated at all in the agenda dominance of other powerful voices. Yet even here, it's hard to imagine a more meaningful kind of remedy than one that seeks to democratise media ownership, and thereby make it harder for *anyone* to monopolise a public megaphone.

It's worth emphasising at this point a key distinction between media owners and media *ownership*. Whereas the former is often invoked to highlight the influence of powerful media figures over public conversation, the latter draws our attention to the forms of governance, laws, regulation and institutional cultures associated with particular ownership structures. This leads me ultimately to consider these questions: What kind of media ownership structures can best preserve independence and autonomy? What forms of governance can best insulate journalists and creative workers from the full range of institutional pressures that may filter down via media owners, managers and editors?

Above all, this book seeks to bring ownership back to the centre of questions about media power. Rather than viewing it in isolation, media ownership is considered here as integral to wider concerns about surveillance, privacy, net neutrality and the implications of changing journalistic practices. Although I am not suggesting that all questions of media power are reducible to questions of ownership, we cannot begin to grasp its full significance in today's media environment without considering the ways in which it cross-cuts with these wider issues.

This book is also steeped in the radical critical tradition that broadly conceives of media ownership as an ideological force, privileging the agendas and narratives of powerful interests in often subtle but systemic ways. But it aims in some small way to move this tradition forward by considering media ownership not as one of several forces or filters that shape the ideological character of the media (Herman and Chomsky, 2002 [1988]), but as a mechanism that is intimately connected to a whole range of pressures that ultimately impact on journalist autonomy. In a similar vein, it reconsiders media concentration as a problem that is central to enduring and emergent concerns around media plurality and diversity, rather than as a problem that has diminished in the wake of new technologies of communication (Napoli, 2011a).

Overall I want to persuade you that, nearly a decade on from Baker's seminal analysis, media ownership *still matters*. It matters because "the way in which the media are organized has a significant impact on what the media report" (Aalberg and Curran, 2012, p. 193); it matters because professional media institutions retain a powerful presence in the new information environment; and it matters because those institutions are still *needed* to support meaningful democratic and cultural expression (Couldry, 2013). Their enduring publicity power provides access to the public consciousness, a window to reflect it back and, potentially, a common space in which to convene and converse as citizens.

But to begin with, I want to suggest that in the context of media ownership, we can think of invisible power in two broadly overlapping ways, each of which bears a close relation to the theory of power that Lukes developed. The first concerns the visibility of media owners themselves, their interactions and inter-relations with other powerful figures and institutions, as well as the nature and extent of their editorial control. The second relates to the visibility of manifest control in the containment of news agendas. Here the scandals and crises that routinely feature in media output may offer the misleading impression that such power is non-existent or in decline. Over the following two chapters, we will consider each of these aspects of invisibility in turn. Part I then concludes with a summary and outline of the book's scope and conceptual framework.

Note

1. For instance, whereas Glasser (1984) suggests that competition in radio can mask a lack of diversity, research by Di Cola (2006) attributes homogenised radio programming to ownership consolidation.

Chapter 2

Behind Closed Doors

The Meaning of Control

To own, in media terms, is to control. As already suggested, control of media institutions is not solely a function of majority shareholdings in any given media entity, or formal aspects of governance. Throughout this book, our concern is rather with the notion of de facto control in respect of media organisations, which opens up a much broader conception of how vested interests can exert a commanding influence over media output. Ofcom, the UK media regulator, established guidelines in 2006 for how it defined this:

> Even where a person does not have a majority interest, he is regarded as controlling a company where it is reasonable, having regard to all the circumstances, to expect that he would (if he chose to) be able in most cases or in significant respects, by whatever means and whether directly or indirectly, to achieve the result that affairs of the body are conducted in accordance with his wishes.
>
> (2006, p. 3)

This requires us to pay attention to the broad range of contextual factors that determine the power *behind* any given media organisation, which often extends beyond the formal voting rights attached to shares. For instance, suppose I own the majority of shares in a given media group, but I sold a minority stake to a company that is also a major advertiser and source of funding for my media outlets. My decisions regarding things like editorial appointments might then be ordinarily swayed by the preferences of the minority shareholder who would, effectively, exercise de facto control. But what if that minority shareholder's interests are themselves structurally dependent on a third party? Then, de facto control may be exercised by an individual or entity without any formal or direct stake in the media group at all.

Although the key to unravelling the source of control is often to follow the money, in the complex world of transnational finance and offshore havens, this can be a daunting task in itself (Dragomir and Thompson, 2015). In spite of Ofcom's elaboration then, getting to the bottom of who exercises de facto control of media companies can be extraordinarily complex, especially in light of the unique inter-play of commercial and political interests that are often at stake in large cross-media holdings. The significance of media ownership as an instrument of power therefore has the potential to be obscured even before we consider the impact of digital communications in empowering audiences and diversifying media voices. Both the means by which control is exercised in large media groups—and the ends to which it is directed—are rarely simple and transparent.

From Barons to Tycoons

This complexity evolved over the course of the late twentieth century, when a new ownership figure emerged from the press baron era: the media tycoon. It is a figure that has been villainised in popular fiction from Sherlock Holmes to James Bond. Its referents are a very few individuals able to command control of news organisa-tions across platforms and borders, often seeming to secure ever greater influence over both the public and policy agenda. One of the most extreme incarnations was Silvio Berlusconi, the four-time prime minister of Italy since 2000. Over the course of his political and business career, Berlusconi assumed control of Italy's three largest television channels, with a combined 90 percent share of national audience and advertising revenues, along with the country's largest publisher and a daily national newspaper.

The only substantial challenge to Berlusconi's near-total grip over the national news audience stems from Sky Italia, effectively controlled by Rupert Murdoch, whose News Corporation owns over 800 media companies in more than 50 coun-tries. Unlike Berlusconi, Murdoch has never himself sought political office. But his newspapers have long been accused of 'winning' elections for their owner's preferred candidate. After the British election in 1992, the *Sun* newspaper even went as far as to claim the credit for itself, declaring infamously, " 'twas the Sun wot won it" (Kay, 1992).

But far from basking in the glee of victory, the paper's editor allegedly faced a "hell of a bollocking" from his boss immediately after the headline ran. In Mur-doch's own words, "it was tasteless and wrong for us. We don't have that sort of power" (Dowell, 2012). In truth, media tycoons have long been at pains to down-play their agenda influence, preferring to portray themselves as entrepreneurs who direct the political leanings of their outlets merely to reflect rather than shape the views of their audience. Of course, we don't have to look hard to find examples of editorial control that seemingly flies in the face of this commercial logic.[1] But the 'strictly business' rhetoric is a distinct characteristic of modern media tycoons, in contrast to their press baron predecessors.

Over the last decade, however, this rhetoric has been confounded by the declin-ing profitability of newspapers. As a senior fund manager from one of News Corp's major institutional investors remarked in 2011: "I'd like [News Corp] to sell all the newspaper businesses," adding that "it's a digital world now and the competitive advantage that newspapers had has been competed away" (Blackden, 2011). Such pressure eventually led Murdoch in 2013 to spin off his publishing assets into a separate company. But his refusal over many years to ditch even loss-making titles like the *Times* suggests something other than purely commercial motivation.

As we will see, the declining profitability of newspapers has fostered a new narrative that positions both the owners and the titles themselves as increasingly power*less*. Ironically, this decline has also led in many countries to a resurgence of press barons. The power vacuum left by evaporating profits and retreating corporate investors has put many newsrooms back in the hands of wealthy individuals, from local oligarchs in Eastern Europe hoping to capitalise on opportunities for political influence (Open Society Foundations, 2014) to dot-com billionaires in the US seeking to redefine the business of news (Freedman, 2014).

Off Limits

What remains constant is the instinct among media proprietors to dissociate themselves from any kind of political influence. This finds its logical extreme when the owners of media go to determined lengths to ensure they are themselves invisible to the public eye (Crauford Smith and Stolte, 2014). As already mentioned, complex financial structures are a key mechanism by which the ultimate beneficiaries of media groups can remain in the shadows. This explains why much of Ukraine's TV, for instance, continues to be bankrolled by non-disclosed offshore sources in Cyprus, in spite of a new law on media ownership transparency that came into effect in 2013. A report by Freedom House notes that although the new law prohibits the financing of broadcast companies from offshore zones, it is

> easy to evade by creating a chain of three or more shell companies with a Ukrainian broadcasting company on one side and an offshore company on the other. Indeed, offshore companies have not been removed from corporate structures of Ukrainian TV channels as a result of the law's enactment.
>
> (Freedom House, 2013, p. 7)

In those countries where the structures of media ownership are relatively transparent, the political influence of media owners remains unclear, even when intimate ties between media and political elites are exposed. During the Leveson hearings in 2011 and 2012, we learned about a club at the top echelons of political and press power in Britain that operated both as an exclusive social clique as well as a professional alliance:

> The relationships within which lobbying can take place are not the everyday relationships of journalism and politics. They are the relationships of policy makers (actual or potential) and those who stand to benefit directly from those policies. That is a limited category, comprising (on the one hand) a

small number of relevant Government decision-makers and those who credibly aspire to those positions in the future whether from within governing parties or their rivals in opposition, and (on the other) the proprietors, title editors and executive decision-makers of the press. In these relationships the boundaries between the conduct of Government business with its formalities and accountabilities on the one hand, and informal 'political' or 'personal' interactions on the other, are not clear, and inevitably so.

(Leveson, 2012, p. 28)

The dual aspect of such relationships was epitomised by the very personal text messages exchanged in 2009 between then *News of the World* editor Rebekah Brooks and the soon-to-be prime minister, David Cameron. They revealed a shared love of horse riding and a close friendship that extended to their mutual partners and families. But one text in particular provided a simple and telling insight into the *professional* dimension of that relationship (BBC News, 2012). It was sent by Brooks following the speech that won Cameron the leadership of the Conservative Party and read simply:

Brilliant speech. I cried twice. Will love 'working together'.

The timing was auspicious. Just weeks prior, Murdoch's newspapers had switched their allegiance to the Conservative Party following more than a decade of support for successive New Labour governments. What is perhaps especially insightful here is the enclosed speech marks around the phrase 'working together'. It suggests a kind of co-operation over shared interests that is understood without being spelled out explicitly. But although the implications of such a text may seem obvious, it still leaves a great deal to the imagination as to the extent of cross-influence and institutional corruption at the nexus of media-political power. Even when the veil on media-political elite interactions was so dramatically lifted, we were left without a tangible sense of what 'working together' actually entailed.

In a bid to demonstrate its commitment to transparency, the British government has since 2010 proactively published lists of external meetings involving senior ministers or officials and, among others, media owners and editors. But during research for this book, a freedom of information request for further details of such meetings was met with obfuscation and rejection by the Cabinet Office. A subsequent review by the Information Commissioner found in the government's favour, noting that "confidential engagement with the media at a senior level is appropriate as an aspect of government."[2] This amounts to the state asserting its right to have secret dealings with the media above and beyond off-the-record journalistic briefings. In spite of heightened public disquiet over press freedom and accountability in recent years, and the government's own declared transparency agenda, secrecy remains the default strategy in its interactions with media at the highest levels.

It is worth remembering, however, that such secrecy would not even be required to mask the machinations of media power in the 'third dimension'. In reflecting on the nature of relations between media and political elites, Leveson remarked that the former are "highly skilled, at the level of some proprietors, editors and senior executives, at subtle and intuitive lobbying in the context of personal relationships and friendships." What this means is that the very existence of such an elite club dissolves the *need* for deal making or active lobbying. Even a nudge and a wink over lunch or in the corridors between meetings may be more than is necessary. In the third dimension, the mere presence or proximity of powerful actors is enough to ensure that their will prevails.

In part IV, we will examine in more detail the web of connections that characterise this kind of elite hub and bear a strong resemblance to the power elite theory developed by C. Wright Mills (1959). For now, it's worth highlighting one of the first and few attempts to empirically link invisible power to agenda control, when Matthew Crenson (1971) examined how the media and policymakers responded to the emergent issue of air pollution in two comparative US cities. What he found was that in Gary, Indiana, the reputation of US Steel was a key factor in keeping the issue off the public agenda, without the need for active lobbying. In contrast, no single company had such a strong presence in East Chicago, which had similar levels of air pollution. As a result of this, the issue of air pollution was able to surface in public and policy debate in one city leading to progressive reforms, whereas in an adjacent city in the same state, it remained a 'non-issue'. For Crenson, it was the powerful presence of US Steel in Gary, with its hold on local jobs and contribution to tax revenues that enabled it to exert influence, crucially, "without taking any action" (Crenson, 1971, p. 69).

This is agenda control. But it is a particular form of control that lacks any identifiable agency. In contrast to propaganda, it need not involve any act of conscious manipulation, censorship or even active persuasion. There need not be any threats, or bribes, or deals; no offers that cannot be refused; no calling of the shots by media owners or their pay masters. Those who represent powerful corporate or state interests can legitimately claim to play no part in cajoling editors or enforcing their will on the editorial line. In the third dimension, the powerful do not shape the agenda: it merely bends in accordance with their will.

A similar condition may apply *inside* the newsroom, whereby editors or journalists do not need to be 'leaned on' in order to comply with the interests of owners or managers. In reflexive moments, journalists often attest to the silent and even unwitting conformity of self-censorship. For some, it is a problem that has increased in line with growing resource pressures, and is manifest in newsrooms that are less frictional and less prone to resistance from below. As one senior BBC news editor told me in 2011:

> We definitely have more of a yes man or woman culture now [. . .] There's a generation of people now that are very keen to rise, will do what they think the editorial bosses want them to do, and are less awkward in terms of how they interpret directives from the top. So all of that doesn't add up to a particularly

healthy picture I think. You end up with an output that is too homogenised, too reactive and I think probably not questioning enough.

(quoted in Schlosberg, 2013, p. 132)

Crenson's study certainly suggested that agenda control is *sometimes* exercised without agency. But it is difficult to infer from such isolated examples how extensive or pervasive this kind of invisible power is, much less the precise role of media ownership in facilitating it. Clearly, powerful individuals and institutions do at times actively lobby the media. Alan Rusbridger—former editor of the *Guardian* newspaper—has attested to the persistent complaints, harassment and threats he received from the British government over coverage of the national security files leaked by Edward Snowden in 2013. In an interview for this book, Rusbridger told me:

There were two meetings [with the Cabinet Secretary] in this office. In both meetings their position was we shouldn't have this stuff and they wanted it back. So the first meeting I said we hadn't finished with it, we were still working on it, we couldn't give it back and the second meeting there had been a change in tone. They claimed there was more urgency and we ended the meeting [. . .] we left it that we would think over the weekend. I said if your anxiety is about the security of the material please come in and advise us because it's in neither of our interests to lose it. But something then over the next four days changed and their position hardened. They said they need it back or they needed it destroyed. I asked them explicitly do you mean you're going to go for prior restraint and they said we will if you don't do what we say.[3]

On the flip side, we also know that some newspaper owners actively seek to use their voice in lobbying government through both formal and informal channels. One of the most striking examples was revealed in a recently declassified account of a secret lunch between Rupert Murdoch and Margaret Thatcher in 1981 (McSmith, 2012). Following the meeting, Thatcher overrode the Monopolies Commission and waved through Murdoch's purchase of the *Times* and *Sunday Times*, doubling his ownership of British newspapers overnight.

Nor is it a secret that some media owners adopt a hands-on approach to running their news outlets, intervening regularly in editorial decisions even after appointing compliant editors. So in thrall was the *Daily Express* to the interests of its owner, Richard Desmond, that when he published his autobiography in June 2015, the paper reserved its first three pages for the headline story 'businessman writes book' (Ponsford, 2015), complete with five-star reviews and information on where to buy a copy.

We might well ask, in what sense does this kind of interventionist pressure or active lobbying reflect exemplary power over the agenda? After all, the fact that governments feel compelled to apply pressure on media outlets (and vice versa), or that owners seek to use their outlets to advance their own interests, is to some degree in step with the view that the agenda is not a given but the outcome of some form of struggle—a struggle in which battles may be won or lost—but the information war does not necessarily swing permanently and irrevocably in favour of a unified establishment elite.

Stage Management

But this is not the whole story. One of the great complexities of hegemonic power in the sense considered by Lukes is that its effectiveness depends on it never being absolute and always at least *appearing* to be contestable and open to challenge. Consider, for instance, all of the public inquiries, police investigations, arrests and trials associated with the phone hacking scandal between 2011 and 2015. After the revelations hit the headlines, Rupert Murdoch and his son James were hauled before a Commons Select Committee hearing on a day he famously described as "the most humble" of his life (*Daily Telegraph*, 2011). He subsequently closed the *News of the World* title at the centre of the furore; dropped a controversial bid to buy out other investors in the satellite broadcaster BskyB (since renamed Sky); siphoned off his newspaper assets from his other global media interests in an effort to stem the tide of share price decline; and ordered his newspaper staff to hand over reams of emails and other communication records to investigating authorities on both sides of the Atlantic.

The Leveson Inquiry, which then came in the wake of the scandal, produced a report that made a series of recommendations for root-and-branch reform of press regulation, subsequently enacted by Parliament via a Royal Charter in 2012. And as a result of police investigations and prosecutions, 10 journalists were found guilty of associated crimes, including Andy Coulson, the former editor of *News of the World* and former communications strategist for Prime Minister David Cameron. Rebekah Brooks—Coulson's predecessor at *News of the World* and one of Murdoch's closest confidantes—stood trial alongside him.

The revelations also triggered an investigation into both News Corporation and its sister company, 21st Century Fox, by the US Department of Justice. Aside from prosecution, this threatened the prospect of license withdrawal for Fox News, one of Murdoch's most lucrative and (arguably) influential broadcasting assets. Perhaps most ominous of all, the Crown Prosecution Service announced in August 2015 that it was considering criminal charges against Murdoch's UK newspaper publisher for which he himself could be charged under legal provisions concerning the criminal liability of directors (O'Carroll, 2015).

All of this was clearly reflective, on one level, of a complete loss of agenda control. In spite of determined efforts to suppress the story over many years, the phone hacking scandal had erupted and culminated in a series of official investigations, prosecutions and convictions that threatened irreparable damage to Murdoch's media empire. Yet it was not long before Murdoch appeared to have successfully weathered the storm. By the end of 2015, both the Department of Justice and the Crown Prosecution Service had announced decisions not to bring corporate charges against either Murdoch or his companies, and Brooks had been acquitted and rewarded with promotion to chief executive of Murdoch's UK newspaper operations (BBC News, 2015). Meanwhile, according to an article in the *Economist* magazine, the Murdoch family had more than doubled its wealth since the scandal broke (Schumpeter, 2014).

As for press regulation reform, the vast majority of UK national newspapers had opted out of the system of 'recognised' press regulation according to the terms recommended by Leveson. The UK government had even signalled its willingness to reconsider implementing the financial incentives designed to lure newspapers into the new regulatory system (Hickman, 2015). And as if to underline the sense of a return to business as usual, analysis of government meetings data suggested that the special access afforded to News Corporation was showing no signs of abatement (Media Reform Coalition, 2015). Far more than any other media group, News Corporation executives met with government ministers, officials or advisors on 10 separate occasions in the year leading up to the end of March 2015—at least eight of them attended by Murdoch himself.

Whether all of this amounted to an ultimate victory for Murdoch is a matter of opinion. Nor can we be certain that the positive outcomes were a result of calculated moves aimed at regaining some measure of agenda control. But one email disclosed during the trial of Rebekah Brooks seemed to provide a glimpse of precisely this kind of crisis management philosophy. It was sent by Brooks to James Murdoch at the height of the scandal, and recounted an hour-long phone conversation Brooks had purportedly had with former Prime Minister Tony Blair. In the email, Brooks summarised Blair's instructive advice to form an independent unit to investigate allegations "and publish a hutton style report" (BBC News, 2014), referring to the controversial inquiry in 2003 that absolved Blair's government of any wrongdoing in the death of intelligence whistle-blower David Kelly. What's more, the report was to be published "as the police closes its inquiry," and although it will clear Brooks, she will have to "accept short comings and new solutions and process."

Implicit here is the notion that, provided Brooks was prepared to accept a limited degree of culpability, she could carefully stage-manage the accountability process and predetermine its outcomes. We may never know how extensive or effective such stage management was in the aftermath of the phone hacking scandal. But the email does suggest that we need to look beyond what often looks on the surface like a complete loss of agenda control by powerful elites, in order to consider the strategic ways in which control can be *regained.*

In summary, we can think of agenda control both in the structural sense invoked by Crenson (control without controlling) *or* in a more instrumental sense typical of the kind of crisis management alluded to by Brooks. The key point is that in both structural and instrumental contexts, the mechanics of control are invisible, and this is likely to be the case even from the vantage point of those who exercise it. We have seen how in structural contexts, control can manifest through self-censorship without the need for powerful figures to actively push for their preferred agenda. In these contexts, the limits of the media agenda appear natural and consensual, rather than the consequence of pulling any editorial or political strings. But even when media owners, political actors or corporate elites resort to *active* efforts to exert influence, such pressure may be legitimised by appeal to a contestable news agenda in which the outcome is not necessarily prefigured. This enables powerful elites to claim—with some degree of authenticity—that the agenda is not theirs for the taking, but rather shaped by a complex interplay of competing ideas and interests over which their ascendancy is not always achieved and never guaranteed.

But it obscures the more subtle and potentially far-reaching power to stage-manage their own accountability and thus to regain control of the agenda at pivotal moments. In the following chapter, we consider in more depth how such surface agenda openings can mask the ultimate limits of agenda resistance.

Notes

1. During the build-up to the 2003 invasion of Iraq, for instance, Murdoch's 127 news-papers around the world gave full backing to the war, in spite of overwhelming public opposition outside of the US.
2. See Freedom of Information Decision Notice, 23 July 2015, available at https://ico.org.uk/media/action-weve-taken/decision-notices/2015/1432183/fs_50556590.pdf (last accessed 14 April 2016).
3. A. Rusbridger, research interview, June 2014.

Chapter 3

The Art of the Impossible

The Origins of Openness

From an optimistic perspective, the media are widely credited with *increasing* the visibility of power in ways that have widened opportunities for resistance and diminished potential for agenda control (Thompson, 1990). In this respect, there is nothing especially new about new technologies of communication. The invention of the printing press in 1516 brought about profound change in the way that humans communicate (Downing, 2000; Garnham, 2000; McLuhan et al., 2011 [1962]). It marked the birth of the author and the death of the oral tradition; it introduced a new record of history; fostered an information explosion and unprecedented spread of knowledge; gave rise to a new wave of scepticism that catalysed social change; and provided the foundation for the emergence of a public sphere (Habermas, 1962).

Some 300 years later, physicists working in Germany and other parts of Europe laid the foundations of the first telegram sent by Samuel Morse in 1838. What followed was a global communication system that transmits and receives signals in accordance with a code of electrical pulses, giving rise to the first 'instant message' and replacing pigeons, horses, trains, boats and ships in the transmission of long-distance communication. The sheer speed of long-distance communication that the telegraph enabled fostered the development of time zones, the futures market and world wars. It was greeted as the first in a series of history-ending technologies leading up to the internet (Mosco, 2004).

The telegraph was a point-to-point system of communication whose twentieth-century variants included the telephone and email. But it was the invention and spread of broadcasting technologies in the early twentieth century that spawned the phenomenon of electronic mass media. Although the mode of communication was limited to one-way and few-to-many, radio and television became integral features of the modern public sphere. They created a virtual space for the shared consumption of culture in real time (Scannell, 1996) and gave fuel to the anti-war movement, civil rights and second-wave feminism (Fiske, 1996).

Pre-digital technologies of communication thus embodied much of the empowering and emancipatory potential attributed to the digital. Even when the technology itself was deemed insufficient to fulfil this promise on its own, a range of checks and balances developed to ensure that power over the media was contained in the interest of audience-publics. Such checks and balances included formal regulation, market competition, public service or community media sectors, and the professional ideology and ethics of journalism. As a result—in the liberal tradition at least—the media have always been seen as, on balance, a force for transparency, accountability and progressive social change.

But there is one feature above all that marks the internet apart as an information medium. Unlike other modern platforms of communication across time and space, the internet was developed as an open network with only a limited capacity for centralised control. Ironically, this was a legacy of Cold War thinking and the desire of US military planners to develop a communications infrastructure that would be intrinsically resistant to nuclear attack. But it was not just about protecting a communications system for its own sake. Military planners realised that a network infrastructure that lacked a central node or a command-and-control hub could be the last line of national survival in the event of a nuclear holocaust (Benkler, 2006).

In practice, the absence of a central node meant that the actual technology of digital communication became embedded in the receiving 'ends' of the network (Lessig, 2001). In other words, the users of the network—the *people*—were to have shared control of its destiny. This feature gave rise to an unlikely marriage of worldviews during the early phases of the internet's development. Scientists and engineers enlisted by the Pentagon brought the foundations of the internet onto university campuses that were subsumed by anti-war protest and the culture of freedom and openness synonymous with the hippy movement (Curran et al., 2012). It was not long before these values began to be inscribed in the development and spread of internet technologies, and gave rise to a new movement that was the antithesis of military command and control: open source.

At the heart of the open source movement is the idea that information *wants to be free*, and arguably its greatest disruptive impact has been on newspapers whose very business model was always predicated on information scarcity. Once the vanguards of the news agenda, newspapers have been cast as the first casualties of the information age, the agenda influence of their owners seemingly irrelevant in the face of participant audience-users, as well as digital superpowers like Google and Facebook.

This is a narrative adopted above all by the owners of major news brands, and especially newspapers. As News Corporation stated in a written submission to Ofcom in 2011:

> The dynamic media environment, in the UK and internationally, in particular the increasingly important role played by the internet, is leading to a much more plural media environment in which consumers can and do easily access a multitude of news sources. Consumers are also increasingly exposed to

news content via social media sites such as Facebook and Twitter which also allow consumers to influence the wider news agenda.

(News Corporation, 2011, p. 4)

I mentioned earlier that media tycoons in the late twentieth century sought to downplay their political power by emphasising the commercial drivers behind editorial decisions. But faced with the declining profitability of the news industry in general—and newspapers in particular—the commercial logic of editorial decision-making carries increasingly less weight. In its place, twenty-first-century media owners have embraced digital evangelism as a way of negating their own power and lobbying successfully for still further liberalisation of ownership rules. It is a discourse that puts media moguls in an unlikely alliance with hacktivists and the general tide of digital civil society. The common belief—predicated on buzz phrases like 'multi-sourcing' and 'networked gatekeeping'—is that press power no longer matters and that new technologies have signalled a game change in the information struggles between publics and elites.

Explosions

In part II, we will explore the narratives of dispersal, which embrace this logic and collectively suggest that the influence over the information environment once wielded by or through media institutions has dissipated, and their power dispersed among an increasingly active and participatory audience. Much of our attention is devoted to unpacking and critiquing this narrative for its overestimation of audience empowerment and neglect of the ways in which press power over the agenda is consolidating in the digital realm.

But it is not without substance and we need to first consider why it offers such a compelling account of how things are changing. What seems certain is that the nature and make-up of the news agenda—even within the confines of the mainstream media and professional journalism—has indeed undergone a profound shift in recent decades. In Britain, this has seen institutional corruption at the highest levels of state-corporate power exposed at a breathtaking rate since the turn of the millennium. From stories about widespread banking fraud to mass surveillance, the contemporary news agenda in liberal democracies rarely *looks* like it is subject to any kind of an elite hold, and increasingly less so (McNair, 2012).

In a recent case study analysis of such media 'explosions', Amber Boydstun argued that although "policymaker attention is indeed a significant influence on media attention," the news is nonetheless "very difficult to control, even for the most powerful elites" (2013, p. 204). Once the momentum of crisis gathers pace in the media, the diversity of debate expands beyond elite frames, seemingly offering a powerful platform to voices of resistance and dissent. This was the case in Britain, for instance, during the build-up to the Iraq War in 2003, which produced an uncharacteristic skew in the mainstream—and even the right-wing press—in favour of the anti-war movement (Freedman, 2009).

But the anomaly proved to be short-lived, as much of the anti-war press began to fall into line post-invasion. The BBC—widely perceived as falling foul of the government *after* the war—was very much embedded during the actual combat phase (Lewis, 2006). This raises the difficult but important question of what *counts* as a meaningful agenda opening—that is, one that extends beyond a superficial and ephemeral demonstration of watchdog journalism. Does it matter, from an accountability perspective, if social media platforms are able to produce and spread a counter-narrative to that which dominates the mainstream news agenda, without having a substantive influence on that agenda? Does it matter if, within the mainstream news agenda, voices of dissent feature at the margins or even at the centre but are co-opted, short-lived and ultimately muted? If so, agenda openings may not only do very little to support agenda resistance, but may actually reinforce control by rendering its mechanisms less visible and less open to critical scrutiny.

Containment

Indeed, for all the chaos and explosions in global headlines over recent years, Western media have been implicated in a succession of accountability *failures*, some of which concern the very exposés for which the 'new model of journalism' is credited (Dunn, 2013). Consider, for instance, the case of Cablegate in 2010, when major news outlets around the world partnered with the digital whistleblowing platform WikiLeaks to publish a series of secret US diplomatic cables. This unprecedented media event was welcomed as the fruit of a new 'networked fourth estate' that synthesised the best of old and new approaches to watchdog journalism (Benkler, 2011). Yet from another perspective, it symbolised the abject failure of the mainstream press and professional journalism to deliver on their watchdog promise, and their ultimate complicity in the very strategies of agenda control that they claimed to resist. Whereas stories of high society gossip dominated the headlines, crucial revelations of systemic corruption went largely unnoticed (Schlosberg, 2013). These included communiqués that suggested Britain's long-running and controversial Iraq war inquiry had been systematically undermined by government officials from the outset; that legal loopholes had been cynically exploited by British and American governments in order to maintain a stockpile of US cluster bomb munitions on British territory; or that British military personnel were involved in the training of a Bangladeshi paramilitary group in Bangladesh, dubbed a 'death squad' by one human rights group (Human Rights Watch, 2011). Such stories attracted no more than a brief mention in any of the BBC's television news output. When its most senior foreign correspondent was asked by a news anchor to reflect on the impact of the leaks, he remarked simply:

> An awful lot of it is really not much more than refined tittle-tattle and the only thing that I've really raised my eye brows at is the suggestion—and you've

got a put a question mark over it—that a Chinese diplomat said to a South Korean diplomat 'we don't really care if Korea is united under South Korean control' [. . .] If true, that is potentially important.[1]

Professional journalism has also been roundly criticised for its failure to predict—and even prevent—the global financial collapse of 2008 (e.g. Fraser, 2009; Schechter, 2009; Tambini, 2008). But it was during the aftermath of this crisis that incompetence began to look more like complicity in the reassertion of control. Following the collapse of Lehman Brothers in 2008, with some of the world's largest banks poised to follow suit, governments on both sides of the Atlantic were faced with an imminent decision of whether and how to intervene in order to contain the crisis and stem the damage caused to the wider economy. The debate that foregrounded this decision and that was articulated by at least one highly influential newsroom was, as Mike Berry (2013) has shown, systematically contained within boundaries that marginalised or excluded alternative solutions.

For instance, the bailout package proposed by the UK government was generally preferred by banking executives and other financial elites, and in the weeks leading up to the decision, these were the most prominent sources featured on the BBC's *Today Programme*, widely recognised as a leading influence over the 'serious' news agenda. The bailout package promised a huge injection of public funds into the most endangered banks in return for preference shares (rather than voting shares) and without any guarantees about lending to the wider economy or controversial remuneration structures for bank employees. The cost to the taxpayer was to be a generation of austerity.

At least one alternative to the government's bailout plan was nationalisation; an option endorsed by Joseph Stiglitz—a Nobel Prize–winning economist and one of the world's leading commentators on the financial crisis—among others. But Berry demonstrates how proponents of this alternative were not featured at all on the *Today Programme* during the weeks leading up to and immediately after the bail out. Although some degree of debate was admitted, this fell far short of nationalisation being considered at any point as a credible option.

Such is the ideology of 'There Is No Alternative'—or 'TINA' as the phrase has become known (Downing et al., 2014). Originally popularised by Margaret Thatcher in her repeated dismissal of arguments against economic liberalism, its sentiment was echoed in Francis Fukuyama's declaration of the "end of history" following the collapse of Soviet Communism in 1989, signalling "the end point of mankind's ideological evolution and the universalization of Western liberal democracy as the final form of human government" (Fukuyama, 1989, p. 3). It was also revived by David Cameron in 2013 to justify the programme of public spending cuts that duly followed the bailout, triggering a fall in the living standards of the poorest not seen since the Great Depression: "If there was another way I would take it. But there is no alternative" (Robinson, 2013).

This fostered an arena of debate that was largely restricted to a choice between moderate austerity and 'austerity max', with the mainstream media reflecting and reinforcing the boundaries of political consensus across Europe (Mercille, 2013; Mylonas, 2014; Sousa and Santos, 2014). In defence of TINA, the dominant framing attributed the causes of austerity to the excesses of government spending on public services during the decade or so leading up to the crash (rather than the unprecedented and unparalleled spending on the bailout that followed it). It thus obscured the excesses of a deregulated banking system and, in a remarkable ideological twist, austerity became a correction to *too much* government (Callinicos, 2012).

Another arena in which the mainstream media have been implicated in accountability failure is national security. In June 2015, amid the continuing fallout from the Snowden leaks, the Murdoch-owned *Sunday Times* newspaper launched a front page exclusive titled 'British spies betrayed to Russian and Chinese' (Harper et al., 2015). Masquerading as investigative journalism, the article offered a verbatim repetition of government claims that the Snowden leaks had been intercepted by both the Russian and Chinese authorities. Aside from factual errors subsequently retracted, no evidence for the claims was sought as a basis for running the story, no 'alleged' qualification added and no right of reply offered to Snowden or others who might have challenged the government's claims. For Glenn Greenwald—one of the first journalists to gain access to the leaked material—the article was symptomatic of a disease of deference to the national security state, endemic in the mainstream media:

> That is the tactic of how major U.S. and British media outlets "report," especially in the national security area. And journalists who write such reports continue to treat self-serving decrees by unnamed, unseen officials [. . .] as gospel, no matter how dubious are the claims or factually false is the reporting.
> (Greenwald, 2015)

For its part, the newspaper stood defiantly by its article asserting that the story was "another example of the *Sunday Times* setting the news agenda" (Snow, 2015). And on that point at least, the paper appears to have got it right. The story was more or less duplicated in a BBC television news report, and in the following days, coverage related to Snowden across both mainstream and social media was dominated by the controversy hanging over the feature.

Critics of Greenwald's view will point to the barrage of criticism it received from other journalists, including those working for mainstream news outlets like the *Washington Post*. The way that the story played out, from this perspective, reflected the failure of both Murdoch's journalists and official sources to control the narrative. It's certainly hard to imagine that the authors and editor behind the story were not caught off guard by the degree of backlash it prompted.

But from another perspective, all of that noise merely served to obscure the fact that attention was skewed in favour of an issue that played ultimately to the establishment's hand. The opportunity cost was an absence of attention to what else was going on amid the continuing fallout from the Snowden leaks.

In particular, just three days prior to the feature, an independent and highly respected lawyer published a report describing the confusion surrounding the government's legal powers of surveillance as "undemocratic, unnecessary and—in the long—intolerable" (Anderson, 2015). But instead of talking about the need for and shape of reforms, the media spotlight had shifted towards whether or not the leaks had damaged national security, and whether or not mainstream journalists were too in hock to the authorities. That this secondary coverage admitted a great deal of criticism towards the government and the *Sunday Times* does not discount the story's potentially crucial impact in redirecting the lens of attention.

After all, agenda control is not equivalent to editorial control. Establishment interests may determine the range of issues that surface on the agenda, and even to some extent how those issues are defined. But this does not mean that the coverage itself will be perennially biased in their favour. In this sense, agenda control is by no means incompatible with genuine controversy and the fierce political debate that is routinely played out before and through the professional news media.

The Trouble with Hegemony

This touches on a paradox that has dogged critical media inquiry for almost as long as it has existed, and is perhaps best captured by the release of Orson Welles's first feature film in 1941, *Citizen Kane*. Produced by Hollywood's RKO Pictures, the film attracted unprecedented controversy—as well as acclaim—for its portrayal of a newspaper magnate whose early career idealism evolves into a ruthless pursuit of profit and power. The character was based loosely on the American press magnate William Randolph Hearst who, upon the film's release, imposed a blanket ban on any mention or advertising related to the film across his newspaper and radio empire. But Hearst's influence extended far beyond his own media outlets. A synopsis of a 1996 documentary about the film provides a glimpse into the sheer range of strings pulled by Hearst in an effort to suppress it:

> Hollywood executives [. . .] rallied around Hearst, attempting to buy *Citizen Kane* in order to burn the negative. At the same time, Hearst's defenders moved to intimidate exhibitors into refusing to show the movie. Threats of blackmail, smears in the newspapers, and FBI investigations were used in the effort.
>
> (PBS, n.d.)

The producers of the documentary add that "Hearst's campaign was largely successful. It would be nearly a quarter century before *Citizen Kane* was revived—before Welles would gain popular recognition for having created one of cinema's great masterpieces." Yet despite all his efforts, Hearst did not succeed in shutting down the film, nor did he prevent its achievement of some degree of critical acclaim and modest box office success, even during its first year of release.

Did this failure demonstrate the futility of attempts to ultimately control the agenda, even by some of the most powerful figures in the media? Did it betray deep divisions within the media-political establishment that undermine conceptions of a power elite? Did it demonstrate very real opportunities and spaces for dissent even within mainstream popular culture?

Or was it merely the exception that proved the rule, perhaps even serving to legitimise a system that perpetuates agenda control by making it look and feel like nothing of the sort? In their critique of the cultural industries three years later, Adorno and Horkheimer asserted that the film posed "no big threat, because its calculated deviations from convention serve all the more strongly to confirm the validity of the system" (Adorno and Horkheimer, 1997 [1944], p. 129).

This view was taken up by others associated with the Frankfurt School in the post-war period (e.g. Marcuse, 2002 [1964]). They dismissed any kind of apparent subversion of popular culture as not so much insignificant, but rather an essential component of a mass media system designed above all to indoctrinate and pacify. It was essential because the key to ideological domination in this sense was not to project control (a point missed in feudal and totalitarian societies) but to mask it behind a veil of credibility. Provided dissent was kept within the margins of popular culture, or contained within periodic moments, it served an essential purpose in legitimising the system of cultural production at large. In other words, they were essential because they made ideological domination look less visible.

Echoes of this view are found in contemporary radical critics of the media who sharpen the focus of their critique on the so-called liberal press, precisely because these outlets enjoy a reputation for relative independence and fourth estate values of speaking truth to power. In the words of veteran muckraker John Pilger:

> The most effective propaganda is found not in the *Sun* or on *Fox News*— but beneath a liberal halo. When the *New York Times* published claims that Saddam Hussein had weapons of mass destruction, its fake evidence was believed, because it wasn't *Fox News*; it was the *New York Times*.
>
> (Pilger, 2014)

But this doesn't seem to capture the reality that the liberal media *have* at times posed a real threat to establishment power and have been instrumental in catalysing social change. From *Citizen Kane* to *Anarchy in the UK*, from coverage of the Pentagon Papers to the national security leaks of Edward Snowden, it is difficult to accept that the media and cultural industries in capitalist democracies have always been broadly if not entirely faithful servants of the established order. The unprecedented steps taken by the British government to curtail coverage of the Snowden leaks is perhaps a case in point here. Aside from the threats of prior restraint already mentioned, security officials entered the *Guardian*'s offices in July 2013 to oversee the destruction of a hard drive containing source material. Even more controversially, a month later police used terrorism legislation to arrest and detain David Miranda, the partner of the story's lead reporter Glenn

Greenwald (Rusbridger, 2013). Such moves hardly seem in keeping with a 'calculated deviation' from the consensus agenda.

For Stuart Hall (1982), these critical junctures serve as a reminder that beneath the surface of news discourse lies an underlying and historic struggle over meaning. Drawing on Gramsci's idea of hegemony, Hall argued that there are indeed infrequent *redefining* moments that surface in the mainstream media, to the extent that they bend or prise open the existing boundaries of the debate, especially during periods of crisis. But over the long term, such ruptures can also have a stabilising effect on the hegemony of elite worldviews, precisely because they make hegemony less visible. This is the paradox at the heart of Gramsci's analysis that Hall sought to reconcile, but in a more nuanced and less fatalistic way than the Frankfurt School. In particular, Hall did not think of the expression of dissent as necessarily a calculated deviation designed to legitimise the system. At least on occasion, he considered such expressions in mainstream media or popular culture to mark a genuine break with and challenge to dominant narratives. Instead, the force or act of legitimation consists in the way in which such episodic moments are *overstated*—especially in the discourse of those who work for or own mass media institutions. In the context of journalism, they are presented as the modus operandi of the news media consistent with the liberal ideals of the fourth estate and watchdog reporting:

> Such institutions powerfully secure consent precisely because their claim to be independent of the direct play of political or economic interests, or of the state, is not wholly fictitious. The claim is ideological, not because it is false but because it does not adequately grasp all the conditions which make freedom and impartiality possible. It is ideological because it offers a partial explanation as if it were a comprehensive and adequate one—it takes the part for the whole (fetishism). Nevertheless, its legitimacy depends on that part of the truth, which it mistakes for the whole, being real in fact, and not merely a polite fiction.
>
> (Hall, 1982, p. 85)

This suggests we need to avoid opposing conceptual traps when attempting to understand the nature of agenda control. The dismissive pessimism of the Frankfurt School critics is inadequate because it does not acknowledge the hidden struggle behind the agenda that manifests in occasional but real moments of crisis and resistance. On the other hand, the dismissive optimism of those who perceive media institutions as ever more scrutinising and challenging of establishment power overlooks the often subtle ways in which such scrutiny is contained, and challenges mollified (Schlosberg, 2013).

The point about invisibility in this sense (and one that ties it intimately to the third dimension of power) is that the less contained the media agenda *looks* from the audience's point of view, the more effective it is likely to be in shaping what issues people think about, as well as how they think about them. This paradox is underlined by research that demonstrates the sensitivity of audiences to perceived interpretive cues or prompts in the media. For instance, one study on the media's 'priming' effects—the association between issues and/or political actors that can influence audience judgements—showed that such effects are most significant when the prime is unnoticed or overlooked by audience members (Srull and Wyer, 1980).

Hall's analysis suggests that in order to gain a deeper understanding of agenda control, we need to ask not whether the agenda is open to contest, but to what degree. This requires us to pay close attention to not only the frequency and intensity of disruptive news narratives, but also the extent to which they may be marginalised or contained at pivotal points. In my previous book, I attempted to demonstrate this containment in the coverage of high-profile controversies, especially within public service television (Schlosberg, 2013). What seemed clear at first glance, for instance, was that corruption in the British arms trade was for an extended period (2006–2010) a recurring and relatively prominent theme in public service news. This provided opportunities for journalists to act on public service and watchdog values in a way that was not reducible simply to ideological 'repair work' (Bennett et al., 1985). Although much of the coverage was confined to particular points within the schedule (especially minority audience news programmes), the most significant aspect of containment was manifest in a spectacle of accountability that precipitated the end of intense coverage. For instance, rather than interrogate the legitimacy or proportionality of a plea bargain settlement that enabled BAe Systems to avoid prosecution, the coverage tended to adopt the framing of both BAe and the government in presenting the settlements as a humbling moment for the world's largest arms manufacturer.

As we have seen, when the press themselves became the centre of the story during the phone hacking scandal, the peak of coverage intensity surrounded a similar hands-up moment in which Rupert Murdoch described himself as 'humbled' amid the exposure of rampant criminality within his newsrooms. Such spectacles resonate with Blair's advice to Brooks and embody the paradox that agenda disruptions can be at once a challenge to an elite hold, but also obscure the reality of that hold. In recent years, we have become accustomed to witnessing the humbling of powerful figures in public inquiries ranging from spies to bankers to prime ministers and media owners themselves. On one level, these crisis moments are testament to the fact that agenda control is rarely a given but has to be *won*, a point that is widely acknowledged in sociological studies of journalism (Ericson et al., 1989; Deacon and Golding, 1994; Schlesinger and Tumber, 1994). But what is less acknowledged is that for victory in this sense to be achieved, it must often be presented as defeat.

In his meditation on the *Contradictions of Media Power*, Des Freedman shows how—just like capitalism itself—the structures of media power are inherently vulnerable to periodic crises and moments of instability (Freedman, 2014). According to this view, the surfacing of dissenting views in mainstream public discourse, however occasional and ephemeral, presents unrivalled opportunities for social change. Rather than dismiss the significance of such crises, Freedman insists that scholars and activists should remain alert and responsive to them.

It's hard to contest such a view, especially in light of disclosures during the Leveson Inquiry, which focused unprecedented attention on the politics of media ownership. Although we might well question whether disclosure is enough to produce meaningful accountability and reform, history suggests that it is the cumulative and gradual effect of recurring crises that matters. The three million anti-war demonstrators who took to the streets of London in March 2003 did not stop the invasion of Iraq, but they might well have made it immeasurably harder for subsequent governments to launch offensive military action, especially in the absence of a popular mandate.

In a compelling analysis, Freedman shows how the demonstration of 13 March was symbolic of the potential for dissenting voices to reshape the news agenda in the midst of such crisis periods. The important lesson he draws is that although these periods may not of themselves produce substantive accountability outcomes, they can nevertheless serve to expose the machinations, concentrations and abuses of power to a much wider audience than is ordinarily possible. In other words, the distinctive feature of agenda openings is that power becomes *more* visible and *more* open to challenge. In contrast to radical functionalist accounts (e.g. Herman and Chomsky, 2002 [1988]), Freedman's analysis suggests that such critical junctures must reflect at least some degree of a counter-hegemonic force, however exceptional and ephemeral they prove to be.

But there is always a risk in reflecting on such crises that we overlook the subtleties of hegemonic power and confer greater openness to the media agenda than is empirically demonstrated. This matters from an activist standpoint because the narrative most widely adopted by media owners is that agenda openings constitute the rule rather than the exception. If we fail to subject them to critical scrutiny, we risk falling into the legitimation trap that Hall illuminated. In Boydstun's analysis (2013), for instance, media explosions are held to signal the finite capacity of elites to exercise meaningful control of the agenda. But we might just as well think of this in the inverse, that it is the dissipation of media explosions that signals the limits of agenda *resistance*. By focusing on explosion at the expense of stabilisation, these studies are led to conclude that the values of professional watchdog journalism are more of a countervailing force than is often the case.

But radical functionalist accounts have also tended to overlook the significance of agenda closure in this sense, painting instead a relatively static picture of control. One exception was a study in 1985 that examined the response of professional journalists to an event that threatened to disrupt what the researchers called a 'news paradigm' (Bennett et al., 1985). Thanks to the active repair work of journalists, they argued, a story about a man who set himself on fire to protest against unemployment quickly became a story about the irresponsibility of journalists who exploited his actions for their own gain. In other words, professional journalists were, on the whole, complicit in reworking an anomalous news narrative to fit within the dominant paradigm.

But this study predates the increased intensity of media explosions that have surfaced over recent decades. What's more, the very fact that the narrative was transformed so quickly and effectively suggests that the case did not bear the hallmarks of a truly explosive story in the sense considered by Boydstun (2013), and which is captured by long-running crises like the phone hacking scandal or Snowden leaks. The challenge we are left with is to identify *both* the 're-defining' moments that may surface in such news discourse, as well as the complex and subtle ways in which control can be regained, often leaving the promise of meaningful accountability or substantive reform unfulfilled. Equally, we need to recognise both the opportunities for ideological and cultural resistance that agenda openings present *as well as* their potential to obscure the underlying mechanics of control; and to acknowledge both the important contributions that professional media organisations can make in destabilising elite agendas, as well as their complicity in restoring them.

Above all, it requires us to be sensitive amid agenda openings and explosions to 'the dog that isn't barking'. This is critical because, as Crenson (1971) showed in his comparative analysis of environmental reforms in two US cities, the liberal pluralist vision of democracy begins to unravel when we ask not what is included in the agenda, but what is left out and why. The power to set the terms of debate may not guarantee an easy ride for the powerful. It may not even amount to the structural advantage of news definition widely attributed to elite sources in critical media theory (Sigal, 1973; Hall et al., 1978; Gans, 1979). But it does prescribe limits on potential solutions to policy problems, and thus determines the nature and scope of reform. From a radical perspective, this is the epitome of hegemonic power: the mechanism by which some alternatives are omitted from the consensus framework and as such, excluded from the realm of what is possible, realistic, or *common sense* (Miliband, 1973; Chibnall, 2001 [1977]).

Conclusion and Scope of the Book

We began by suggesting that the concept of invisibility is fundamental to critical questions about media ownership in the information age. In particular, it requires us to look beyond the linear and surface control typified by the press barons, and consider media ownership as a structural condition that is central to the machinations of power in post-industrial societies. But ownership only *matters* to the extent that the professional media are still considered instrumental in defining the scope of public and policy debate. This focuses our attention on the question of agenda control, with particular reference to the very few platforms and outlets that reach across fragmented audiences and interests characteristic of the new information environment.

It was further suggested that in order to understand the full significance of media ownership in the power structure of post-digital societies, we have to penetrate two layers of potential obscurity relating first to the actual means and mechanics of control, and second to the manifest outcomes of control. To this extent we have looked at the different ways in which media owners—in tandem with other powerful interests—may distance themselves from the editorial output of their media assets, and negate their potential for leveraging political influence. And we have considered how the power equation itself can become erased from questions of media ownership by reference to a diversified and contestable agenda, while the omission of certain frames or perspectives at key moments may contribute to the stabilisation of agendas in the interests of elite power. Amid the fluidity of knowledge and ideas characteristic of the information age, these layers of obscurity may collectively manifest in powerful interests being *heard* but *not seen*.

So far, however, our focus has been implicitly restricted to media groups that exercise editorial control—traditionally the press and broadcasters—rather than so-called digital intermediaries, or websites that list, aggregate or otherwise feature news and information content produced by third parties. As we will see, the political and agenda influence of intermediaries is in many ways even more opaque than that of mainstream news institutions. And it is no secret that companies like Google and Facebook have amassed a degree of market power that traditional media groups can only gawp at. Much of the book's attention is therefore directed to critically scrutinising their agenda power, but not in isolation of editorial news organisations. In the realm of media policy especially, this can create significant blind spots and has fostered a misplaced assumption that the agenda power of intermediaries is increasing at the expense of news producers. The distinct approach taken by this book is to interrogate the *interdependencies* that have developed between dot-com giants and major news publishers, and the impact this is having on both the 'head' and 'tail' of news distribution.

But the book does adopt a relatively restrictive focus in its preoccupation with news and current affairs. This is not to negate the profound influence that other genres and other cultural industries can have on public or policy agendas. Indeed, one of the central arguments developed in chapter 13 has resonance for cultural forms beyond news; namely, that the way in which the media landscape is evolving may be making it harder for radical or subversive ideas to permeate the boundaries of fragmented audiences. But the focus overall is restricted to news because of its potentially unique contribution to democratic life and its centrality in media policy debates. More acutely, the news has an immediate and intimate connection to the way in which issues and problems that affect society as a whole are defined, and the extent to which they impact on the consciousness of the public or polity (Carpentier, 2014).

Finally, the book is biased in its focus towards the UK and US, especially in the context of media policy. It is also informed partly by case study research on coverage of the national security files leaked by Edward Snowden in 2013, as well as the election of Jeremy Corbyn to the leadership of the British Labour Party in 2015. However, many of the themes discussed have strong parallels in other countries and contexts. As already mentioned, the close alliance of media and political elites is a feature common to a wide range of media and political systems around the world (Open Society Foundations, 2014).

Building on the conceptual terrain established here, Parts II and III navigate through the complexities of news circulation today that have produced competing narratives of change. Part II introduces the core concepts of gatekeeping and agenda setting; two overarching and related theoretical traditions that capture the book's central problematic. The discussion takes a forensic look at the latest research within these fields, along with various arguments that suggest the gatekeeping and agenda setting power once vested in media owners is increasingly dispersed among audiences and users. In part III, attention is turned to digital intermediaries and their purported roles in the collection, storage and commodification of personal data; in encasing users within 'filter bubbles' or 'echo chambers' in ways that undermine the public sphere; in collaborating with state censorship and surveillance; and above all, in usurping the power of agenda control from traditional media.

Part IV tries to make sense of these competing narratives through a critical examination first of long tail theory. Here I will attempt to show why the lengthening of the 'tail' in the digital distribution of news and culture underpins some of the ideas synonymous with dispersal, but has done little to detract from a relatively constricted agenda captured by the 'head'. Attention is then turned to power elite theory as a basis for exploring the interdependencies of old and new media gatekeepers, as well as their interlocking connections to the wider structure of state-corporate power.

Overall, the arguments developed in the book revolve around two core contentions. First, that there remains a relatively coherent and cohesive mainstream or aggregate news agenda that is still vulnerable to control by powerful interests—ineradicably connected with media ownership—at key points and moments, and in spite of a sense of agenda chaos that pervades periods of relative openness. Second, that the agenda power attached to major media groups is enduring and evolving in spite of—and to some extent because of—failing news business models, the rise of intermediaries, and the vast sea of information noise that has swelled in the digital sphere.

This calls for a holistic policy approach that addresses both old and new sources of gatekeeping while recognising that they require distinct forms of regulation. To this end, part V concludes by mapping these sources and elaborating policy remedies. They are collectively goal oriented towards nurturing the redistribution of communicative power in ways that preserve rather than dissolve public spheres, and enhance rather than threaten the sustainability of professional newsgathering and publishing.

Note

1. BBC *Newsnight*, 3 December 2010.

Part II

Dispersal

Chapter 4

Dismantling the Gates

In the 1980s, journalists at the *Observer* newspaper began to investigate allegations of bribery and corruption centring on BAe Systems—one of the world's largest weapons manufacturers—and its arms sales to Saudi Arabia. What they did not know at the time was that they were embarking on a story that would endure for the better part of 25 years, focusing unprecedented light into the murky world of the British arms trade. Although BAe eventually managed to see off any prosecution for bribery or corruption, the story's legacy was writ large in prestigious journalistic awards and a $400 million fine imposed on BAe by the US Department of Justice.

Yet the trigger for those initial investigations was not a journalistic hunch or leaked documents or a whistle-blower coming forward, but rather a specific request by senior management at the newspaper. According to one of the journalists working on the story at the time, this request had come through "the channels of Tiny Rowland," the paper's then owner, who also had an interest in Dassault, one of BAe's main European competitors (Schlosberg, 2013). This begs two thought-provoking, if unanswerable questions. First, would the story ever have emerged at all had it not been for the alleged request filtering down the management and editorial chain? Second, what other headline-worthy stories of systemic corruption go untold in the absence of such requests?

The factors that determine what stories, issues or frames are included in the news agenda have long been the preoccupation of gatekeeping theory. In its earliest formulation, this theory focused on the subjective personality of the editor as the main driver of news selection (White, 1950). Since then, it has developed and expanded to reflect a much wider range of influences and account for the nuances and complexities of editorial decision-making (e.g. Galtung and Ruge, 1965; Gans, 1979; Manning, 2001). This also led to the emergence of different levels of analysis, examining gatekeeping as a function of individual agency, communication routines, organisational behaviour, social institutions and the social system as a whole (Shoemaker and Reese, 1996).

Because there is always more news than is fit to print, judgements about newsworthiness are an intrinsic and routine feature of journalistic life. Of course, powers of selection synonymous with gatekeeping do not tend to be evenly distributed in newsrooms. The role of the editor is clearly paramount in this respect, and in collapsing different levels of gatekeeping into one generic role we risk disguising power relations within news institutions. But even with an expansive range of selection criteria, and differentiated levels of analysis, the gatekeeping paradigm has not tended to produce critical responses to the question of power *behind* the media agenda, focusing instead on the manifest qualities that guide news selection. This is surprising given that the very notion of gatekeeping seems to invest significant cultural power and information control ultimately in the hands of those who own and control mass media institutions.

In attempting to address this problem, White (1950) suggested that so long as newspaper editors were more immersed in the communities they serve than the power structures in which they operate, journalism can fulfil its monitorial and representative role (albeit imperfectly and incompletely). The gatekeeper thus "sees to it (even though he may never be consciously aware of it) that the community shall hear as a fact only those events which the newsman, as the representative of his culture, believes to be true" (White, 1950, p. 390). Later explanations pointed to the professional norms, codes of conduct, routines and values that act as an insulation buffer, ensuring that "the news is not simply a compliant supporter of elites or the Establishment or the ruling class; rather, it views nation and society through its own set of values and with its own conception of the good social order" (Gans, 1979, p. 62).

Thus the central problematic of news selection is often resolved by gatekeeping studies that suggest the limits of the media agenda are not generally imposed but emerge naturally as a function of community allegiances or shared news values. Even if limited to providing a public 'alarm' system, according to which journalists are charged with signalling only those issues "requiring urgent attention" (Zaller, 2003, p. 122), journalists ultimately serve citizens over and above the vested interests of their owners or powerful sources. In these terms, gatekeeping is not only a relatively harmless practice, but a necessary and desirable filter that guides citizens towards the issues that matter, and provides a regular, coherent and digestible diet of news in the public interest.

Critical challenges to gatekeeping theory have stemmed from a broad spectrum of viewpoints. Accounts influenced by post-structuralism have tended to view newsgathering as a process of reality construction rather than selection (e.g. Tuchman, 1978; Schlesinger, 1987; Baudrillard, 1995), whereas radical critiques have long considered the act of news filtering an essential component of ideological work (e.g. Sigal, 1973; Herman and Chomsky, 1988; Manning, 2001). Yet one of the earliest and profound challenges stemmed from a different corner altogether, and one that shared with gatekeeping theory an essentially optimistic view of journalism's social role: media populism.

From this standpoint, the driving force behind the news agenda was not so much the professional judgements of journalists or media and cultural producers at large, but the growing influence of audience tastes and preferences over the course of the twentieth century. This audience empowerment was intimately tied to the commercialisation and liberalisation of media ownership (Curran, 2002). In Britain, for instance, the introduction of commercial television in 1955 and commercial radio in 1973 were seen as pivotal moments in forcing the BBC to abandon its paternalistic approach and redefine its public service mission along lines less condescending towards its audience. So entrenched was this culture within the BBC's formative years that one station controller was moved to justify an exceptionally late broadcast in 1929 as something of a rare treat for well-behaved viewers: "as a general rule, people should not be encouraged to sit up till all hours, but we feel that one special occasion will not hurt them."[1]

In fact, the origins of media populism stretch back further to the early days of the original press barons. They were the first to commission regular surveys of their readers, and to respond by prioritising crime and human interest stories over hard news topics such as politics, foreign affairs and the economy (Curran and Seaton, 2003). This led to the beginnings of what populists argue was a progressive democratisation of the news agenda, widening access beyond a metropolitan white male elite, and favouring issues and topics that resonated with the lives of ordinary people (Fiske, 2010). It was also a process that arguably reflected and supported the social and professional advance of women. According to Mick Temple (2008), the associated "rise in consumer and lifestyle coverage could be interpreted as reflecting a 'new visibility' for what are often derogatorily referred to as 'women issues'." Above all, the rise of populism marked a *diversification* of the news agenda, with the effect that "serious electoral news, and thoughtful coverage of policy debates remains strong and flourishing, along with the tabloid trash" (Norris, 2000, p. 312).

Thus, the seeds of what was to be seen as an epic power shift in the digital era were sown by the commercialisation and liberalisation of media channels during the second half of the twentieth century. In the digital realm, the empowerment of audiences became not only a function of commerce, but also the *commons*[2] (Lessig, 2001). The rise of content sharing platforms and social networking sites was seen as the key driver of a news agenda increasingly shaped by people power rather than profit. The phenomenon of 'networked gatekeeping' in particular was to become a catalyst in the ability of audiences to decide for themselves what is newsworthy and represented, for many, the last nail in the coffin of agenda control.

Unspun

In 2012, a school bus chaperone from New York State and victim of intense bullying by the students she was responsible for became an unlikely news hero (McGee, 2013; Jaffe, n.d.). When a video capturing her abuse was uploaded to YouTube, it was immediately picked up by a user of Reddit, a news social network, and quickly became the most popular ranked story on the site. At that point the moderators of the site removed the story due to concerns about the identities of young people exposed in the video. But this only fuelled its spread to other networks, including 4Chan and Indiegogo. So strong was the outpouring of public sympathy for Ms Klein that a crowdfund of $750,000 was raised in her name and, eventually, the story was picked up by major news outlets including *People* magazine, the *Washington Post* and ABC.

This is networked gatekeeping, and reflects the supposed new role of the audience and the crowd in redefining and shaping the wider news agenda (Barzilai-Nahon, 2008). It has echoes in notions such as 'gatewatching' (Bruns, 2011) and the 'fifth estate' (Cooper, 2006; Dutton, 2009)—terms that denote a form of journalism that is preoccupied with scrutinising the mainstream news agenda and exposing its limitations, biases and inaccuracies. It is also closely aligned with broader conceptions of networked forms of resistance articulated by the likes of Manuel Castells (2009) and Yochai Benkler (2011), among others. At root here is a conviction that the linear, editorial gatekeeping power once in the hands of journalists, editors and proprietors has been progressively subverted by the spread of participatory news platforms. These platforms engage users directly in the production and sharing of content, and thus the business of story 'selection' is no longer the preserve of the newsroom. It has been especially invoked with reference to the political uprisings that took place across North Africa in 2011. From Tunisia to Egypt, social media platforms appeared to play an instrumental role in mobilising protest, circumventing censorship and influencing the global news agenda (Castells, 2009; Meraz and Papacharissi, 2013; Hermida et al., 2014).

Some have articulated this power shift as a relegation of the professional news function from editorial control to amplification and guidance. In this new dynamic, the unique contribution of journalists lies in helping users navigate the new news terrain, as opposed to determining the terrain itself; marking a switch "from the watchdog to the 'guidedog'" (Bardoel and Deuze, 2001, p. 94). Others suggest, conversely, that the role of professional journalists is now limited to that of newsgathering, while audiences have assumed responsibility for determining which stories achieve salience and prominence (Dylko et al., 2012; Singer, 2014). Either way, the professional media still play a part in agenda creation, but it is now a supporting rather than lead role. This point was made emphatically by Henry Jenkins when he argued:

> The power of participation comes not from destroying commercial culture but from writing over it, modding it, amending it, expanding it, adding greater diversity of perspective, and then recirculating it, feeding it back into the mainstream media.
>
> (Jenkins, 2006, p. 257)

Yochai Benkler articulated a similar idea in what he called the 'networked fourth estate'. Here, professional news institutions offer not only publicity power but also journalistic skills and experience that, in combination with networked participation, can yield powerful emancipatory effects. This kind of collaboration was epitomised by the relationship that WikiLeaks forged with its mainstream media partners prior to publishing diplomatic cables leaked from the US State Department in 2010. Although the relationship between WikiLeaks and the *Guardian*—as well as the *New York Times*—quickly descended into an acrimonious and very public split, the impact of the story on the global news agenda was nevertheless held as testament to the new balance of agenda power (McNair, 2012; Shirky, 2011).

For Brian McNair (2006, 2012), all of this amounts to what he calls 'cultural chaos'—the inherent unpredictability and uncontrollability of news flows that also underlines Boydstun's conception of agenda 'explosions' (2013), discussed in part I, and which he contrasts with the 'control paradigm' associated with the mass media age. Its roots lie not only in technological change but also in the epochal social and cultural shifts that have coincided with it. Thus, the collapse of social deference towards elites, the end of the Cold War consensus, and the fragmentation of audiences and society have all contributed to a general opening up of the cultural paradigm (see also Entman, 2004). Episodes like WikiLeaks' Cablegate exemplify the incapacity of elites to censor, pressure or otherwise lean upon particular outlets in order to leverage influence over the agenda at large.

What all of these ideas share in common is a core conviction that media ownership is no longer a useful mechanism or lever of agenda control. Gone are the days when media owners or other elites could direct or manage the news agenda in any generalist or systematic sense. Even if mainstream agendas persist and remain malleable to some extent by elites, they are increasingly checked and scrutinised by alternative channels and the wisdom of the crowd.

This notion of an emergent fifth estate carries some weight in empirical and anecdotal evidence. One of the most striking examples appeared to surface in 2015 following the election of Jeremy Corbyn as leader of the British Labour Party. As a committed socialist and voice of the radical left, his unexpected and grassroots mandate marked a profound break-up of a mainstream bipartisan consensus that had prevailed for at least a generation. Not surprisingly, it also prompted a chorus of warnings by the Tory government and backbench MPs, the mainstream press and, in a manner that broke with constitutional precedent and basic democratic norms, significant voices from the military and security establishment. Mainstream broadcasters like the BBC and Sky provided an echo chamber for a mantra repeated with such consistency as to suggest the response was very much coordinated. But this seemed only to produce an outpouring of criticism and ridicule across social media and new news channels, reflecting a deepening cynicism and ideological polarisation between traditional and new media platforms.

It began prior to Corbyn's victory, when the two most powerful people in UK government each wrote an article for the Murdoch press over two consecutive days, preparing the ground for a narrative that positioned Corbyn as not just a political outlier, but a comprehensive security threat (Gunter, 2015). Prime Minister David Cameron's piece for the *Times* used the word 'security' on six occasions in response to Corbyn's unexpected poll lead, while the Chancellor of the Exchequer George Osborne mentioned it eight times in his article for the *Sun* newspaper. In the days that followed Corbyn's victory, ministers and backbench MPs tweeted and spoke in almost complete unison about the threat the Labour Party now posed to "our national security, our economic security, and your family's security" (Cameron, 2015). As if to give some sort of credence to the clamour, a senior military official was quoted in the *Sunday Times* newspaper as predicting something "tantamount to a mutiny" if Corbyn was to become prime minister (Mortimer, 2015), a sentiment later echoed by an outgoing chief of defence staff who expressed to the BBC his "worry" about the prospect of a Corbyn premiership owing to his views on nuclear weapons (Waugh, 2015).

Interestingly, analysis of press coverage showed that ideological bias was even more pronounced in actual news reports compared to columns and opinion editorials (Ridley, 2015). Yet it was not long before this bias became a story in itself, rippling across Twitter and Facebook and amplified by new news entrants such as BuzzFeed. For these outlets, the meaning of the 'security threat' story became fundamentally subverted. What's more, this counter-narrative did not just target the Conservative Party government or its cheerleaders in the right-wing press, but rather a class of out-of-touch elites. As one tweet put it, "The Labour party is now a threat to a dying group of elitist dinosaurs hell bent on taking us all to the edge of extinction" (Silver, 2015). For *Guardian* columnist Owen Jones, the state's PR offensive was "the sort of rhetoric you'd expect from a tinpot dictatorship" (Jones, 2015).

Such tweets seemed to capture the sense of exasperation that characterised the prevailing social media response—exasperation over what looked like yet another attempt to deploy the security threat narrative for ideological purposes. In chapter 3, we discussed the controversy surrounding government claims of a threat to national security caused by the Snowden leaks, which were 'reported' in the *Sunday Times*. Once again, the government was seen as exploiting national security for ideological purposes, and a compliant press was implicated in regurgitating its exaggerated or fabricated claims.

The framing of Corbyn as a threat to the national interest seemed to colour much of the attendant political debate around issues such as the monarchy, Britain's nuclear deterrent and economic austerity, all of which Corbyn opposed. But its derisory treatment in social media and new news channels represented something more than just an oppositional voice: it marked a profound resistance to the very framing of the debate. At least for a significant and potentially growing minority of news consumers, the story was comprehensively unspun.

Of course, meaningful exposure requires a critical mass audience, one that is large enough to impact on the public consciousness. As we will see, for all the subversive noise generated by news participatory platforms, they remain the preserve of an engaged minority whose reach into the public psyche still cannot compare with that of established news brands. What's more, social media agendas are, on aggregate, still largely 'cued' by mainstream press and broadcasters who have an established and expanding presence on the likes of Twitter and Facebook.

Notes

1. Roger Eckersley letter to Bernard Shaw, 1929, as cited in Conolly, 2009, p. 43.
2. This refers to the internet as essentially public space where communication and participation is subject neither to state nor corporate control.

Chapter 5

Proliferation

Parallel to the spread of participatory platforms, a separate development has empowered a potentially wider section of the audience, and is thought to have advanced the cause of democratic populism far beyond the promise of commercialisation *per se*. Its roots lie in the multichannel era ushered in by the rise of cable and satellite television in the 1970s and 80s. This had critical implications for media ownership because with the end of channel scarcity, the need for scrutiny of ownership practices appeared to be dissolving. According to Bruns, "the power and influence of editors over the news agenda is inversely proportional to the number of available news channels" (2011, p. 119).

With digital platforms, the proliferation of sources dramatically expanded the horizon of choice and gave rise to unparalleled opportunities for audience selectivity (Castells, 2009). Although news consumption has largely consolidated around traditional news brands, recent years have seen the rise of significant new entrants including Huffington Post and BuzzFeed (Newman et al., 2015). This has resulted in an intensification of competitive pressures that have forced editors to pay ever closer attention to the demands of the audience (Lee et al., 2014).

At the same time, online news platforms share few of the space and time constraints characteristic of broadcasting and print, enabling those institutions that have invested significantly in online news to produce a vastly more diverse offering than was ever feasible on traditional platforms. This requires us to think of proliferation not just in terms of a growing number of channels, but also an expanded news space within existing channels. By way of example, during a three-month period starting in November 2013, the BBC produced a total of 13 television news reports on the national security files leaked by former National Security Agency (NSA) contractor Edward Snowden.[1] But in the same period, it published over a hundred in-depth news articles on its website covering the story from a full range of perspectives, many of which were made available alongside raw video footage or recordings of television or radio interviews. This level of coverage is all the more remarkable given that it was in essence a single story that had long since outrun its headline status.

In part IV, we examine news proliferation in more depth and through the conceptual lens of long tail theory in an effort to assess patterns of concentration in online news consumption. Here our concern is chiefly with its impact on the relationship dynamic between editors and audiences. Clearly, the expanding news space has enabled editors to cater to a wider array of niche interests while also providing a framework by which to determine newsgathering priorities and the prominence of particular stories in response to audience metrics. Rather than relying on periodic surveys or focus groups conducted by market research agencies, editors now have access to real-time indicators of audience preferences for particular types of news (Napoli, 2010; Vu, 2014). Aside from the direct responses of users captured by comment threads, the impact of a given article can be measured precisely, instantly and comprehensively at any point in time through a vast array of consumption data. This might include not just the number of people who have accessed an article, but also how they accessed it, when they accessed it, what led them to the article, how long they spent reading it and how active they were in commenting or sharing it with others—not to mention the host of personal user data that may be collected at various points in the news consumption chain, either directly or via partnerships with affiliate sites.

It is inevitable that the constant availability of such rich information about user trends will have a profound influence on story placement (Lee et al., 2014)— all the more so in an environment where the proliferation of news channels and sources has fostered a hyper-competitive struggle to attract audiences. This is critical because, as we saw in the last chapter, responding to audience demand is a hallmark of the way in which the editorial influence of media owners tends to be negated. By giving the readers what they want, journalists and editors are supposedly pandering to the whims of the market rather than proprietors.

So strong is the pull of audience demand in the online domain that journalists are said to suppress their own content preferences in deference to the "agenda of the audience" (Anderson, 2011). In a study that spanned several continents and varied news brands, Boczkowski and Mitchelstein (2013) identified a consistent gap (during periods of relatively normal political activity) between the news content preferences of online journalists and their audiences. In particular, they drew attention to the generalised preferences of journalists for 'hard' news content, particularly in respect of current and public affairs, as compared with users who were generally more inclined towards soft news including celebrity, crime and human interest stories. In the new news environment, this disjuncture is often visible on the home pages of websites that list the most popular stories at any given time alongside those recommended by journalists.

But the assumption that audiences are generally disinclined towards political news content online is problematic for a number of reasons that will be discussed in the following chapter. For now, it's important to stress that the declining influence of editors has not necessarily produced a more diverse news offer after all. On the contrary, as Boczkowski (2010) has shown, "in the age of information plenty, what most consumers get is more of the same" (p. 6). In response to the profound changes in the way that news is both produced and consumed, along with an intensifying climate of uncertainty, journalists and editors are increasingly looking over their shoulders and deferring to the selection decisions of their competitors, as well as what is perceived as the common denominator of user preferences.

This argument is reminiscent of public sphere concerns that have long been voiced in respect of the commercialisation and marketization of the news product. Over recent decades, many have lamented what they saw as a progressive tabloidization of the media—privileging entertainment over information—and undermining the public sphere with a growing tendency towards sensationalism, spectacle and homogeneity (Habermas, 1962; Franklin, 1997; Barnett, 1998). In this brave new media world, marketization has put celebrity, sport and lifestyle above politics, foreign affairs or economic issues, and the capacity for the media to nurture citizenship and hold power to account was eroding in its wake. Some feminists also argued that the rise of 'women's issues' was at least as much to do with ghettoisation as emancipation, and the reinforcement of a socialised gender order (Djerf-Pierre, 2007).

Dissolving the Agenda

In contrast to what has become known as the 'dumbing down' critique, a different set of public sphere concerns focus on the fragmentation of audiences into cultural and partisan niches (Karppinen, 2013). According to this view, the proliferation of channels has indeed produced a more diverse news offer, but not in the way that benefits democracy and citizenship. On the contrary, it has meant that fewer people are actually *exposed* to diverse perspectives as a result of their increasing capacity to self-select their media diets. Cass Sunstein (2001) first articulated this problem by invoking the concept of 'echo chambers' to reflect the polarising and fractious impact of the Daily Me on the public sphere. In a later account (2009), he argued that increasing atomisation of news consumption threatens entrapment of individuals within what he called information 'cocoons'.

This critique has found voice among those who argue that the media are no longer capable of playing an agenda setting role, at least not in the ways that pre-digital studies suggested (Bennett and Iyengar, 2008). Ever since McCombs and Shaw's seminal study at Chapel Hill (1972), decades of agenda setting research has tended to confirm its central conclusions and echo what Bernard Cohen had first hypothesised in 1963: that the press "may not be successful much of the time in telling people what to think, but is stunningly successful in telling its readers what to think about" (Cohen, 1963, p. 13).

Agenda setting thus became the corollary to gatekeeping. Whereas the latter was concerned with the effects of editorial decisions on news output, agenda setting theory interrogated the effects of news output on the public consciousness. Later studies also addressed the media's agenda setting role within policymaking communities, as well as agenda building strategies by sources and journalists (McCombs, 2004). It thus became a key site through which to examine holistically what makes the news *matter*.

But like the gatekeeping tradition, agenda setting studies have tended to overlook or take for granted critical questions of media ownership and ideology. This is the case even after later research found that effects went further than was first thought (e.g. Kim et al., 2002). If the first level of agenda setting research compared the prominence of issues in the news media to the level of importance attached to them by audiences, the second level matched prominent frames or 'attributes' within a given story to the way that issues were understood by audiences. In this sense, agenda setting theory became intimately tied up with news definition; the power to determine not just what issues people think about, but also *how* they think about them.

In spite of this and echoing the sentiments of gatekeeping theory, the media's role in setting the agenda was seen as not only unavoidable but also desirable. It provided a much-needed filter for our window on the world, helping us to focus on and make sense of issues that are *important*. Embedded in the narrative of some agenda sceptics is therefore a concern for the social and cultural consequences of a dissolving public agenda. Rather than democratising the media, the twin forces of proliferation and fragmentation are deeply undermining both citizenship and social cohesion—especially in those countries without a public service media tradition. In the new hyper-competitive media landscape, news providers are driven to become politically partisan in an effort to attract and sustain niche audiences. The commercial success of *Fox News* is held as testament to this supposed new reality in which 'partisan selective exposure' on the part of individuals becomes the key agenda driver (Van Aelst and Walgrave, 2011).

There are broadly three inter-related developments that underpin this view. First, as with gatekeeping theory, agenda sceptics point to the end of channel scarcity (along with the explosion of news and information sources and the lengthening tail of content distribution) as having a diluting effect on the media agenda as a whole. It stands to reason that without a coherent agenda of its own, the mass media can hardly be expected to define or determine a public or policy agenda. Second, agenda sceptics highlight the changing patterns of news consumption—especially in the context of mobile, social media and rolling news channels. According to this view, the real-time news cycle coupled with the growing influence of peers has undermined the role of traditional agenda leaders such as prime time television or national daily newspapers. Finally, the public agenda itself is thought to have dissolved as a result of audience fragmentation and "the continued detachment of individuals from the group-based society" (Bennett and Iyengar, 2008, p. 708). If the media have any agenda setting role at all in this new environment, it is reduced to the level of the individual rather than the aggregate (Shehata and Strömbäck, 2013).

Agenda sceptics thus paint a much more sobering picture compared to the celebrants of networked gatekeeping. But they also share common ground in one important sense: both intellectual camps conceive of audiences as no longer passive recipients of news but active agents of their own agenda, self-selecting their media diet according to their personal and political identities and affiliations. Above all, agenda sceptics and networked gatekeeping theorists share a belief in the erosion of the mass media paradigm according to which major news brands—for better or for worse—play a pivotal role in fostering public debate and defining its boundaries.

This conviction can be traced back to the central tenet of media populism: that commercialisation, liberalisation and proliferation have fostered the inexorable rise of audiences and placed them in the driving seat of news selection. It has also been shared by media policymakers who have presided over an accelerated pace of ownership deregulation since the early 1990s (Doyle, 2002; Freedman, 2008). In the US and elsewhere, the narrative of media populism—bolstered by technological utopianism—has led the deregulatory charge. According to this logic, the market speaks for itself and new technologies are delivering a promised land of plurality and diversity. Rather than dictate from on high, it should be left to media firms "to determine the wants of their audiences through the normal mechanisms of the marketplace" (Fowler and Brenner, 1982). Anything else risks descent into paternalism or worse, an incursion on media freedom and speech rights. The underlying assumption is that media firms operating in a marketplace will always respond exclusively to the content preferences of consumers, rather than that of their owners. Indeed, its logic implies that the content preferences of owners are predicated on those of consumers, and their interests entirely consonant with maximising consumer welfare.

Note

1. Data based on case study research conducted for this book. Specifically, key word searches were cross-referenced between Google and the online and broadcasting news archives held at the British Library.

Chapter 6

Endurance and Resurgence

A number of political communication scholars have sought to reconcile the apparent waning of a unified public agenda with a lingering sense that news producers still have a crucial influence over the *policy* agenda (e.g. Kepplinger, 2007). According to Davis (2003), for instance, among the multiple fragmented audiences and agendas is one that provides a forum for the negotiation of power among elites, in which professional journalists are not just moderators but active participants. Here agenda control manifests not through exclusion of particular types of content so much as exclusion of particular types of audience. It is reminiscent of a tiered conception of news proliferation, according to which exposure to diverse and critical perspectives becomes the preserve of an elite public sphere (Bourdieu, 1998). This nuanced line of critical thinking draws our attention to the fact that while audiences may be fragmenting, not all fragments are created equal, and this has important implications for the capacity of publics to engage meaningfully with policymaking. But it still takes for granted the notion that a news or public agenda in any generalizable sense no longer exists, or at least not to the extent that it once did. And this is the underlying assumption that I think demands closer scrutiny.

For a start, actual examples of popular news stories that have emerged and spread in ways that circumvent professional news institutions are few and far between. Cases like the Karen Klein story (the school bus chaperone and victim of intense bullying referred to in the previous chapter) are anecdotal and the stories themselves tend to be short-lived, rarely having the kind of sustained resonance that the theory of networked gatekeeping suggests (Asur et al., 2011). Even the new communicative spaces opened up by the so-called Arab Spring turned out to be ephemeral in a way that casts doubt over their capacity to nurture progressive social change (Christensen, 2011).

What's more, research has tended to support the view that most of the news circulating on content sharing platforms and social networking sites is produced by professional news institutions, and an overwhelming majority of these belong to the so-called legacy media—mainstream news brands that predate the internet (Shoemaker and Vos, 2009; Abell, 2011; Asur et al., 2011; Newman, 2011). Even one study that drew positive conclusions about the waning of an 'elite hold' over the news agenda at large, nevertheless found that "a few elite actors are in control of the majority of source influence throughout the entire network of traditional media and citizen media blog links" (Meraz, 2009, p. 691).

This makes sense because although online news consumers are relatively active in the sharing of content, very few actually engage regularly in production: blogging, reporting or uploading of content specifically for a news audience (Boczkowski and Mitchelstein, 2013). Even those that do participate in the amateur blogosphere tend to take their lead from content produced by legacy media (Hindman, 2008), just as those who contribute to comment threads on articles are limited to a purely reactive role in news participation.

It also makes sense because producing and marketing a daily international news service is still an expensive cost centre on any platform. In spite of struggling business models, established news brands have had the capacity and scale to invest and innovate in digital news delivery. As we will see in chapter 14, this barrier to market entry is reinforced by Google's news search algorithm, which emphasises the volume of stories produced by any given source in its determination of page ranking (among other criteria that favour bigger players).

But there is something else at play here that is less obvious and has drawn less attention, but seems to be a major driver of consolidation in the online news market: brand loyalty. This is odd because public trust in professional journalism has consistently ranked among the lowest of public service professions (Ipsos MORI, 2015). Yet in the online domain, established news brands seem to signal a degree of news authority that cuts above the near-infinite horizon of news sources. In a survey of online news consumers across nine countries in 2013, the vast majority of respondents in all countries said that they tended to access news from websites that they know and trust (Levy and Newman, 2013). This translates into a surprisingly small number of news sources, with the same researchers noting in their 2014 study that "although the number of sources available is almost infinite, the average user tends to access fewer than three sources each week, with the British and Japanese using just over two" (Levy and Newman, 2014, p. 42).

Faced with an ever-expanding sea of information noise, rumour, opinion and spin, it is perhaps not surprising that users gravitate towards the professional and the familiar. News organisations may not be trusted in many contexts, but they are at least recognised as genuine news providers. Researchers have coined this phenomenon 'gatekeeping trust', defined as trust that "the news media selects stories based on judgments of the relative importance of social problems" (Pingree et al., 2013, p. 351). In other words, it is a form of trust intimately connected to both news selection and agenda setting power. Journalists may not be trusted to tell a story accurately or fairly, but gatekeeping trust signals a prior recognition that the stories they do tell are at least worthy of telling.

In a fascinating experimental study conducted in 2014, a sample of students was unwittingly exposed to a set of news issues artificially presented either as stories carried by mainstream news brands, personal blog entries, reports by recognised non-governmental organisations (NGOs), or crosswords with an associated news or gaming site brand (Carpentier, 2014). What the researchers found was that the association of a major news brand (*New York Times* or *Washington Post*) with any of the issues was likely to cue relative judgements of issue importance. So for instance, participants exposed to a particular story with a recognised newspaper brand were more likely to consider the issue important compared to those exposed to an exact copy of the same story presented as a personal blog entry or NGO report.

This phenomenon casts doubt over the supposed erosion of the mass media paradigm when it comes to news consumption. For all the talk of multi-sourcing by policymakers and commercial media lobbyists (see chapter 16), there clearly remains a small number of major news brands that reach across fragmented audiences and thus continue to provide a potentially far-reaching lever of agenda control. Indeed, the growing competitive and commercial pressures on newsrooms may have *increased* the tendency for editors to enforce the bottom line when it comes to appeasing advertisers or deferring to owners (Fenton, 2010). This was certainly the sentiment captured in 2014 by Peter Oborne, former political editor of the *Daily Telegraph*. According to his published resignation letter, Oborne quit the role after alleged pressure to curtail coverage of the tax scandal embroiling HSBC, one of the paper's biggest advertisers. Significantly, he pointed the finger not just at his former bosses, but at what he perceived as a more general malaise in journalist autonomy:

> It is not only the *Telegraph* that is at fault here. The past few years have seen the rise of shadowy executives who determine what truths can and what truths can't be conveyed across the mainstream media.
>
> (Oborne, 2015)

But it was Ben Bagdikian who was the first to draw a link specifically between media ownership and news selection. In the *Media Monopoly*, he argued that ownership is intimately connected to the power to prioritise or marginalise, a power distinct from the kind of hands-on control associated with press barons:

> Most owners and editors no longer brutalize the news with the heavy hand dramatized in movies like "Citizen Kane" [. . .] More common is something more subtle, more professionally respectable, and, in some respects, more effective: the power to treat some subjects accurately but briefly, to treat other subjects accurately but in depth, or in the conventional options every medium has of taking its own initiatives, carefully avoiding some subjects and enthusiastically pursuing others.
>
> (Bagdikian, 2000 [1983], p. 16)

In contrast to earlier gatekeeping theories, Bagdikian critiqued what was often taken for granted as a normal and necessary function of journalism; to filter and distil information into accessible news formats. Baker (1997) argued similarly that the commercial interests of media owners are never straightforwardly synonymous with the demands of the audience. As such, in contrast to the policymaking consensus and the narrative of media populism, the commercial logic of 'giving the audience what it wants' is not and has never been the exclusive driver of editorial decisions in the media marketplace. It is clearly constrained, for instance, by the fact that certain stories may have a negative 'external' impact on the interests of owners or advertisers irrespective—or indeed *because* of—their newsworthy appeal.

This suggests a far more complex picture of the drivers, triggers and incentives that shape editorial decisions compared to that invoked by either media populists or dumbing down theorists. We can imagine, for instance, a whole range of commercial considerations—often conflicting—that may impact on a decision of whether or not to run with any given story. Aside from the desire to keep major advertisers on side, proprietors might also consider trade-offs between satisfying readers on the one hand and policymakers on the other, perhaps with a view to leveraging influence over policies that have direct commercial implications for their media or wider interests. By a similar token, proprietors may be willing to sustain loss-making titles because of the associated brand prestige (especially in the 'serious' news space) or because of the special access it provides to politicians and policymakers—both of which may offer indirect but potentially lucrative returns in respect of wider commercial interests.

Baker (1997) and others (e.g. Garnham, 2000) have also pointed to a number of peculiar features of media products that mean that media markets do not tend to operate in the way that standard economic models predict. For instance, media products tend to be non-rivalrous to the extent that consumption by one person does not reduce the supply available to others. This leads to the creation of artificial scarcities in the form of box office sales, copyright and subscriptions that can result in potentially significant unmet audience demand for particular media products. These products are also characterised by a relatively high degree of novelty value, making demand inherently difficult to predict. The net effect is that media markets are relatively prone to concentration as firms seek to combine in order to offset the risks associated with novelty. Where competition remains intense, the risks of novelty are offset by producing more of what is known to be popular at the expense of content that is unexpected. Competitor firms thus end up relying on formulae and precedent, imitating each other's content offer (Boczkowski, 2010), while latent or manifest audience demand for 'different' content remains unfulfilled.

As Boczkowski and others have shown, the development of digital news has, if anything, intensified those characteristics that are said to make the market an insufficient means of fostering media diversity, especially at the level of exposure (Napoli, 2011b). The phenomenon of personalised news in particular seems to work against the production of content that is *surprising*. In chapter 9, we will discuss the implications of personalised news for gatekeeping practices and agenda effects in more depth. For now, it is worth stressing that surprising or serendipitous news content has special resonance for the public sphere concept central to deliberative democracy, which calls for the *intersection* as opposed to just the availability of diverse viewpoints (Curran, 2011). But it is also foundational to the marketplace of ideas upon which more pluralist visions of democracy are based. According to this logic, media consumers must be exposed to diverse viewpoints in order to be adequately informed as citizens at the ballot box. Both these sets of arguments tend to stress the social benefits or 'positive externalities' associated with content that challenges preconceptions and that audiences "would not have chosen in advance" (Karppinen, 2013, p. 67).

Another problem is that audiences themselves have always constituted media products in their own right, and are systematically commodified, packaged and sold to advertisers in ever more explicit and intrusive ways (Bermejo, 2009). According to this view, far from reflecting audience empowerment, the growing responsiveness of news producers to market research or analytics is really about the ever-greater *control* of audiences (and by extension, the news agenda) exercised through that process. Implicit here is the notion that rather than simply responding to audience demand, commercial media producers, along with advertisers, are engaged in a complex feedback loop in which audience preferences are reinforced and to some degree shaped by the demands of the market. These conditions may also hold for public service providers who are entrapped within the logic of markets as a result of intensifying competition with commercial players (Murdock, 1982; Born, 2003).

But what does all this mean for the phenomenon of networked gatekeeping and the so-called new era of minimal effects? As we have seen, both of these schools of thought share an implicit assumption that owners and editors no longer hold sway over the agenda in any meaningful sense, and that the very existence of a generalised news or public agenda is increasingly open to question. In the following chapter, we interrogate further the assumption that news selection is increasingly driven by the demands of the user-audience, for better or for worse.

Chapter 7

Two-Sided Preferences

Even within mainstream professional news institutions not all editors have been susceptible to the growing pressures of audience selection. Gans (2004), for instance, found that print newspaper editors routinely ignored audience feedback on editorial choices, whether expressed qualitatively in letters to the editor or quantitatively through market research data. Even in the digital environment, some editors and journalists express disdain for the wisdom of the crowd when it comes to editorial choices. As former *New York Times* editor Douglas Kellner remarked: "We don't let metrics dictate our assignments and play, because we believe readers come to us for our judgment, not the judgment of the crowd. We're not 'American Idol'" (Peters, 2010).

What does seem to be happening, however, is that *more* editors are pandering to the selective choices of audiences than was the case when they had much less accurate and more infrequent indicators of audience preferences, and faced less immediate competitive pressures. In other words, digital media have dramatically intensified the rate and extent of newsroom responses to audience feedback. But aside from normative perspectives of whether this represents commodification or democratisation of the news agenda, the apparent rise of audience sovereignty requires closer scrutiny.

For a start, audience preferences are not fixed but subject to dynamic shifts, not least in response to crises or varying intensity of political activity (Boczkowski and Mitchelstein, 2013). What's more, if I have a tendency to select celebrity stories over political news, this does not necessarily mean that I am more interested in celebrity news than politics. It may be that I find the issues or language of political news stories on offer not particularly engaging, resonant or accessible, or written from a gendered point of view that I do not relate to. Or it may be because I am more exposed to celebrity stories because they tend to rank more highly on some of the most popular news feeds and aggregators.

News analytics also fail to take account of news consumption across digital and traditional platforms. Perhaps I tend to consume non-political news on my mobile phone or tablet via short, frequent updates when I am waiting for a train or drinking a coffee. But I might opt to watch political news coverage on television during the evening, and devote comparatively more time and attention to it. Television is, after all, still by far the most popular news medium in most parts of the world (Open Society Foundations, 2014).

Of course, none of this proves that online news consumers do *not* have a general preference for say, celebrity over political news stories. Consumer market research often tries to fill the gaps by combining actual consumption data with survey responses that give a broader picture of news consumption habits. But when we look at what kind of content people *say* they prefer in response to survey questionnaires, the picture can become even murkier.

The Value of Importance

In 2013, the Reuters Institute for Journalism based at the University of Oxford asked over 11,000 people across nine countries which types of news are most important to them (Levy and Newman, 2013). The category of entertainment and celebrity news was the lowest ranked throughout the sample. What's more, this was relatively constant across the spectrum between heavy online news consumers and those who consume news from traditional sources only. In the UK, where entertainment and celebrity news attracted the most positive responses compared to other countries in the sample, it was still ranked only 10th out of 11 categories (ahead of arts and culture news). The biggest differences were observed in the gender and age gaps with a stronger preference for entertainment and celebrity news expressed by women and younger people. But even here, women ranked entertainment and celebrity news as the eighth most important genre with just four categories below it—science, business, sport and arts. Young people were even less enthusiastic, valuing only business and arts news less than entertainment.

Surprisingly, this strikingly low value placed on celebrity and entertainment by all segments of the audience was not highlighted anywhere in the actual report. Instead, the authors merely drew attention to this fact:

> Political news is much more valued overall, but it is clear that entertainment news is much more polarised. People either love it or hate it. Interest is driven by women far more than by men and by the under 45s.
>
> (Levy and Newman, 2013, p. 35)

So what's going on here? Part of the explanation may lie in the so-called social desirability bias that can distort the data collected from such questionnaires. This means that rather than giving their *actual* preference or views in response to survey questions, respondents often give the answers they think are more socially acceptable. The obvious explanation here would be that people in general *do* prefer celebrity and entertainment news over political news, but they don't like to admit it.

Yet this explanation would be inadequate, partly because of the particular way the question was phrased. In asking respondents which types of news they consider *important*, the researchers were addressing a specific type of preference, one that is concerned with the kind of news thought to be *beneficial* (to society at large) as opposed to just enjoyable. It's akin to the difference between asking people which kind of news they would like to see more of and which kind of news they actually consume more of. In this context, there would be no inherent contradiction if I express a general preference for political over entertainment/celebrity news, but choose to consume more of the latter in my actual news diet.

In phrasing the question in this way, consumers were effectively being asked about the kind of content they value as *citizens* rather than as consumers, and there is good reason to believe that these represent two different faces of media value (Sunstein, 2000). Consumer media value is inherently private, individualistic and instantaneous. We are thus more likely to be willing to pay for it directly and at the point of consumption. But citizen-valued media benefits society more broadly. It amounts to *public* value and may accrue over time and cumulatively through the sustained availability of certain types of content. Although we may be less willing to pay for this content at the point of consumption, we may be more inclined to demand it from public service or community media, even if we don't consume much of it ourselves. In his seminal essay on 'Television and the Public Interest', Cass Sunstein put it thus:

> In short, there is a pervasive difference between what people want in their capacity as viewers (or "consumers of broadcasting") and what they want in their capacity as citizens. Both preferences and values are a function of the setting in which people find themselves; they are emphatically a product of social role. In these circumstances, it would be wrong to think that the choices of individual viewers are definitive, or definitional, with respect to the question of what individuals really prefer.
>
> (Sunstein, 2000, p. 520)

It seems plausible that owners, editors, journalists, market research consultants and policymakers have long been preoccupied with only one half of the audience demand equation. Consumer demand is certainly more easily captured by ratings and news analytics, and clearly offers less risk from a commercial point of view. But this preoccupation has nevertheless marginalised the question of *citizen* demand for particular types of media content and produced a kind of groupthink that has distorted debates about media policy, particularly in the context of ownership and plurality. It has also distracted attention away from the role that media producers can play in *shaping* audience preferences, and the way that consumer market survey questions can be framed to trigger expected responses and reinforce prior assumptions about audience tastes.

But we should avoid overstating the distinction between consumer and citizen type preferences. Clearly, there is much overlap between them when it comes to news, and it would be an oversimplification to assume that any citizen-oriented content is inherently non-commercial. Witness the launch in 2014 of a dedicated news investigations unit at BuzzFeed, a website predominantly aimed at young people. With a business model based on content that has maximum shareability across social media platforms, it's perhaps not surprising that it began with a focus on entertainment, gossip and 'weird' news stories, packaging them into formats like 'listicles', with multimedia content that maximises viral potential (Klein, 2013). But its recent shift into the serious (and much more expensive) news space seems at odds with some of the prevailing assumptions about the kind of online news that is popular with young people in particular. Yet as BuzzFeed's founder and CEO recently remarked, "News is the heart and soul of any great media company [. . .] News might not be as big a business as entertainment, but news is the best way to have a big impact on the world" (Rieder, 2015).

What this suggests is that the return on investment in expensive newsgathering is not necessarily measured in clicks or likes, but a less tangible and potentially more far-reaching impact on brand value. This is because serious news may well matter more to people than audience metrics or survey data suggest. If I consume more entertainment news than political news, it does not necessarily mean that I *value* the former more than the latter. As the blogger and *Washington Post* columnist Ezra Klein (2013) pointed out:

> Brand matters quite a bit, as does the underlying type of content. That's one reason both Gawker and BuzzFeed are expanding aggressively into long form articles. Sacrificing your brand for more social page views often isn't a good business play.

In one respect, with its rapid growth and new emphasis on original newsgathering, Buzzfeed clearly marks a diversification of the online news market and thus, a dilution of concentrated media power. But its move into the serious news space also suggests that new journalism business models are not simply reducible to following a click-driven agenda. In terms of news selection, arguments that sound the death knell of the owner-editor-journalist-gatekeeper thus seem premature, and overstate the degree to which their agenda power has been usurped. By extension, the supposed dissolution of mass media power and of 'aggregate' agenda effects should be treated with caution. The digital news landscape is evolving rapidly: the nature of news content is changing, along with the ways that it is packaged, distributed and consumed; new entrants are gaining ground, and some traditional brands are ceding it. But when it comes to agenda power, the tables have not quite turned—and are not quite turning—in ways that make the user-audience sovereign and consign 'old' questions of gatekeeping and agenda setting power to the dustbin of history.

Conclusion

I have argued that the narrative of dispersal is adopted in different ways by both networked gatekeeping theorists and agenda sceptics. Although in many ways oppositional, these schools of thought collectively paint a picture of news institutions increasingly sensitised and responsive to audience demand and, accordingly, omit little or any place for media ownership as an enduring instrument of agenda control.

We have also seen how these arguments bear some resemblance to earlier narratives of media populism and tabloidization, respectively. In the digital environment, they have taken on new force, and have been widely adopted by an unlikely alliance of activists, scholars, commercial media lobbyists and policymakers, the latter two in efforts to rebut calls for greater regulation of media ownership. But they do not account for the role in which mainstream media organisations may continue to play in both *shaping* audience demand to fit a highly cost-efficient news product, as well as suppressing demand for news that is inherently more risky and, potentially, subversive.

This is because the core assumption underpinning narratives of dispersal rests on shaky foundations. For a start, it does not take adequate account of the enduring and expanding reach of a small number of major news brands in the online sphere. Although the door may be opening to one or two significant new entrants like Buzzfeed and Huffington Post, this does not necessarily mark an expansion of the news agenda or even a pluralisation of news voices, especially given cutbacks and closures in the legacy media. Above all, narratives of dispersal tend to wrongly equate the content choices of audiences—as measured in survey and/or analytics data—with content *preferences* in a general sense. The role that professional producers may continue to play in shaping the news agenda is thus implicitly or explicitly negated without sufficient evidence or theoretical foundation.

When it comes to questions of media ownership and agenda control, this leaves us in some very muddy waters. Clearly, both the gatekeeping and agenda setting power of large media groups is profoundly altered in the new information environment. News consumers have access to a widening array of news sources and at the very least, they are intervening at the level of *distribution* in ways that suggest the owner or editor is no longer the exclusive arbiter of news salience. On the other hand, original newsgathering is still largely the preserve of professional institutions, and newsroom pressures may be fostering greater journalistic conformity to an organisational or institutionally defined agenda. In the following chapter, this picture will be further problematized when we examine the emergence of a new type of gatekeeper altogether: the digital intermediary.

Part III

Transferral

Chapter 8

Directing the Flow

The War over Words

It was a devastating display of invincible bargaining power. In August 2013, the German government approved draft legislation granting an extension to the intellectual property rights afforded to the press. Specifically, it required digital intermediaries to obtain a license from publishers in order to feature cached content from their articles in search listings or news feeds (Pfanner, 2012). But a law intended to make Google pay for the use of such snippets quickly became a law that forced publishers to agree *not* to be paid.

Nevertheless, for a brief moment at least, the law's enactment was a broadly successful and long-awaited outcome for German publishers after years of intensive lobbying and advocacy. Theirs was by now a familiar tale of industrial woe. Once the dominant purveyors of news and information, with control over both production and distribution points in the supply chain, newspapers had become the undisputed underdogs in the new titanic struggle for eyeballs and advertisers. The stratospheric rise of the new media monopolies had been driven in no small measure by the near-wholesale migration of advertisers from print media to online pay-per-click campaigns, decimating the business models of newspapers along the way. As if to rub salt into the wound, digital intermediaries now seemed to be extracting additional value from the unauthorised use of their copyrighted news content.

For the bill's advocates, this was not just a problem for publishers. Because digital intermediaries do not, in the main, produce original news themselves, the future of the free press as a vital contribution to democratic life was at stake. If audiences had long since become accustomed to getting their news and information for free, and advertisers increasingly demanded the kind of traffic volumes that only large intermediaries like Google or Facebook could offer, the burning question became who will pay for journalism in the public interest, beyond the state or private philanthropy. Long-form and investigative reporting—a traditional pillar of watchdog journalism—was especially under threat in this brave new world of news.

The ancillary copyright law—or *Leistungsschutzrecht* as it became known—was thus greeted by publishers as a token nod to their suffering in the face of technological disruption and monopoly power. But for Google and a number of information rights activists, the bill's passing marked "a black day for the internet in Germany" (Schmerer, 2012). They argued that the new rules were at odds with the free flow of information and the internet commons, undermining innovation and creating dangerous precedents that threatened to erode fair use exemptions to copyright.

In the end, neither the hopes of publishers nor the fears of intermediaries were realised. Prior to the law's enactment, Google simply informed news publishers that it was reversing the default opt-out for inclusion of snippets in its listings, with the effect that publishers now had to opt *in* by agreeing to a royalty-free license. But in the final hours the bill was changed to allow the 'smallest' use of text excerpts in search listings without a license, precipitating chaos and confusion over what the smallest actually amounted to (Kucharczyk, 2013). Amid the ensuing uncertainty, VG Media—a collecting society representing some of Germany's largest news publishers—sued Google for what it claimed was the continued unlicensed use of its members' content, in violation of the new law.

Google's response was to immediately stop including *any* snippets of text in the listings of sites represented by VG Media. But the effect on publishers was catastrophic. Germany's largest news publisher—Axel Springer—announced soon after that it was issuing Google a royalty-free license to start including the snippets again, after traffic to its websites plummeted following its exclusion from Google's news listings (Axel Springer, 2014). A number of other publishers promptly followed suit, as it became clear that those who refused to play by Google's rules faced the prospect of banishment to a cyber-wilderness. The very companies that had lobbied tirelessly for the new law were now effectively rendering it redundant.

But the farcical episode didn't end there. In 2015, VG Media submitted a formal complaint to the German competition authority, this time arguing that by refusing to use snippets by publishers who did not agree to a royalty-free license, Google was abusing its dominant market position. It did not take long for the regulator to dismiss the complaint out of hand on the simple logic that you can't *force* someone to use your copyrighted content in order to get paid for it (Bundeskartellamt, 2015).

Other European countries have pursued divergent paths in dealing with this issue. In France, for instance, publishers agreed to lay their claims to rest after Google promised a fund for supporting digital innovation in journalism (Stupp, 2014). In Spain, on the other hand, legislators passed a much tougher version of Germany's ancillary copyright law in 2014, making it illegal for publishers to opt in and extending copyright restrictions to cover *any* amount of copyrighted text or hyperlinks. Google's response in that case was to simply shut down its Spanish news service altogether (Google, 2014).

Perhaps in anticipation of these problems, the issue has gained little traction among either publishers or policymakers in many other countries, including the UK. Nevertheless, it has played into a wider narrative that is carrying increasing weight in media policy debates. Its overarching message is that far from dispersing among the crowd, the market and gatekeeping power once wielded by traditional media has *transferred* into the hands of digital behemoths like Google and Facebook. At its heart is a concern for the unchecked power of Silicon Valley that has enabled internet giants to circumvent local laws, notably in the areas of privacy, corporation tax and copyright. But above all, it reignites age-old concerns about the potential for major media corporations to control information and, ultimately, thought. It does so in a context and language that is deeply fashionable and resonant with wider discursive themes that suggest the digital revolution is not so much about emancipation, as a *change of guard.*

Open and Closed

But what exactly is the extent and direction of control exercised by intermediaries when it comes to the news agenda? The immediate answer to this question is simple: we don't really know. In markets that are as dynamic and rapidly evolving as the technology that drives them, algorithmic codes are competitive jewels for internet companies who, unsurprisingly, do not tend to disclose their ingredients in any great detail. This has presented something of an empirical black hole for scholars, regulators and activists seeking to interrogate the nature and extent of intermediary power over the information environment. Many have resorted to theorising about the *possible* ways in which intermediaries can manipulate information flows, as Robin Mansell warned in 2014:

> Search activities may result in referrals to specific content through corporate tie-ins leading to cross selling of products and services. The intermediaries' interest is in aggregating content and shaping traffic by managing agreements between content providers, advertisers and network operators. When intermediaries close off or steer their customers through subscription access to news outlets, for instance, then no matter how trustworthy they are, or how much they promise to protect their customers' privacy, they are managing the content that their consumers are most likely to see. Platform providers can screen out desirable content without the citizen's knowledge just as they can screen out undesirable content. It should not simply be commercial operators that decide what is and is not desirable.
>
> (Mansell, 2014)

Yet the very notion of 'closing off' is inimical to the corporate ethos and strategy of companies like Google, whose business empire was founded on the open architecture of the internet and the unencumbered flow of content across the network. As Tim Wu (2010) observed, Google is a monopoly like no other. Its fortune was built not on the foundations of ownership and control, but rather "a set of ideas— or more precisely, a set of open protocols designed by government researchers" (Wu, 2010, p. 280). Its empire occupies the valley between the twin peaks of telecoms and content. It is wholly dependent on both, but not significantly invested in either. Without any stake in the intellectual property that sustains content and technology businesses, or the network infrastructure that underpins the telecoms industries, Google can be squeezed-in theory, at least-by all sides.

This is because most telecoms and media companies still operate according to the 'closed' logic of the old economy; a logic based on proprietary code, corporate aggrandizement and network control. Google, on the other hand, has always peddled the rhetoric of openness, collaboration and interconnection synonymous with the new economy and the internet commons. The same can be said to varying degrees of social networking sites like Facebook and Twitter, content aggregators like Yahoo, as well as online retail sites like eBay and Amazon that provide consumer-to-consumer and business-to-consumer services. They are intermediaries precisely because they *intermediate* in some way between content providers, network operators and users. They may not do it purely on the basis of point-to-point interconnection in the way that a search engine functions (for instance, if they host third-party content in full). But their primary service is best described as one of facilitating and optimising the distribution of content across the network.

Of course, this distinction is rapidly blurring as communications industries become increasingly vertically integrated. But for now, it is still useful to think of the new media ecosystem as essentially made up of those whose core business is either content (publishers, studios, record labels, software and hardware companies, etc.), network operation (internet service providers, mobile operators, telecoms, etc.), or intermediation (search engines, social networking sites, aggregators, auction sites, etc.). Not surprisingly, those who fear for the future of the internet commons have tended to side with the latter—in spite of the enormous monopoly power amassed by the likes of Google—against the closed world order represented by content owners and network operators alike.

And this is perhaps the most unique and puzzling characteristic of intermediaries—Google especially, with its academic roots as a side project of PhD students at Stanford University and its long-standing commitment to the openness ethos. Although it has faced sustained attack from 'disrupted' industries like news publishers, Google has managed to maintain its reputation among many open rights activists and digital evangelists as a big friendly giant. In a paradox that sometimes verges on doublespeak, it is thought to have secured its monopoly power precisely because it embraced and led "the openness movement," its commercial success a product of a very non-commercial philosophy. As Wu put it:

> At some level, the apostles of openness aspire to nothing less than social transformation. They idealise a postscarcity society, one in which the assumption of limited resources dictating traditional economic theory are overturned, a world in which most goods and services are free or practically free, thereby liberating the individual to pursue self-expression and self-actualisation as an activity of primary importance.
>
> (Wu, 2010, p. 294)

The Limits of Neutrality

Such sentiments, embodied by Google's corporate motto of 'don't be evil' and directly opposed to the narrative of transferral, have risen to the fore of debates over net neutrality—a principle based on the idea that there is a strong public interest in maintaining the neutrality of any communications network "as between competing content and applications" (Wu, 2003, p. 141). If internet service providers (ISPs), for instance, are able to charge websites higher fees for the use of certain applications like video, or implement tier pricing based on different levels of bandwidth allocation, this would amount to what proponents of net neutrality call 'content discrimination'. Although its undesirable effects have largely been considered by policymakers in terms of distorting competition (Curran et al., 2012), it also threatens to inhibit innovation (Lessig, 2001); foster 'private censorship' (Marsden, 2014); and place a differentiating filter on the kind of news and information that users are exposed to, or can readily access.

Not surprisingly, one of the most vociferous advocates of net neutrality regulation when it first emerged as a public policy issue was none other than Google itself. In 2006, a senior policy counsel stated the company's line explicitly:

> Google believes that forcing people and companies to get permission from, and pay special fees to, the phone and cable companies to connect with one another online is fundamentally counter to the freedom and innovation that have defined the Internet.
>
> (McLaughlin, 2006)

In the end, it was to be another nine years before the US Federal Communications Commission (FCC) formally imposed net neutrality rules. But by this time Google had long since lowered its profile in the net neutrality debate, preferring to lobby the FCC and lawmakers directly (Jopson and Waters, 2015). Some have speculated that the company's silence was part of a strategy to ensure that its ultimate success looked more like a victory for the open rights movement than a victory for itself (McMillan, 2015). The FCC's decision certainly seemed to suggest that it considered telecoms and cable companies the only gatekeepers requiring regulation in the digital domain (McCarthy, 2015).

This is odd, because Google itself actively discriminates between content arguably in ways that extend far beyond the capacity of ISPs. Indeed, Google may already have breached many of the new net neutrality rules it helped to bring about, at least in spirit if not the letter. Since 2010, the company has been the target of ongoing antitrust investigations by the European Union that began over allegations that its search algorithm actively discriminates against rival online shopping services, and has since expanded in response to similar complaints of abuses through its mobile app platform as well as map services (Davies, 2015).

On the other side of the coin, Google pays network operators in order to ensure that its services are afforded preferential treatment. In 2014, for instance, it paid

Apple $1 billion to retain its status as the default search function on Apple's mobile operating system (Rosenblatt and Satariano, 2016). It also regularly enters into negotiated deals with ISPs in order to secure a dedicated path into their networks (Brodkin, 2015). Although such deals do not amount to paying for higher speeds directly, they can enhance the performance of Google's services and afford a structural advantage over competing services (McMillan, 2014). After all, at the heart of the net neutrality principle is the idea of access *equality*. If content providers or intermediaries are able to pay for preferential treatment from ISPs, that distorts the level playing field even if the traffic speeds of other content and services are not actually slowed down as a result.

And here's where things start to get hazy. On closer inspection, Google's silence on net neutrality during the build-up to the new ruling was not absolute, nor was its support for regulatory oversight unequivocal. Shortly before the new rules were announced, Google wrote a stern letter to the FCC demanding that it rein in the scope of its regulation to exclude what it called 'interconnection' agreements between ISPs and 'edge providers' like itself (Brodkin, 2015). This was based on a somewhat obscure argument that the FCC would, by including such deals within its framework, give legal authority to the principle of charging both end users *and* content or edge providers for access to the network. It threatened to legitimise what Google called 'double recovery'—ISPs getting paid twice for providing the same service—and the FCC promptly amended its plans accordingly.

Let's pause for a moment. Google's impassioned public support for net neutrality back in 2006 was based on a clearly stated conviction: companies should not be forced to pay or get permission from network operators to connect with end users. This is what Google believed ran "fundamentally counter to the freedom and innovation that have defined the internet" (McLaughlin, 2006). Yet here it was, in the eleventh hour of the FCC's ruling, demanding that companies be left alone to *continue* paying for preferential access, provided such payments are negotiated in ad hoc deals rather than set in the form of tier pricing.

The really puzzling thing is that the FCC's original plans allowed it to intervene only in response to complaints from content or edge providers of unfair treatment by ISPs. They did not prohibit ad hoc interconnection deals or provide a blank cheque for regulatory meddling. So why would Google not want the FCC to intervene in negotiated deals with ISPs and network operators, only at the behest of content or edge providers like themselves? One plausible explanation is that Google does not want to be put on an equal footing with competing services—which is exactly what the FCC would seek to ensure under the new rules. Although it may be structurally unintegrated and undefended (Wu, 2010), Google wields enormous market power by virtue of its substantial cash reserves and brand clout. The billion-dollar deal with Apple in 2014 certainly suggests that Google is willing to pay—and pay big—in order to secure preferential access to customers on networks that it does not itself control (and incidentally, we only know about that deal because of a court disclosure that Google's lawyers tried very hard to suppress). We therefore have to at least consider the possibility that

Google wants to deploy its weight in order to negotiate access deals that secure its dominant presence across the internet, without the interference of regulators. Such a prospect may not fit with long-standing perceptions of Google as a champion of openness and open rights. But as we will see, neither does Google's gatekeeping and censoring practices in a wide range of other contexts.

Putting the User First

Clearly, any kind of divergence from net neutrality principles has special significance for news agendas. The less freely, openly and equally content flows across the network, the more users' exposure to information becomes subject to certain controls. But Google is an intermediary rather than a content provider. Its preferential access would not be much of a problem provided that Google's own services—particularly search—did not distort the user's exposure or access to content in ways that run contrary to the values of openness, plurality and diversity—values that the corporation has always aligned itself with. But this is exactly what many critics have accused Google of doing.

In order to get come to grips with the substance of these critiques, we need to be clear about what the function of search does in the digital mediascape. As web pages proliferated during the 1990s, the act of crawling or surfing via hyperlinks became an increasingly laborious and inefficient means of finding content. The very purpose of search engines was thus to redress this problem and make it easier for users to get to where they wanted to go. This purpose in itself presupposes the need for some kind of filtering mechanism that—in response to a search query—sifts through billions of web pages in order to select, rank order and display those that are relevant to the user's search. The important question then becomes not whether the likes of Google engage in filtering practices, but *how* and with what *effects*.

For its part, Google has always maintained that its algorithms are designed exclusively with a view to maximising the user experience, highlighting the content that he or she is trying to find, not the content that Google—or any of its advertisers and partners—wants them to find. The underlying logic seems obvious enough: it is ultimately in the interests of intermediaries, as well as their advertisers and partners, to maximise user volume and engagement. And that can only be achieved by designing and developing algorithms exclusively with the end user's interests in mind. This notion of putting the user first was vividly captured by the testimony of Eric Schmidt, Google's chairman, to a US Senate committee in 2011:

> At Google, we've always focused on putting consumers—our users—first. For example, we aim to provide relevant answers as quickly as possible, and our product innovation and engineering talent deliver results that we believe users like, in a world where competition is only a click away.
>
> (Schmidt, 2011)

But there are a number of conceptual problems with this argument, not least that it presupposes users are in the driving seat of search queries, and that Google's algorithm is designed merely to seek and respond as opposed to guide, tailor or even censor. Above all, the rhetoric of 'user first' obscures the potentially subtle ways in which the interests of the user are both *interpreted* as well as *shaped* in line with commercial exigencies. Prior to Schmidt's Senate testimony in 2011, Google's search algorithm had already started on a process of adaptation that was making it increasingly interventionist in guiding users towards particular types of content. Schmidt himself told the *Wall Street Journal* in 2010 that "I actually think most people don't want Google to answer their questions. They want Google to tell them what they should be doing next" (Jenkins, 2010).

This is clearly a very different sentiment to that conveyed in Schmidt's Senate testimony a year later. Although a more interventionist search function is not necessarily in conflict with the principle of putting users first, the shift from 'answering questions' to 'telling people what to do next' clearly signals a profound change in the order of power assumed over the flow of news and information. According to Eli Pariser (2011), this change has indeed produced powerful closing off effects. In a disturbing account of the rapidly developing 'personalised internet', he argues that not only adverts but virtually everything that we encounter online will soon be individually targeted:

> The basic code at the heart of the new Internet is pretty simple. The new generation of Internet filters looks at the things you seem to like—the actual things you've done, or the things people like you like—and tries to extrapolate. They are prediction engines, constantly creating and refining a theory of who you are and what you'll do and want next. Together, these engines create a unique universe of information for each of us [. . .] which fundamentally alters the way we encounter ideas and information.
>
> (Pariser, 2011, p. 9)

In chapter 5, we saw how the enhanced capacity of users to self-select their media diets has caused concern about the disintegration of the public sphere into partisan niches and individual 'cocoons' (Sunstein, 2009). Sunstein's notion of a personalised cocoon is related to what Pariser calls the 'filter bubble' but different in one important sense. Cocoons are weaved by moths and other insects as a protective cover for their pupae. In the online context, they are webs of personal enclosure weaved by users themselves who actively *choose* to engage with issues and viewpoints that they share a personal affinity with, and disregard or overlook others. Individual agency is thus the key driver of personalisation when navigating the ever-expanding horizon of informational choice. With the emergence of the filter bubble, however, the process of personalisation is now said to have been taken out of the user's hands and is controlled by automated algorithms.

To help us see the implications of this, Pariser points to examples of different users performing identical key word searches on Google with often radically different search results. The implication is that we are no longer exposed to diverse viewpoints and are thus deprived of even the *opportunity* to engage with opinions that do not match our own, or issues that do not have an immediate personal resonance. This may not be such a problem when we are searching for information about yoga classes or football results. But if we are searching for information about climate change, for instance, or stem cells, the results are likely to be shaped by an ideological bias that comports with our previous searches, clicks, purchases, communications and connections.

The problem for Pariser is not just personalisation per se, but that both its development and application have gone largely unnoticed. This has produced something akin to an invisible revolution in the way that we access and engage with news and information online. And much of it is down to the way that Google presents and articulates its social role, not just in terms of putting the user first, but also in embodying the spirit of openness and championing the cause of the commons. There may be good reasons to believe Google is fundamentally different in the way it operates compared to other media and tech giants. But we should be equally mindful of the power and control it wields over both the market and the flow of information. Perhaps even more importantly, we should remain vigilant to the ways in which that power and control is negated with reference to the open architecture of the internet.

Chapter 9

Getting to Know You

In the previous chapter, we noted the contradictions between Google's professed commitment to the values of openness synonymous with the internet commons, and the closing-off practices inherent in its personalising algorithms. But to what extent does personalisation amount to agenda control, as considered in the wider context of this book? Although personalisation is in essence a filtering mechanism, it is clearly distinct from the kind of closure manifest in political censorship exercised by authoritarian states, or practiced by traditional media owners in their capacity to direct the attention of editors away from certain stories or issues (Bagdikian, 2000 [1983]). At the aggregate level, personalisation does not work to systematically marginalise or exclude certain types of news altogether. As I am a broadly left-wing activist, Google has no interest in steering me away from causes or issues that may interest me, even if I am directed to content that may be explicitly or implicitly critical of Google itself. On the contrary, Google's search algorithm actively seeks to *prioritise* whatever content makes the best fit with my personal user profile. Although I may place some value on being challenged by alternative viewpoints, or being exposed to content that deepens my understanding of issues or broadens my political horizons, there are few guarantees that this kind of content will immediately satisfy my searching impulse. And in a world where, in Eric Schmidt's words, "competition is only a click away," immediacy counts above all.

What Google wants, then, is for me to experience a sense of fulfilment from the content I am directed to such that I will return to use its services again and again (which I do). And the more I use its services, the more likely I am to click on one of its sponsored links—the bread and butter of Google's $70 billion of annual revenue. But there is a prior reason why Google wants to prolong and enhance my engagement, which is more of a means to realising the commercial value of my search than an end in itself. Google knows that the longer I spend and the more that I do on its networks, the more opportunities it has to *learn* about me. And the more of my personal data Google can collect, the more it can tailor both its content and adverts according to what it thinks I will be most interested in.

Of course, there is something of a circular logic here. While Google's filtering decisions are intended to reflect—at least in part—my prior content choices, the longer I am retained within its sphere of influence, the more my content choices will start to reflect its own filtering decisions. This is because the value of personalisation algorithms hinges on their power to *predict* my content choices without me having to exert time and effort in actually making those choices. But the less active I am in choosing content, the greater the risk that algorithmic predictions become self-fulfilling prophecies.

Nevertheless, in the world of intermediaries, personal data is what copyright is to content owners: gold dust. Few companies are more conscious of that and more active in the collection of personal data than Facebook. Like Google's search function, Facebook's news feed algorithm filters and orders stories and informational content in line with the social and demographic profiles of its users. And as with Google, this filtering process is barely noticeable from the vantage point of the user. When I land on the home page of the *New York Times*, it's pretty clear to me that the ordering and wording of its headline stories are the products of editorial decision-making. But when I log on to Facebook, the stream of posts and shares I am presented with looks more like the chronological order of choices made by all of my friends and pages I have 'liked', rather than the selective priorities of intricate personalisation metrics. According to one recent study, 62 percent of Facebook users were unaware that their newsfeed was 'curated' by Facebook in this way (Eslami et al., 2015), whereas another study suggested that up to 72 percent of posts by friends and subscribed pages are routinely hidden from a user's news feed (Herrera, 2014).

Just like Google, Facebook's personalisation metrics are also trying to predict the news and information that will most interest users, in the hope that they return to the Facebook universe more frequently and for longer periods of time. According to Greg Marra, one of the engineers that designs Facebook's news feed algorithm code, this process is explicitly *not* editorial:

> We don't want to have editorial judgment over the content that's in your feed. You've made your friends, you've connected to the pages that you want to connect to and you're the best decider for the things that you care about.
>
> (Somaiya, 2014)

In other words, it is the user who steers Facebook, not the other way round. Embedded in this mantra is once again an emphasis on consumer sovereignty, but it is also imbued with a *civic* rationale. In an environment awash with information noise, the likes of Facebook are helping citizens to find, identify and understand the news and information that matters to *them*.

In reality of course, the interests of users—either as citizens *or* consumers—do not necessarily accord with Facebook's algorithm development in the way that the company suggests. In 2015, for instance, Facebook used such a 'user first' justification when it announced changes to its news feed algorithm that would prioritise content shared by individual users compared to pages belonging to groups and organisations. Clearly, this change bolsters Facebook's bottom line by effectively forcing organisations to start paying—or to pay *more*—in order to sustain their existing user base. As journalist David Holmes pointed out, this has potentially profound implications for plurality and diversity:

> Changes like this create a "pay-to-play" paradigm wherein only the most well-funded news organizations are afforded the enormous reach Facebook can offer. This state of affairs tends to crowd out smaller outlets—many of whom are smaller because they value journalistic bravery over brand-friendliness.
>
> (Holmes, 2015)

There is of course nothing unexpected or untoward about this in and of itself. The priority of commercial companies is to maximise profits and deliver returns to their shareholders, not to serve citizens in a democracy. However, the problem for democracy once again comes down to the disjuncture between rhetoric and reality. If Facebook was completely open and transparent about the commercial expediency of its algorithm changes, it would not be a good look for a company that, whether we like it or not, has become a central pillar of the global public sphere. Holmes concludes that such changes "are aligned with its endeavours to boost its revenue and influence and not, as Facebook innocently claims, to create a 'better user experience'."

On closer examination, those who extol the social value of personalisation tend to do so in a way that recalls liberal accounts of news gatekeeping as discussed in part II. The language might have changed, but the citizen's need for orientation in a world of chaos and confusion is entrenched in the discourse of putting the user first. If, as Eric Schmidt suggested, we do indeed want Google to tell us what to do next, it is because we have come to depend on the particular gatekeeping role it has assumed. From this vantage point, users have voluntarily entered into a social contract with intermediaries, giving up their personal information in exchange for a service that enables them to consume more relevant information for less time and effort. Like a personal shopper, Google and Facebook simply ask what kind of things we like, and then go out and find them for us.

Along with gatekeeping, there are striking parallels between the civic rationale of personalisation and the normative vision behind media populism. The democratic mantra of giving the audience what it wants clearly reverberates in putting the user first.

But there are also reasons to be cheerful. Clearly, personalising algorithms can help users access alternatives that might otherwise be maligned from the mainstream agenda. And contrary to the often presumed effects of personalisation, several studies suggest that users do not remain rigidly within interest, ideological or partisan communities (Kelly et al., 2006; Gentzkow and Shapiro, 2010; Webster and Ksiazek, 2012). A study by Pew Research (2013) found that Facebook users have a high tendency to read news from sources that do not share their point of view. And there is certainly little evidence to suggest that users are any *more* partisan in their news consumption choices compared to the analogue era (Usher, 2015).

It is also questionable whether personalisation reduces the chances of users encountering surprising or serendipitous content. As Nikki Usher (2015) points out, the best algorithms do more than just cater to prior tastes and interests; they seek to broaden or extend them: "Gradually, a good algorithm not only gives you what you expect, but also helps you discover what you didn't know you wanted to see." As well as giving users what they want, there is also clearly a commercial logic in getting them to *want more*, and this can (in theory at least) push users outside of their cocoons, echo chambers or filter bubbles.

The Data Rush

So far, we have discussed concerns around personalisation in terms of its agenda filtering effects. But by far the most voiced line of critique is aimed at the impact of personalisation on privacy (e.g. Trepte and Reinecke, 2011; Dwyer, 2011; Turow, 2012; Sevignani, 2015). Far from entering into a social contract with users, intermediaries are said to have built their business models on collecting as much personal data from users as they can. And although they have embraced (or co-opted) the rhetoric of radical transparency, they have in practice merely imposed this standard on users while shrouding in relative opacity the extent and methods by which they collect, store and monetise personal user data.

This practice is inextricably linked to programmes of mass surveillance. The national security files leaked by Edward Snowden in 2013 revealed the complexity and duplicity that characterises relations between the Surveillance State and Silicon Valley. Whereas intermediaries expressed outrage in response to revelations that intelligence agencies had hacked into their private servers, other documents suggested that at least some had cooperated with surveillance in ways that went beyond legal compliance and for which they were financially compensated (MacAskill and Rushe, 2013). In particular, the now notorious 'Prism' programme collected bulk communications data through cooperation with at least nine internet companies (Gellman and Poitras, 2013). Ewen MacAskill, defence and security correspondent for the *Guardian* newspaper, reflected on the awkward position in which these companies found themselves during the aftermath of the revelations:

> The initial reaction of those companies was "we've never heard of Prism" and that could be right because Prism was an internal code word. But they did know about the relationship and they've always been kind of cagey about it. There are a lot of details that have still not come out. When you push them on how much money did they get from the NSA for doing this they say, well, there's a big legal cost in providing the information, but they don't give you the figures [. . .] When the stories about Prism came out the big internet companies were—I think they were embarrassed that they'd been made public.[1]

When it emerged that the agencies were also accessing networks *without* the cooperation and knowledge of intermediaries, Google and others reacted with outspoken anger (Carroll, 2013), as well as action to protect user data by encrypting their servers. But the public furore belied the enduring and intensifying collaboration between Silicon Valley and the security and intelligence sector in other areas, a point that we will return to in chapter 14.

To be fair, it is not clear or certain how far intermediaries have collaborated with the National Security Agency (NSA) and other security agencies in programmes of mass surveillance. Part of the problem is rooted in the professional and technical jargon as well as semantic ambiguity of key words and phrases like 'direct' and 'back door'. All companies implicated in the Prism programme revelations have strenuously denied complying beyond what was required by law (Lardinois, 2013), but this may not have included measures to make legal compliance more efficient and secure (Miller, 2013). In respect of Google, any degree of cooperation also has to be considered against prior efforts to increase the transparency of its compliance. Since 2010, the company has published regular transparency reports on requests for user data from governments around the world, as well as the extent of its compliance with such requests. Although there have been notable gaps in the reports, these may well be the result of court orders that effectively gag the company rather than anything that amounts to voluntary cooperation. As a lawyer for the non-profit Electronic Frontier Foundation remarked in 2013,

> Google might have very well fought a valiant and difficult fight to keep the NSA away from it, but there is only so much it can do as an American company if you get a valid United States court order.
>
> (Stern, 2013)

The important point for now is that bulk data collection and mass surveillance programmes have been made possible—or at least much easier—by the development of personalisation. It is the *coincidence* of commercial and intelligence value in bulk data that has enabled authorities to tap into personal communications with little more than the click of a mouse. Personalisation is thus a form of gatekeeping power that has implications beyond the news agenda. But issues to do with privacy and surveillance are also integrally connected to the way in which personalised agendas are shaped. One of the great ironies of the big data era is that the more information that is collected about *you*, the more filtered your own access to information becomes.

These issues are also intimately associated with concentrated market power. In chapter 14, we will examine the particular aspects of capital accumulation in the intermediary world. But it's worth highlighting the obvious: that it would be much harder for authorities to enlist or enforce the cooperation of internet companies in the collection of bulk data if they had to deal with a multitude of smaller market players rather than a handful of giants with extensive scale and reach. And the more powerful the corporations, the more symbiotic those relationships are likely to be. According to Tim Wu (2010), the resurgence of AT&T as a renewed monopoly power during the early 2000s owed something to the mutual backscratching that developed between the corporation and the administration under George W. Bush. The timing was certainly auspicious. In 2002, the president signed a secret executive order that authorised the NSA to monitor telephone conversations and internet transactions of US citizens without a court warrant. Such monitoring would have required the co-operation of AT&T both in facilitating the wiretaps and in maintaining secrecy around them. For its part, AT&T "manipulated regulatory regimes to eliminate competition" (Wu, 2010, p. 239).

Market dominance has also enabled Google to prevent newcomers redressing the imbalance of power over user data. Consider the case of Disconnect.Me, a privacy app developed by former Google employees designed to protect users from unwanted and invisible tracking by mobile advertisements. In 2014, it was twice banned by Google on its mobile app store, Google Play. Along with Apple's App Store, Google Play constitutes one-half of the duopoly that dominates the global app market. In defence of its actions, Google claimed that its policies prohibit "apps that interfere with other apps (such as by altering their functionality, or removing their way of making money)" (Lunden, 2015). In other words, it is fine to post apps that interfere with the privacy of users, but you can't interfere with other apps that interfere with the privacy of users. And it is precisely because Google controls such a significant gateway to the app market that it can prevent new entrants from interfering in this way.

Note

1. Interview conducted for this book, October 2015.

Chapter 10

The Tyranny of Automation

One important distinction of intermediary gatekeeping lies at the root of contemporary plurality concerns. According to the narrative of transferral (and in contrast to radical accounts of news gatekeeping), it is the *absence* rather than mobilisation of news values that should worry us in the information age, particularly when it comes to questions of news selection. Although algorithms are always the products of human intention and design (Diakopoulos, 2015), they partly displace much of the discretionary judgement exercised by journalists and editors in day-to-day editorial decisions (Thurman, 2011).

Even if we adopt a cynical view of news values, the scope for discretionary judgement creates conditions for anomalous decisions, or *lapses* of judgement. This can lead to the surfacing of stories or issues on the agenda that fit neither with a standard conception of audience wants nor with owner interests, opening the door to content that has serendipitous value or that challenges an ideological paradigm (Bennett et al., 1985). The example cited at the beginning of chapter 4 is an illustration of how some controversies in the news owe their share of the media spotlight to what seems to be purely coincidental factors. Had Tiny Rowland not given the nudge to his journalists at the *Observer* newspaper to investigate BAe Systems—a corporate rival of Dassault in which he had a personal interest—decades of disclosures about corruption in the British arms trade may never have materialised.

But in the world of automated news selection, there is no scope for such accidents or anomalies. This is thought to be especially problematic because the intermediaries that design and control personalisation filters are not guided or sensitised by professional news values that can, at least in liberal accounts of the media, act as a counterweight to purely commercial judgements or the potentially corrupting influence of owners and powerful sources. The importance of maintaining a clear distinction between reporting, commentary and advertising has, for instance, long been at the core of professional journalism codes of conduct. But in the world of online news and targeted pay-per-click advertising, this distinction is becoming increasingly blurred. If you happen to land on the home page of Yahoo—one of the world's leading news aggregators—you will likely find a lead 'advertorial' among the headline news stories distinguished only by a fine print, light-coloured font that qualifies the article as 'sponsored'.

Automation can also result in inadvertent censorship that *looks* like it is driven by an ideological agenda but is in fact a product of the intricate features of algorithmic filters. Arguably the closest proxy for a news agenda in the social media world is the list of trending topics featured on Twitter. These highlight the most popular issues discussed on the social network in any given locality or region, at any given time, as denoted by the hashtag label for particular topical discussion threads. In 2011, considerable controversy was stirred when activists from the Occupy movement—a global direct action protest network born out of the fallout from the 2008 financial crash—noticed that the hashtag for Occupy Wall Street (OWS) never seemed to make it on to the trending topics list in New York (Poell and Van Dijck, 2014). This seemed particularly bizarre because OWS was at the heart of the movement that was attracting significant attention from mainstream media at the time. The hashtag #OccupyWallStreet had also been trending regularly all over the world, but never actually in the city where its direct action and protest activity was taking place. What's even more bizarre is that the exact same thing was happening with the #OccupyBoston hashtag, which was regularly trending in cities and regions *other* than Boston but never in Boston itself.

Not surprisingly, the social network was accused of co-operating with local authorities in efforts to suppress the movement. But this seemed at odds with Twitter's role in, and reputation for *supporting* protest movements, not least during the spontaneous uprisings across North Africa and the Middle East in 2011 that earned the widely used moniker of the 'Twitter revolutions' (Axford, 2011). Part of the suspicion stemmed from the fact that the technical apparatus of trending topics has always been hidden from public view. But in a brilliant reverse engineering data analysis, Gilad Lotan (2011) showed how the anomalies in Boston and New York were not the function of any intentional manipulation by Twitter or the authorities, but rather the unintended consequences of a particular algorithmic feature.

Contrary to what might ordinarily be assumed, Twitter's determination of trending is not based exclusively on the volume of tweets attracted by any given hashtag at any given time. This is because one of Twitter's principle concerns with trending—as the term suggests—is to do with 'newness'. So its algorithm rewards particular terms and topics that experience spikes in user attention and participation, rather than those that attract consistent and prolonged activity. The reason that #OccupyWallStreet and #OccupyBoston had never trended in their respective cities was because they had, from the start, attracted a gradual and *sustained* growth of attention in their local areas, as opposed to just spiking around particular events that attracted broader mainstream media focus. As Lotan (2011) remarked, "There's nothing like a Police raid and hundreds of arrests to push a story's visibility."

So this was not, after all, censorship—or at least not in the way that many had suspected. But it did reveal an important feature of Twitter that has potentially profound implications for the news agenda at large. Trending topics have become a key mechanism by which certain ideas or perspectives gain visibility in the digital domain. They have become a symbol of *newsworthiness*. But rather than offering a challenge to the editorial agenda set by mainstream media, trending topics serve in many ways to reinforce that agenda. By virtue of algorithmic design, they favour spikes in attention given to any given topic or issue, over and above volume and in place of consistency. There can be little doubt that one major catalyst for such spikes is the immense publicity power that mainstream news brands continue to deploy.

In one sense the opposite problem occurred in 2013 when Hurricane Sandy hit New York. In that case the vast majority of Twitter activity centred on Manhattan, which made it look like the epicentre of the storm. But as Kate Crawford (2013) pointed out, some of the worst affected areas beyond Manhattan were significantly under-represented. This was due in part to the relative affluence and associated 'connectedness' of Manhattan residents compared to those in the worst affected areas, an imbalance that was exacerbated by the infrastructural damage caused by the storm. Crawford calls this a "signal problem" and concludes that the visibility of news on Twitter is fundamentally skewed by the digital divide: "Data are assumed to accurately reflect the social world, but there are significant gaps, with little or no signal coming from particular communities."

The Blame Game

Perhaps the most talked about way in which algorithms are said to have unintended and undesirable effects on the news agenda recalls the dumbing down thesis discussed in chapter 5. Facebook's news feed algorithm in particular has been accused of disproportionately favouring stories that are highly emotive, trivial and partisan (Goel, 2014; Yglesias, 2014; Anderle, 2015) over political and 'serious' news in general. The problem here is not just related to individual exposure. Given Facebook's dominant position as a driver of news traffic (Lafrance, 2015), its favouring of particular types of news content is thought to be having a negative impact on both editorial decisions and newsgathering priorities *at large*.

Indeed, the trivialisation of news in the Facebook age is something that the company's founder and CEO seemed resigned to when he famously remarked that "a squirrel dying in your front yard may be more relevant to your interests right now than people dying in Africa" (Usher, 2015). Yet curiously, Facebook officials have begun to both express and respond to concerns about news standards. In 2013 the company announced that it was tweaking its news feed algorithm in order to promote what it called 'high-quality' content (Kacholia, 2013), based on a survey of users that asked questions like "is this timely and relevant content?" and "is this content from a source you can trust?" This was followed in 2014 by an experiment in prioritising 'hard' news during a pre-election period for a sample of its users. The result, according to Facebook, was a significant increase in voter turnout (Goodman, 2014).

But rather than assuaging fears by demonstrating Facebook's capacity to nurture democratic citizenship, this only seemed to raise new alarms about its engagement in 'computational politics' (Tufekci, 2014). Added to that, the quality metrics introduced in 2013 appeared to do little to stem the groundswell of entertainment and titillation in the digital news sphere. The following year Facebook's head of product, Mike Hudack, went on the offensive bemoaning the dearth of serious and long-form news, and singling out new entrant Vox.com:

> I hoped that we would find a new home for serious journalism in a format that felt Internet-native and natural to people who grew up interacting with screens [. . .] instead they write stupid stories about how you should wash your jeans instead of freezing them [. . .] someone should fix this shit.
>
> (Hudack, 2014)

His post triggered a blogging war with journalists who retaliated by shifting the blame back onto Facebook. As one put it, "if Facebook executives don't like a world in which those are the kind of stories people read, they should do something about it" (Yglesias, 2014). But Hudack was having none of it, and hit back with a sentiment that recalled the long-standing dumbing down critique of professional journalism:

> I call bullshit. They do the link bait to make money. They do real journalism as a hobby if they do it at all. And once they realize that it's a cost center that isn't going to pay back their venture investors they shut it down. Just like their mass media forebears.
>
> (Ingram, 2014)

Arguments on both sides of this debate rest on an implicit assumption that the sum of news value (from an audience perspective) can be measured entirely in clicks and likes. This is a marketing dictum that may hold some weight when it comes to measuring the commercial return on individual articles, but as we saw in chapter 7, it does not take account of crucial factors like depth of attention and consumption across digital and traditional platforms. It is perhaps in view of these other aspects of value—which are intrinsically harder to capture with click data—that new entrants like Buzzfeed and Vice have indeed branched out into serious investigative news.

Whether or not Facebook's evolving algorithm will lend greater support to this kind of content remains to be seen. What is certain, however, is that news matters to Facebook—as much as it does to Google, Yahoo, Twitter and others. And by extension, news *quality* matters. Facebook has a particular interest not just in promoting the most viral or popular news but also news that users engage and spend time with. A core and common principle of social media business models is that the longer we spend on any given page, the more likely we are to click on an advert. In this sense, casual likes and shares do not do as much for Facebook's bottom line as what it calls high-quality content.

But the ultimate move towards a more hands-on involvement in news curation for intermediaries came in 2015. After months of negotiation with publishers, Facebook announced its introduction of 'instant articles', based on a revenue-sharing model that enables the social network to host news articles directly (Baughan, 2015). It was a move that prompted Google, Twitter and Apple to quickly follow suit (Kafka, 2015). Irrespective of whether this spells the death or salvation of digital journalism, the knock-on effects for the news ecosystem are likely to be wide-ranging. It will, for instance, accelerate the disaggregation of news content, much as iTunes did for long-playing albums. The phenomenon of instant articles essentially devalues the news 'package' and, potentially, makes it even more difficult for individuals to encounter news and information with which they have not been individually targeted. It will also favour larger and more established news providers who have the resources to produce regular and high volumes of content, as well as the brand clout to attract users en masse.

The Editor's Code

Above all, the launch of instant articles marks another step change in the gatekeeping power that intermediaries are assuming, and which their critics have been warning about for some time. But what is less obvious is whether this power is *editorial* in a way comparable to traditional media. It's a question that has critical implications for media policy and for how we understand the complexities of news gatekeeping in the digital era. For some, the business of selecting and arranging stories in a newsfeed (however automated and personalised) is ultimately little different from the role played by traditional editors. After all, the exercise of voice—the critical dimension of media plurality concerns—consists not just in the expression of words and pictures of a given news story, but in the aggregation of stories and design of the news package, whether it be on paper, on air or on screen.

It is certainly true that in one sense, computerised algorithms are the equivalents of the news desk for what looks like a growing number of online consumers who get their news not from the source but from hosts like Yahoo and, increasingly, Facebook. The role of aggregation here—packaging and prioritising news stories—is certainly reminiscent of the traditional role played by editors. But there are three crucial distinctions that make algorithmic gatekeeping less about exercising editorial voice and more to do with adjusting the *volume* of other editorial voices.

First, as already suggested, news algorithms are limited in their gatekeeping capacity to practices of selection and arrangement of content that has already been produced, and usually already published. For all the complex weightings imbedded in news algorithms that enable them to make ever more nuanced and interpretive judgements, they do not get involved in the business of news production. This is different from human editors who, in the process of selection and arrangement can make changes to copy, rewrite headlines or paragraphs (or order them to be rewritten), and pen opinion editorials to accompany the reports.

The second distinction is based on the *reactive* qualities of traditional gatekeeping, such that an owner or editor of a conventional news outlet can direct changes in focus, language, style or political leaning in response to real-time developments and events. For all the regularity of algorithmic tweaks they still involve complex engineering of code, often followed by lengthy applications to update their patents. Automated news selection may be inherently faster than a conventional news desk at the point of selection, but changing the priorities and weightings of its judgements is, somewhat ironically, a much slower process. From a practical perspective, this makes it harder for intermediaries to 'editorialise' in the sense of favouring or rejecting particularly political groups, actors or policies like going to war or raising taxes.

The third distinction is that even if intermediaries did seek to editorialise in this way, it would be antithetical to their business models. As we saw in the previous chapter, the logic of personalisation rests on the principle that content is tailored to the individual's preference. That is what keeps us coming back for more. And even though I rarely click on a sponsored link or banner ad, the mere fact that I continue to use Google and Facebook on a daily basis contributes to their bottom line, because my presence adds to the volume of their user base that attracts their advertisers in the first place.

There are of course exceptions to this, and trade-offs between catering to individual preferences and meeting legal obligations over things like copyright, privacy, libel, protection of minors or hate speech; moderating for other types of offensive content; or co-operating with states over political censorship. Witness the extent of Google's collaboration with Chinese authorities over wide-ranging censorship between 2006 and 2010, which drew stern criticism from human rights groups and protest movements (e.g. Human Rights Watch, 2006).

In the following chapter, we will examine in more depth the 'super' gatekeeping roles played by intermediaries, and the extent to which their judgements about whether or not certain material is legal or offensive may have a chilling effect on journalism and free speech. But the point I want to bring home now is that although intermediaries may not exercise *editorial* control, they play a profound role in determining the prominence and accessibility of those who do. And much like in the traditional news space, algorithmic gatekeeping is a power that is largely unacknowledged and to some extent hidden behind the veil of personalisation. The fact that intermediaries do not even identify themselves as media companies—preferring the label of tech companies instead (Napoli, 2014)—points to a new aspect of obscurity when it comes to questions of ownership, gatekeeping and agenda power. This picture is further complicated by the war of words over news quality, reflecting a brewing tension in which both journalists and techies disown their gatekeeping roles and blame each other for a perceived decline in news standards. In reality, if we are indeed witnessing such a decline, it is likely the product of *both* intermediaries and digital news providers pursuing their respective bottom lines. And in spite of the combative rhetoric, the advent of instant articles reflects the growing inter-reliance of news providers and intermediaries, a theme that occupies the focus of chapter 14.

Chapter 11

Manual Control

Alongside concerns around automated processes of news filtering, intermediaries have faced criticism for being overly cautious in their ad hoc responses to legal threats and complaints. In 2002, for instance, Google blocked links to a website critical of Scientology after being served with a complaint under the US Digital Millennium Copyright Act (DCMA). The incident appeared to underscore concerns that the new copyright regulations posed a threat to free speech and that, in the words of one civil liberties lawyer, "people will attempt to silence critics under the guise of copyright infringement" (Hansen, 2002).

As well as blocking links outright, Google has also engaged proactively in demoting links to content it deems to be infringing on copyright. Although it may well be acting in accordance with legal norms, the problem—as with media ownership concerns more generally—lies in the *potential* for abuse. The structural positioning of Google as an information intermediary, coupled with its enormous market power, has meant that it now acts in a quasi-judicial role in dealing with complaints over alleged rights-infringing content. As Ellen Goodman (2014) observed: "The important fact is that the power exists and the public must take Google's word for the benignity of its exercise."

While recent surveillance reforms in the UK aim to make ISPs responsible for the collection of bulk data on behalf of the state, this outsourcing of monitorial and regulatory power has significant precedent in the development of copyright, privacy and data protection law. It has amounted to what some have called the "privatisation of censorship" (Tambini et al., 2008) and of communications policy more generally (Hintz, 2014), as intermediaries assume responsibility for adjudicating on claims of rights infringement and, effectively, enforcing compliance with the law.

In the realm of copyright, this is partly the consequence of a range of legal protections introduced for digital rights management that have, in sum, "transferred the authority to define, detect and punish alleged copyright infringements to private actors" (Hintz, 2014, p. 350). But it is particularly related to the so-called notice and take down procedures contained within the DCMA and other equivalent legislation around the world at the national or supranational level. Such rules burden both intermediaries and ISPs with liability for the use of copyrighted content by third parties, unless they co-operate with take down requests in the first instance.

In Europe, intermediaries have been placed in a similar position under the 'right to be forgotten', a potentially chilling addendum to data protection laws that came into force in 2014. Since then, a number of news organisations—as well as Wikipedia—have had articles effectively blacklisted by Google as result of requests under the newly defined legal right (Hern, 2014; Curtis, 2015). This amounts to a form of post restraint on free speech that potentially undermines the important historical record that archived news can offer. It also, in theory at least, offers a boon to wealthy and powerful individuals seeking to suppress details of previous malfeasance on public record. Aided by the growing swell in reputation management services offered by law and public relations firms alike, these individuals no longer have to deal with publishers directly, who have a far more vested interest than Google in ensuring that their articles remain as widely accessible as possible. What's more, the new law enables them to go where libel and defamation law cannot, effectively injuncting articles not because they are factually inaccurate or a breach of privacy, but fundamentally because they are *in the past.*

The problem—from the perspective of media ownership concerns—is not with the right to be forgotten as a legal principle. The internet has created a permanent and very accessible public record of personal histories in a way that never existed before, and which can disproportionately and unfairly impact on an individual's career prospects or personal relationships. Nor is there necessarily anything wrong—ethically or legally—with Google's handling of requests for data removal. The problem is rather that, as with privacy law in general, such rights have to be balanced with the public's right to know, and the legal jurisprudence has effectively placed responsibility for this balancing act in the hands of private corporations. In particular, a landmark ruling by the European Court of Justice in 2014 stated that search engines must remove information from the listings deemed "inaccurate, inadequate, irrelevant or excessive."[1] Although Google's decisions under the right to be forgotten can be appealed through the courts (or an ombudsman like the Information Commissioner in the UK), it is still charged with making crucial public interest judgements in the first instance. What's more, unlike court rulings, Google does not have to explain its judgements or be in any way transparent about its reasoning or decision-making process.

But even absent the force of law, intermediaries have become key decision-makers on a range of issues that can impact on the citizenship rights of users. The ability of social networks like Facebook to exclude or otherwise censor specific users or user groups, alongside their powers of personal data collection, has raised concerns that they have become "quasi-governmental actors" (Kim and Telman, 2015). In 2014, for instance, Facebook decided to remove a popular page dedicated to "anti-capitalist, anti-racist, feminist, and pro-LGBT rights" (Dencik, 2014). Although the page was subsequently restored, individual posts and administrators have repeatedly fallen victim to temporary and ad hoc censorship in response to complaints, most likely from ideologically opposed groups or individuals.

Of course, Facebook has a moral as well as legal duty (in some countries) to control hate speech, and much of its censorship activities legitimately target extremist and racist groups. Its 'community standards' policy embodies its stated values of inclusiveness and openness, and reflects its ascendancy as a pillar of global civil society. But without an independent appeals process or any public oversight of its censoring decisions, there is always a risk that they will extend beyond the bounds of hate speech, stifle public debate and impact disproportionately on radical, dissenting and subversive ideas. That appeared to be the case, for instance, when a number of UK protest and activist pages were blocked or suspended around the time of the British royal wedding between Prince William and Kate Middleton in 2011. The blocks coincided with a more general crackdown on protest groups carried out by authorities ahead of the wedding and was seen by some as an indication of Facebook's growing willingness to cooperate in the control of political activism (Malik, 2011).

Such troubling incidents aside, it is easy to overstate the degree to which intermediaries are stifling speech by bowing to the pressure of either rights holders or authorities. In regard to the right to be forgotten, it's worth noting that one year on from when the new ruling took effect, Google had only approved just over 40 percent of more than 250,000 such requests (Curtis, 2015). As for Facebook's censoring of activist groups, there is little evidence that this is part of a general strategic effort to quiet or exclude radical voices, just as the absence of Occupy Wall Street on New York's trending topics was the unexpected—and *unintended*—consequence of its unique algorithm features. There may be a clear branding rationale for restricting hate speech on their networks, but it is hard to imagine that Facebook or Twitter would want to censor radical political voices given that it would alienate such a significant proportion of their user base. Whereas the political economy of social media may serve to restrict the flow of radical ideas in some ways (as we will consider in chapter 13), it amplifies them in others. It has certainly given voice to an emergent fifth estate that, as we saw in chapter 4, can play a crucial role in challenging and redefining dominant news narratives.

But manual overrides can also take the form of editorial bias or self-censorship reminiscent of traditional newsrooms. In May 2016, five whistle-blowers revealed the existence of a specialist 'curating' team within Facebook, housed in the basement of its New York offices and responsible for manually editing its trending topics—the aggregated list of the most popular news stories that feature alongside the user's personalised feed (Nunez, 2016). In news terms, Facebook's trending topics—just like those of Twitter—have been described as 'gold real estate', guaranteeing a substantial boost of through traffic to any of its featured stories. The revelation stirred controversy over an apparent anti-conservative bias in the curating process, although this appeared to be a reflection of the political sensibilities of its staff rather than a top-down driven agenda. What did apparently feed down from management were explicit instructions to take extra caution with news stories involving Facebook itself and to ensure that stories that were attracting substantial coverage in mainstream media and on Twitter were given a boost if they were not trending on Facebook 'organically'.

This raises profound questions about Facebook's role in determining the news that *matters*, not least given its increasing efforts to bring news content within its own walls. Unlike Twitter and Google, Facebook is moving away from its role as an intermediary and appears no longer content with being just the 'switch', connecting users with content hosted by third parties. In news terms, at least, it seems to want to *be the internet*, ensuring that its users not only find content but also consume it within its own walls and according to its own terms.

Conclusion to Part III

The last four chapters have attempted to set out the parameters of an alternative narrative in regards to the agenda power and influence once exclusively associated with media owners. Rather than dispersing among the crowd, this power is said to have been transferred into the hands of internet companies, bringing a host of new and urgent problems for citizens and policymakers with implications for media diversity, plurality and democracy. This is especially prescient given a clear trend towards more interventionist algorithms that to some extent displace conscious decision-making by both users and editors in their content choices. No longer neutral tools with which to find and share information, intermediaries have become crucial arbiters of salience in the formation of personalised agendas. And depending on how you look at it, the growth of personalisation has followed, coincided with, or *resulted* in users becoming increasingly passive in their consumption of news and information.

The most voiced concerns around personalising algorithms relate to the largely unseen ways in which they both gather personal data and apply it through content filtering mechanisms. But like the commercialisation of news more generally, personalisation is never a one-way process of responding only to prior audience tastes and interests. In attempting to understand its implications for agenda control more broadly, we have to consider the potential for personalisation to reinforce and even *shape* audience tastes in turn. Although the process of audience commodification began long before digital media, it has been catalysed and intensified by the development of personalisation filters.

Comparatively less attention has been paid to the ways in which personalisation impacts on the aggregate or common agenda. I have suggested that this can be considered in terms of amplification—promoting some voices over others—and we have encountered examples of how Twitter can systematically favour topics that chime with breaking news stories, or that are reverberated by the mainstream media, or that are shared among relatively more affluent and 'connected' users.

But as with the narrative of dispersal, we have seen that much of the related concerns are not without precedent in the pre-digital era, and it is important to highlight both what is distinct about new gatekeeping practices and what is similar to the those of old journalism. We saw, for instance, strong parallels between the way that algorithms filter news content according to perceived user preferences and the way that editors have long selected stories based on assumptions about audience tastes. Indeed, segmentation and targeting of niche audiences has always been a hallmark of commercial news development, whereas audience selectivity in news contexts—as between different issues, stories, providers and platforms—began with the *rise* rather than the fall of the mass media paradigm.

We have also noted similarities between normative arguments in support of personalising algorithms and liberal accounts of the traditional media's gatekeeping function, as well as the democratising force of media populism. And the parallels extend further: like media populism, personalisation is also associated with a decline in media standards, and this has produced rival narratives between intermediaries and news providers about who is responsible for the decline. But there is little evidence on which to base either set of arguments, particularly given the complexities of news consumption, which means that the most popular or preferred content is not measurable by click data alone.

What has changed is that the power to filter news and information now appears to reside less with professional news editors, or indeed users, and more with internet companies whose core business activity has very little to do with journalism per se. Added to that, the generic model of personalisation is based on the exchange of free content or services, not for eyeballs directed to generalised advertising but for personal data used for *targeted* advertising. This practice is to some extent legitimised by the requests and requirements of states in the conduct of censorship and surveillance activities.

Clearly, all of these issues raise acute concerns for media plurality and agenda control, not least the assumed power of intermediaries to engage in 'computational politics', as well as the power granted to them by legislative authorities in key aspects of copyright and privacy regulation. Nevertheless, the extent of gatekeeping and agenda control exercised by intermediaries may have been overstated, and many of the concerns raised by the narratives of transferral may be driven more by a fear of the unknown than hard evidence. This is partly because empirical research in these areas is still in its nascent stages, and also chasing a moving target as changes in code bring changes in patterns of news content, distribution and consumption. Added to that is the problem of opacity: the code that determines the prominence, visibility and accessibility of digital news is closely guarded by intermediaries, and there has been little attempt by regulating authorities to enforce any degree of algorithmic transparency.

The degree to which intermediaries have been complicit in programmes of mass surveillance also remains unclear, as is the degree to which increasingly complex and interventionist algorithms are producing informational or cultural filter bubbles. There is certainly considerable empirical evidence that casts doubt over such claims.

It is equally difficult to accept that the filtering role of traditional newsrooms was or is intrinsically more transparent and accountable by comparison. The qualities and characteristics of intermediary gatekeeping are certainly in many ways distinct and call for bespoke policy responses (which we will consider in part V). But these particularities do not mean that critical attention to intermediary gatekeeping should come at the *expense* of conventional news providers, or that user access has displaced ownership as the linchpin of plurality concerns.

Finally, there is no evidence to date that algorithms have any inbuilt political or ideological biases extraneous to the pursuit of profit maximisation. In contrast, ever since the days of the press barons, there have always been some newspaper owners and editors who have deployed their agenda power as leverage for political influence. Far from abating in the digital era, there is good reason to believe, as we saw in chapter 2, that these practices have intensified as local oligarchs fill the gap of retreating investors, and editors become more sensitised to the whims of what's left of their advertisers and funders. Critics of intermediaries as news gatekeepers are thus guilty in some ways both of a 'golden age' perspective of traditional gatekeeping practices, and inattention to the ways in which those practices are enduring and evolving.

And here lies the major blind spot in the narrative of transferral: in reserving its concerns exclusively for the new gatekeepers of news and information, it overlooks the ways in which these practices are *impacting* on more conventional modes of gatekeeping. Indeed, the discursive and legal battles between intermediaries and news providers belies the growing interdependence, alliances and areas of overlap between them. News is, after all, the bedrock of digital content. The profits of intermediaries are dependent on this content either directly or indirectly, just as the survival of news providers is dependent on the traffic generated by intermediaries. It is this fundamental interdependency—the details of which we will examine more closely in part IV—that is largely glossed over in the narrative of transferral. We began part III by examining the fallout from ancillary copyright laws in Europe, which had the most dramatic consequences in Spain. But for all its market power, the shutdown of Google News in Spain hurts Google—maybe not as much as news publishers, and not in ways directly measurable in revenue (given that its news listings do not carry ads). But ultimately Google's success is built on the immersive user experience of which its news listings constitute an integral element. When Google set aside EUR150 million to fund innovative digital news initiatives across Europe,[2] it was not just playing a defensive card in the face of a relatively unfavourable political and regulatory climate. It was also investing in the content that drives its core business. For Facebook as well as Twitter, news is even more central to their user experience, and the move towards monetising articles directly is a logical attempt to capitalise on this.

Notes

1. *Google v. González* 2014 C-131/12 (Luxembourg).
2. See https://www.digitalnewsinitiative.com/fund/ (last accessed 18 January 2016).

Part IV

Coexistence

Chapter 12

The Long and the Short of It

17 November 2014

In a dimly lit hall on a sweltering spring day in Melbourne, veteran punk musician and recording 'engineer' Steve Albini stumbled onto the stage. Direct from a flight halfway across the world and dressed in characteristic black T-shirt, faded jeans and round goggle specs, he had come to deliver the keynote address for *Face the Music*, a conference that brought together struggling artists, indie labels, managers, promoters and others navigating the brave new world of the indie music business. But rather than bemoan their fate or lament the consolidation of what are now the big three major labels, he gave an unexpectedly upbeat address that spoke of the renewed vitality, fairness and diversity of the music industry. Gone are the days where middlemen profited off artificially inflated prices and payola. Gone are the days when small independent labels or self-sustaining bands had to pull off the impossible to get their music heard, let alone sold internationally. Gone are the days when not much more than a handful of bosses controlled the gates and 'set the agenda' that determined both the artists that get exposed to audiences and the way that they get exposed (with both artists and audiences excluded from deliberations over their collective interests and fate). At the heart of Albini's message was a conviction that the way that the music industry had evolved in the face of technological disruption was only a problem for shareholders, major label bosses and superstars; the only threat posed by the ascendant peer culture in music was to "the framework of an exploitative system that I have been at odds with my whole creative life" (Albini, 2014).

It was a powerful message; one that resonated with the ideals of both the digital openness movement and the DIY punk ethics that had long been a defining influence on Albini's career. But above all, it was a message that offered an unequivocal and unabashed celebration of the 'long tail'. What was most distinct about the music industry today, Albini (2014) stressed, was the sheer variety of available and accessible music:

> Whether you're into Dusty's Deep Cut reggae, minimal electronics, symphonic pop, Texas blues, Japanese noise, power electronics, children's music, christmas music, Raymond Scott, or Burl Ives, I guarantee there is an online

community where you can connect with other enthusiasts to indulge the minute specificity of your tastes.

The internet had given to the whole world what was once only available to those who inhabited the scene—local music communities usually centred in big cities. Today, virtually anyone (notwithstanding enduring digital divides) can in principle connect with the kind of "punks and noise freaks and drag queens and experimental composers and jabbering street poets" that made up the musical landscape where Albini cut his teeth.

Of course, the superstar phenomenon in popular music has not quite been consigned to the history books. Witness the global mega-sales of artists from One Direction to Adele and it's clear that the change Albini speaks of is far from revolutionary or absolute. But that doesn't matter; so long as the superstar world can't encroach on the subcultures and countercultures that make up the long tail; so long as the system of exploitation that produces them cannot dictate terms for those who prefer to play on the outside.

This is coexistence. Like the narratives of dispersal and transferral, it offers an account of change that centres on the relationship between media ownership and the agenda. In this version, however, the agenda power of media owners (or of those interests and forces able to leverage concentrated media power) endures—*but not over the whole cake*. Its central claim is that the spread of digital communication technologies has fostered an explosion of niches beyond their reach.

A World of Alternatives

At face value, it is a conception that goes some way to resolving concerns about gatekeeping and agenda power, be it the editorial control exercised by content owners or the curatorial role played by intermediaries. Amid this coexistence, users are both exposed to and free to swim in the river of the mainstream, along with the endless creaks that make up the long tail of alternatives.

Much of this near utopia was foretold a decade or so earlier by Chris Anderson, former editor of *Wired* magazine. In a famous article and subsequent book, he articulated the long tail thesis as a novel and in some sense ultimate stage in the democratisation of popular culture. "If the twentieth century entertainment industry was about *hits*," he declared, "the twenty-first century will be equally about *niches*" (2009 [2006], p. 16).

But Anderson was emphatic that the change would not amount to a complete inversion of the superstar paradigm (an important point often overlooked by long tail critics):

> This shift from the generic to the specific doesn't mean the end of the existing power structure or a wholesale shift to an all-amateur, laptop culture. Instead, it's simply a rebalancing of the equation, an evolution from an "Or" era of hits *or* niches (mainstream culture vs. subcultures) to an "And" era. Today,

our culture is increasingly a mix of head *and* tail, hits *and* niches, institutions *and* individuals, professionals *and* amateurs. Mass culture will not fall, it will simply get less mass. And niche culture will get less obscure.

(2009 [2006], p. 181)

This notion of coexistence echoes arguments that focused on the growth of participatory platforms as a key driver of the agenda power shift (Jenkins, 2006; McNair, 2006; Benkler, 2011). As we saw in part II, notions like convergence culture and the networked fourth estate share a conviction that what we are witnessing is a new settlement, according to which imbalances in the control of critical communication resources no longer manifest—at least not necessarily—in concentrated power of voice. It's not that the mainstream has been or will be displaced entirely, but rather that its capacity to determine agenda boundaries at large have eroded. Manuel Castells argued similarly that "in spite of the growing concentration of power, capital and production in the global communication system, the actual content and format of communication practices are increasingly diversified" (2009, p. 136).

Economies of Small Scale

At the heart of the long tail thesis is a core contention that the cultural industries are no longer fixated *exclusively* on mainstream content because the development of digital communications has made niche content increasingly viable. This much seems intuitively obvious. In the pre-digital creative economy, the costs of producing, copying/manufacturing, storing and distributing creative works were all relatively high. If you wanted to make an album, you had to pay for expensive studio space, equipment and skilled people to operate it. To manufacture the physical record you had to pay for a pressing on a cost per copy basis. And if you got that far, you then had to pay for storage of the stock and a distributor to physically sell and deliver the records into retailing outlets, not to mention all the people that were needed to ensure your record was *heard*: radio pluggers, publicists, marketing managers and so forth.

In the face of these costs, big record companies sought to achieve 'scale economies' by vertical integration, acquiring operations in all points of the supply chain from talent scouting to wholesale distribution. But by far the most lucrative scale economies were achieved by the production of hits. This was because most of the costs of making and selling a record were fixed (i.e. selling more units of a given record did not increase the cost of producing it and only marginally increased the costs of pressing, storage and distribution).

Other cultural industries faced similar barriers and costs in bringing goods to market, including journalism. Before even factoring the costs of newsgathering and access to the airwaves, broadcast news required the use of a wide array of costly technical apparatus and specialist trained staff. As for newspapers, they too incurred a per copy cost for printing, as well as the costs of physical distribution to outlets serving a local, regional or national readership. In light of this, it's not hard to see why the old creative business model was focused on bestsellers, blockbusters, hits and scoops. The most cost efficient and profitable strategy in all markets was to produce more of what was most popular and less of anything else.

But it was not just supply-side economics that fostered 'superstar effects'. Consumers too faced relatively high 'search costs' in discovering new products. Channels of exposure were limited and governed by the gatekeeping filters intrinsic in things like headlines, billboards, reviews and playlists. The sharing of experiences and opinion by word of mouth was an exception, but even here search costs were offset when consumer interaction and feedback concentrated on the most popular (Adler, 1985).

The result was a picture of content distribution that tended to exceed the so-called pareto principle or 80–20 rule, which in marketing terms stipulates that roughly 80 percent of sales are concentrated around roughly 20 percent of brands in any given sector. A typical distribution curve that maps this concentration is shown in Figure 12.1.

It's easy to understand why this pattern was thought to have been inverted by the spread of digital technologies, which slashed production costs and virtually eliminated the costs of copying, storing and distributing digitised works. From music downloads to e-books, these conditions favoured both new entrants and an 'economy of abundance' (Jarvis, 2009) reflected in the range of products brought to market. Even for physical products, the efficiencies afforded by virtual marketing and retailing were transformative. Purveyors of rare books, vinyl or fine art

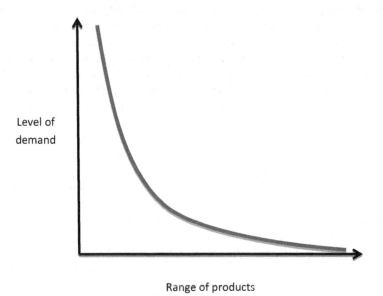

Figure 12.1 The Pareto Distribution Curve

could now reach far-flung audiences with little more than a few clicks of a mouse and, in time, the help of intermediaries like eBay or Facebook.

The resultant long tail of distribution is depicted in Figure 12.2. You can see that as the range of products increases, the distribution curve gradually starts to level off, reflecting the near-infinite range of content that the market now supports.

It was not only now more *feasible* to cater to niche tastes but also increasingly *profitable*. This is partly because 'going niche' promised to unlock latent or unfulfilled demand that could not be catered for in the pre-digital economy, due primarily to the physical constraints of space. We can think of this space in terms of that which was needed to stock products in a retail outlet, as well as that which had to be traversed in order to communicate with and sell to dislocated audiences around the globe. But in the digital environment, there is virtually no ceiling on the range of products that can be sold and catalogued by any given online outlet. And there is virtually no difference in the cost of marketing, selling or distributing to someone who lives on my street compared to someone on the other side of the world. This is what supposedly brought everyone from 'noise freaks' to 'experimental composers' out from the shadows and enabled them to connect with audiences far beyond their local scene.

But what about search costs? We might assume that the elimination of scarcities associated with space constraints would dramatically *increase* the search costs for consumers who now had to navigate an open sea of endless alternatives. What's more, this variety consisted in both the range of content that could be consumed, the range of sources from *where* it could be consumed, and the range of platforms and devices that determined *how* it could be consumed. Yet for long tail optimists like Anderson (e.g. Brynjolfsson et al., 2011), the internet has not only come up with solutions to this problem; it has also made it easier than ever for consumers

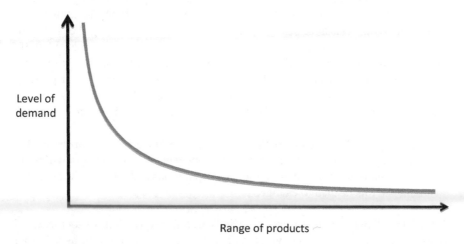

Level of demand

Range of products

Figure 12.2 The Long Tail

to find what they are truly looking for. Rather than succumbing or resigning to the trappings of the mass market, individuals are now guided to the content that speaks directly to their particular views, tastes, identities and values, tailored according to their device, and sourced from content owners directly or via aggregators.

The contexts in which this happens are not dissimilar from the old economy, although the navigational tools are dramatically refined and extended. So, for instance, online retailers organise and label their catalogues to facilitate easier browsing in much the same way as traditional retailers. But they also use complex algorithms to make personalised suggestions and recommendations based on a user's own browsing and consumption history, as well as those who share a similar profile. And whereas traditional radio playlists generalise the most popular music of the day, their digital versions can be personally and individually curated by the user. On top of all that, users have more opportunities than ever to interact with peers through social networking and dedicated forums catering to every conceivable taste and interest. Such forums provide an important vehicle of discovery, often beyond the control of content owners or intermediaries.

From the Barricades

Albini's impassioned speech evoked the particular resonance that long tail theory has for subculture and resistance to dominant social and cultural norms. Dick Hebdige's seminal work (1979) on Britain's youth subculture in the late 1970s examined the aesthetics of punk and other subcultures as fundamentally acts of resistance in this sense. It was the glue that connected white punk with Afro-Caribbean reggae expressed through musical collaborations and the formation of new genres like ska. In the subcultural entertainment world, commercial success has always been something to be avoided rather than chased. As the Brooklyn hip hop duo Gang Starr scornfully put it: "you'd be happy as hell to get a record deal / maybe your soul you'd sell to have mass appeal" (EMI Music, 2009).

This notion of resistance also underlies much of what has always been considered 'radical media' (Downing, 2000). In the digital news sphere, it is explicitly articulated by the so-called fifth estate (Cooper, 2006; Dutton, 2009) or gate-watchers (Bruns, 2011), and reverberates in the discourse of radical transparency associated with the hacker movement. As the website of WikiLeaks—an organisation that embodies the ideals of both hacktivism and the fifth estate—attests:

> In the years leading up to the founding of WikiLeaks, we observed the world's publishing media becoming less independent and far less willing to ask the hard questions of government, corporations and other institutions. We believed this needed to change.[1]

If the long tail phenomenon works especially well for expressions of sociocultural resistance, as well as subversive or radical ideas, this can be seen as a further democratising force. In the absence of a perfect and impossible marketplace of ideas where all opinion and perspectives have equal power of voice, democracies need to support not just diverse forms of expression, but *especially* those that offer a direct challenge to dominant narratives, which is what Castells has referred to as 'counter-power' (2007). Ideological resistance and emancipation are thus imbedded in the subtext of long tail theory. Ideas and perspectives that were (or could be) once suppressed by vested interests or a power elite are now beyond control. As the tail grows, it inevitably starts to wag.

But to fully understand the long tail phenomenon—and particularly why it was thought to work *against* the mainstream—we have to take account of something peculiar about the cognition of cultural consumers. For Anderson, the long tail was not just the result of new opportunities to service latent demand, but the realisation of an active preference among consumers for content that is uniquely tailored to their personal interests and tastes.

It's hard to argue with the logic behind this assumption. Why wouldn't we prefer content that more closely represents who we are and the things we like? There is a rich literature in music sociology, for instance, that explores the intimate relationship between consumption and identity (e.g. Frith, 1996; De Nora, 2000; Hesmondhalgh, 2008). If you've ever dabbled in online dating, you might have clocked how often and how prominently users highlight their favourite books, films and music on their profiles. Such declared tastes function as a unique stamp of individual identity, signalling to others our values and worldviews in ways that go beyond words. As an awkward teenager coming of age in the 1980s and '90s, I relied on the mixed compilation tape as an essential vehicle of self-expression. A mixed tape wasn't just a gift you put together for a friend, boyfriend or girlfriend. It was encoded with a message that said "this is who I am (or who I'd like you to think I am) and if you like these songs then maybe you'll like me too." The more unique our tastes are (i.e. the less they converge around the mainstream and the popular), the more currency they have as tools of self-expression.

An important aspect of long tail theory follows directly from this assumption that consumers, in general, value niche over mainstream content. According to Anderson, this is what makes investment in the long tail not just more profitable compared to the pre-digital era, but more profitable even compared to the head. The redirection of investment thus results in a gradual 'fattening up' or widening of the tail, as expanding niche provision attracts growing numbers of consumers and investors.

It's a crucial piece of the puzzle—from an agenda control perspective—for two reasons. First, the social value of the long tail *requires* a degree of uptake as well as fluidity in niche consumption, as opposed to just an expansion in the availability of diverse supply. A growth in this uptake and fluidity is captured by the widening of the tail as shown in Figure 12.3. The widening tail also offers a response to concerns about cocoons, echo chambers or filter bubble effects. So long as there is an intrinsically group dimension to niche consumption, and so

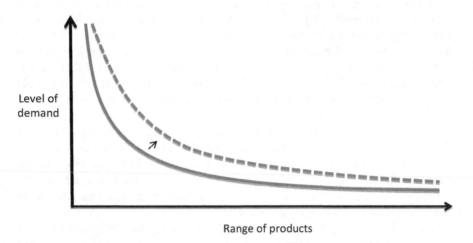

Level of demand

Range of products

Figure 12.3 The Widening Tail

long as the pattern of distribution does not erect un-scalable walls around these groups, then users will remain relatively resistant to the control or gatekeeping practices associated with personalisation filters, just as they will be immune to agenda containment within the head.

Second, such a trend will start to erode the boundary between head and tail. You can see in Figure 12.3 that as the tail starts to thicken, there is an observable effect on the head, which begins to open up and progressively merge into the tail. Self-evidently, such a trend promises to diminish the wider agenda setting role of leading news institutions and inhibit the power of vested interests over the agenda at large. The more users are dispersed evenly across the head and along the tail, the harder it becomes to define and shape even a mainstream agenda.

But the degree to which the tail is indeed widening is highly contestable on both empirical and theoretical grounds. There is also much debate about whether or to what degree the head—representing mainstream media and popular culture—is dissipating, along with the attendant implications for media plurality, ownership and agenda concerns. You have probably noticed that this question recalls much of the discussion in earlier chapters, particularly those in part II. There we interrogated claims that the agenda power of media owners has passed down to users amid the rise of networked gatekeeping and the apparent dissolution of a mainstream news agenda. Indeed, the notion of user empowerment has been intimately linked with long tail theory with the shift from mass to niche equated with a redistribution of power from "them to us" (Jarvis, 2009, p. 67).

I argued in part II that the dominant voice of major news brands has not been overthrown either by the rise of the crowd (through networked gatekeeping and other collaborative forms of news participation) or the empowerment of the individual user (through enhanced opportunities for news selectivity), pointing to the resurgent force of gatekeeping trust and the intensifying commodification of news in the digital environment. In the following chapter we revisit these themes through the lens of the long tail. In particular, we assess whether the tail really is widening and the head dissipating along the lines predicted by Anderson, and reflect on the particular aspects of the emergent cultural economy that favour (contrary to the long tail thesis) mainstream over niche or alternative content.

Note

1. See Wikileaks.org—About. Available at http://wikileaks.org/About.html (last accessed 13 March, 2016).

Chapter 13

Big-Headedness

Is Anybody Listening?

There is little argument that the internet has vastly expanded the supply of niche content in all areas of culture, entertainment, news and information. But the democratic force of plurality dictates that it is not enough for diverse expressions to be accessible in any given media system. They also have to be *accessed* by a sufficient number of people so as to meaningfully impact on the public consciousness. It is, in essence, the difference between the ability to speak and the ability to be heard.

In contrast to the superstar paradigm, ours is indeed an age in which a much wider variety of speakers *can* be heard compared to the days of analogue distribution. To use Anderson's words, "the ants now have megaphones." And we have seen how this theory is based partly on radical changes to the cost structure of cultural production and distribution. But there are other essential qualities of the superstar paradigm that have remained unchanged, and some that have arguably intensified.

In its original formulation (Rosen, 1981), superstar theory was based on a combination of two relatively unique characteristics of cultural and entertainment products. First, notwithstanding the inherent subjectivity in consumption, less talent is generally a poor substitute for more talent. Even if the differences are marginal, there is no reason to settle for anything less than the best from the consumer's perspective. Second, entertainment goods in particular have a high degree of reproducibility: the difference in quality between an original and a copy is marginal and, as we saw in the previous chapter, production tends to incur relatively high fixed costs (and low marginal costs). In a later account of the superstar paradigm (Frank and Cook, 1995), a third characteristic was added: the inherent sociability of consumers of art, entertainment and culture means that they derive added value from consuming the same or similar products to their peers.

Digitisation has done little to change the first of these characteristics, has accentuated the second, and has either diminished or intensified the third (depending on your perspective of social media effects). Added to that, there are strong empirical grounds for challenging the long tail thesis. In one of the first of such challenges, Anita Elberse (2008) argued that at least in the online video rental and music subscription markets, the long tail potential was not being realised and that, if anything, the head of the distribution curve was undergoing something of a resurgence. Writing from a management studies perspective and reflecting on a number of datasets compiled in preceding studies, Elberse cautioned against the presumed investment opportunities presented by the long tail, especially within media and entertainment sectors.

The crux of her analysis rested on a challenge to the core assumption underpinning long tail theory: that users generally prefer niche over mainstream content. Reflecting on data collected from Quickflix (an Australian online video rental service), Elberse pointed out that users who rented both popular and obscure films tended to rate the former more highly than the latter, a finding corroborated in a subsequent study based on consumption data from Netflix (Tan and Netessine, 2009). Elberse acknowledged that this flew in the face of both the long tail assumption about consumer cognition, as well as conventional wisdom:

> We can all easily imagine the extreme delight that comes from discovering a rare gem, perfectly tailored to our interests and ours to bestow on likeminded friends. This is perhaps the most romanticized aspect of long-tail thinking. Many of us have experienced just such moments.
>
> (2008, p. 88)

But her findings were especially important because this assumption—that individuals prefer tailored content—also underlies normative claims regarding the social value of personalisation, as discussed in part III. Indeed, there is an integral overlap between debates about the social implications of personalisation and those of the long tail (Brynjolfsson et al., 2010). Drawing on the work of sociologist William McPhee, Elberse speculated that this unexpected outcome was to do with the fact that users who consume obscure products have knowledge of popular alternatives, whereas most people who consume popular products have little or no knowledge of obscure alternatives. This results in what McPhee termed 'double jeopardy': obscure products not only suffer from an exposure deficit, but are also less appreciated by those who do consume them (compared to those who consume popular products only).

Of course, Elberse was basing her argument here largely on speculation and data collected from a fairly on a limited sample, a point that Anderson (2008) made in response when he questioned "why [Elberse] feels able to extrapolate that to all internet commerce." But the most important findings related to studies that observed trends over time (e.g. Elberse and Oberholzer-Gee, 2006). These suggested that although sales were increasingly spread across a wider range of titles, artists and genres, the volume of sales within the tail was low and actually decreasing, whereas sales were concentrating in the head. The net effect was both a lengthening and *flattening* of the tail and in the music industry, these trends became more pronounced as digital formats and platforms replaced the sale of physical units. Elberse concluded that "digital channels may be further strengthening the position of a select group of winners."

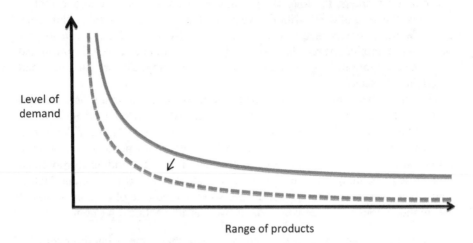

Level of demand

Range of products

Figure 13.1 Long Tail Regression

A more recent study confirmed this pattern of concentration in the music download market across Europe and North America (Duch-Brown and Martens, 2014). Out of 6.7 million songs purchased between 2000 and 2011 (an enormously long tail compared to the pre-digital era), 30 percent registered only a single sale. In Finland—the most digitally advanced country in the sample—this proportion rises to a staggering 67 percent. Even more strikingly, only 0.03 percent of songs downloaded in Finland attracted more than 1,000 sales. That all adds up to a remarkably flat tail and suggests that the development and spread of digital platforms is fostering a *regression* towards a more concentrated market, as shown in Figure 13.1. In this story, the shift to online platforms has an initial long tail effect (illustrated by the solid line curve), but over time the tail becomes flatter rather than fatter.

But what could have caused this regression back to a more superstar-oriented framework? One possibility—contrary to what we might expect—is that the development of social networking has driven users back towards the most popular brands. To glimpse how this might have come about, we need to drill deeper into the phenomenon of niche that is said to have fuelled the growth of the tail.

The Roots of Regression

One of the pillars of the long tail ideal is that digital networking not only facilitates the growth of niche product sales but also the development of niche *communities*. Indeed, the enhanced social interaction around niche interests that digital platforms support is thought to be a key driver of tail growth. In the old days, if you were the kind of person that might potentially be into Japanoise rock but lived in a small town or rural village with people who did not generally share your interests and tastes, chances are you might never have the opportunity to discover that such a genre even existed. This is what economists describe as 'latent' demand and attribute to market inefficiency. But in the networked age, these limitations are in theory overcome not only because Japanoise rock is now accessible to you from a practical point of view, but because you are now able to connect with people who share your general tastes and can help point you to such genres in the first place. Coupled with the personalised recommendations of algorithms, a world of discovery is thus opened up upon joining the network. This is what supposedly results in a net reduction of search costs compared to pre-digital markets, despite the vastly expanded horizon of choice.

But research strongly suggests that word of mouth interactions online can in fact have the opposite effect, favouring mainstream over niche content (Hervas-Drane, 2007; Duch-Brown and Martens, 2014). This is likely due to the fact that search costs for those users with relatively mainstream tastes are reduced *more* through online word of mouth compared to those with relatively obscure tastes. Although it is now easier for people with niche tastes to connect, it is even easier for people with mainstream tastes to find each other, as well as the content that matches their preferences.

But what about personalised algorithms and recommender systems designed to direct users to their preferred content, whatever it may be? Fleder and Hosanagar (2009) suggested that these also, on aggregate, push consumers towards the head rather than tail. The effect stems from 'collaborative filters' that make personalised recommendations based on the purchases of others who exhibit similar preferences. Because more popular products will be more recommended overall, such filters ultimately reward best sellers with even greater market share.

To understand why the long tail effect may prove to have been short-lived (as opposed to non-existent), consider what kind of people were likely early adopters of online communication channels. During the inception phase of the World Wide Web, those with relatively niche preferences had arguably the strongest incentives to join the network, not least as a way to find like-minded souls. This may partly explain the initial widening tail effect of consumer feedback observed in some studies (e.g. Clemons et al., 2006). But as increasing numbers of mainstream-oriented users joined the network, so the culture of 'mass' began to reassert itself. Under such conditions, we would expect producers to respond by reinvesting in content with mass or cross appeal, not least because the enhanced reproducibility of digital content makes best sellers disproportionately profitable.

There is, then, the potential for mutually reinforcing trends to produce an overall regression of the long tail over time, resulting in growing concentration and consolidation around the mainstream. But it's important to stress that such a pattern is by no means conclusive. Indeed, one of the problems confounding the empirical literature on long tail economics is the conflicting trends observed in different studies. So, for instance, whereas Fleder and Hosanagar (2009) suggested that recommendation algorithms have a regressive effect on the tail, Brynjolfsson et al. (2011) found the opposite. And whereas regressive effects have been found in the markets for online video (Elberse and Oberholzer-Gee, 2007) and music downloads (Elberse, 2008), a sustained growth in the long tail has been observed in online book markets (e.g. Peltier and Moreau, 2012).

Many of the discrepancies are likely to do with differences in methodology, as well as the particularities of individual markets studied. It is also entirely plausible that there may be conflicting and simultaneous long tail and concentration effects that result in a depleting share of sales occupied by mid-range products (Duch-Brown and Martens, 2014). One of the few long tail studies to focus on news found a similar contrasting pattern of distribution among articles produced by French online news sites (Smyrnaios et al., 2010). Although their output was voluminous and diverse, article distribution was nevertheless heavily concentrated around a small number of issues that made up the mainstream agenda.

If we shift our analysis to the level of provider, it seems even clearer that the overall trend is towards consolidation of online news markets. This explains the prevalence of mainstream sources in news circulation across social media and the blogosphere. As the audience for online news continues to expand, the general mainstreaming effect observed in other entertainment industries is no doubt playing its part here too. But there are also a number of characteristics specific to the online news sphere that push in the direction of the head.

For a start, as Carpentier (2014) has shown, gatekeeping trust appears to be sustaining the entrenched agenda setting influence of established news brands. As news sources proliferate and the noise of social media grows ever louder, it is not surprising that these brands have become powerful signals of authority and legitimacy in news definition. In the UK, a digital market research company reported in 2016 that "the top 10 publishers make up a huge chunk of the U.K. media market and own more than half of the entire industry" (Schwarz, 2016). The statement was based on data collected over 2015, specifically the number of page visits to 300 selected digital publishers. They found that 65 percent of this traffic was concentrated in the websites of the top 10 publishers. The top five alone attracted more than half of all traffic across the sample.

From a numbers perspective, however, the data could just as easily be read off as demonstrating the pluralising effects of the long tail. For a start, optimists might consider that the mere existence of 300 digital publishers (which is itself far from an exhaustive sample of *all* online publications accessible to a UK audience) reflects the plurality of the digital news sphere, at least compared to traditional platforms. But the list includes many websites that are not really what we would generally think of as news providers. They are much closer to the equivalent of special interest magazines in the print world, focusing on music, film, sport, entertainment and so forth, and it wouldn't make sense to consider their plurality contribution as equivalent to a daily news provider, especially one that covers political news and current affairs.

Starting at the tail end, the lowest ranked news website—*Pink News*—still attracted some 16 million page views. That sounds like a lot. But if we compare page views to unique visitors (as measured by the National Readership Survey[1]), the average ratio works out to around 250:1. So 16 million page views over the course of the year will probably amount to an audience reach of around 60,000. That's still not a tiny amount given that we are at the bottom of the pile here. But in long tail theory, concentration is a relative concept and what matters is not how much attention the smallest outlets attract, but how much *more* attention is captured by the bigger players. The greater the discrepancy, the more gatekeeping and (potentially) agenda setting power is likely to be vested in those at or near the top of the curve.

It is also important to remember the time dimension of long tail theory. Anderson predicted that the imbalance between the head and the tail will, over time, erode under digital market conditions. That's not to say that the head will evaporate entirely, but rather that the *level* of concentration will decline as niches begin to flourish. Ten years on from Anderson's prediction seems like a reasonable period to test this hypothesis, especially given the speed at which digital news markets have grown and the UK being at a relatively mature stage of development. But if we plot the data from SimilarWeb, there is no suggestion of any levelling out of the curve. On the contrary, as Figure 13.2 shows, the curve yields a highly defined head followed by a very flat tail.

But even this picture may still underestimate the true extent of concentration in online news. This is because the data does not capture news consumption via aggregators like Yahoo and social media sites like Facebook. As we will see in chapter 11, a conceptual trap emerges in attempts to measure digital plurality when aggregators and other websites that host the content of wholesale providers are counted as distinct news sources in their own right. This has the inevitable effect of overestimating the plurality of voices in the online news sphere. Conversely in this case, by excluding aggregators altogether, the data fail to capture

Figure 13.2 Top UK Media Publishers and Publications 2015 Index

Source: SimilarWeb, *Index: Top UK media publishers and publications 2015*. Retrieved from Similarweb.com

the added reach that some news brands have through wholesale provision. A much more accurate picture of the 'share of voice' would emerge if we were to include aggregators in the mix but attribute page visits to original or wholesale news providers. In that case, the head of the curve would likely be reinforced still further.

There is yet another conceptual problem from the perspective of gatekeeping power that emerges when data like this are presented. Commercial media lobbyists would be quick to point out that the head of the curve is itself dominated by a single news provider: the BBC. Indeed, the BBC's online news services attracted more than three times the total traffic of its nearest rival, and more than 30 percent of traffic across the whole sample. From this perspective, the existence of commercial competitors within the head looks like a much needed check on the near-monopoly status enjoyed by the BBC. Rather than worrying about the agenda influence of mainstream media in general, some argue that we should be concerned exclusively with the overarching reach and influence of the BBC (e.g. Elstein, 2015).

Issues That Matter

But how far does the BBC's own news agenda reflect or align with that of its commercial competitors? When scholars at Cardiff University set out to investigate this question during the 2015 UK general election (Cushion and Sambrook, 2015), they found a very different picture to that often conjured by critics in the right-wing press. Rather than harbouring a liberal or left-wing metropolitan bias, the BBC agenda appeared to have been consistently led by newspapers editorially aligned with the Conservative Party, who significantly outnumbered left-leaning papers. The extent of this alignment was corroborated by other research conducted at Loughborough University[2] and by Kings College, London (Moore and Ramsay, 2015). These findings showed a strong correlation between the range and rank order of issues covered by both television and the press, and an overall mainstream agenda that played to issues at the forefront of the Conservative Party campaign.

In chapter 2 we discussed the 1992 election in Britain which was widely thought to have been 'won' by the Murdoch press—especially the *Sun* newspaper, which brazenly claimed credit for the Tory victory in a headline that Murdoch himself sought to downplay. One striking parallel with 1992 was that the 2015 election was also one in which the majority of polls prior to the vote failed to predict the result, namely a Conservative majority victory, and which therefore brought questions of press power and influence back under the spotlight (Barnett, 2015). Like 1992, the right-wing press also waged a very personalised campaign against the Labour leader. One study concluded that the extent of partisan bias in the press significantly exceeded that of 1992, with 95 percent of tabloid editorials attacking Labour in the run-up to the election (Plunkett and Sedghi, 2015).

Conservative critics hit back at suggestions that it was the press that 'won it' by drawing attention to declining print circulation and comparatively low levels of audience, and the overwhelming dominance of the BBC across broadcasting and online platforms (Elstein, 2015). But both arguments overlooked the subtle and potentially more far-reaching influence of defining issue priorities, and the extent to which an agenda consensus emerged across mainstream media platforms playing to the Conservative Party campaign.

And this was exactly what happened. In terms of policies, there was a heavy emphasis in the wider coverage on the economy, the near-exclusive policy issue around which the Conservatives crafted their campaign. According to journalist Tim Ross:

> The decision to focus relentlessly on the economic message, at its most basic, is the dominant reason that the Tories won. Every other salvo in the Tories' 'air war' was a variation on this theme: they were the party of economic competence, of the 'long-term economic plan', and all their opponents were emissaries of 'chaos'.
>
> (2015, p. 152)

However, according to monthly public polling by Ipsos MORI,[3] the economy ranked as only the third 'most important issue facing Britain today' throughout most of the campaign, behind the National Health Service (NHS) and immigration. Between February and May 2015, the NHS—an issue at the top of the Labour Party's election campaign agenda—was the number one issue of importance ranked by survey respondents for all but one month, when it was surpassed by immigration.

In terms of election process—to which coverage was skewed over policy in general—both television news and the press focused heavily on the political horse race and the 'threat' of a left-wing coalition between the Labour Party and the Scottish National Party (SNP). This was an issue that again chimed with the Conservatives' agenda, in contrast to the Labour Party that actively sought to avoid or downplay it.

In the election aftermath, a number of journalists reflected on the two-pronged attack of the Tory's central campaign message. According to the BBC's campaign correspondent Jonny Dymond,

> David Cameron had two simple messages in the campaign and he rarely veered from them; the first—the economy is in good shape and the recovery is threatened by Labour. And the second—the SNP would hold a Labour-led government to ransom.
>
> (Dymond, 2015)

But at no point did he reflect on why these two issues also happened to be the most widely covered on the BBC and elsewhere. Did journalists have a sixth sense of what issues mattered most to people that was more accurate than the surveys conducted by Ipsos MORI? Or were the BBC and other broadcasters led by a predominantly right-wing press agenda?

It was not just traditional media platforms that were entwined in this way. An analysis of political influencers on Twitter (based on the number of followers, tweets, and other data suggestive of a user's prominence) showed that the agenda here was also largely reflective of the mainstream media (Moore and Ramsay, 2015). The difference, however, is that Twitter influencers were more likely to challenge mainstream media on the issues, particularly with reference to things like inaccuracy and bias.

As we saw in chapter 4, such challenges offer a potentially cogent check on the dominance of mainstream media narratives. But in spite of its expansive reach, Twitter remains an unrepresentative forum of public debate, with its members drawn heavily from younger age groups and relatively privileged socioeconomic backgrounds. According to a recent survey, 12 percent of people in the UK use Twitter for news, compared to 75 percent who use television for news (Newman et al., 2015). What's more, challenging the mainstream media on how it covers issues does not have the same counter-hegemonic force as *redefining* the issues that matter. In this sense, influential Twitter users still seem to be taking their cues from the agenda set by mainstream media.

One vivid illustration of both the scope and limits of this resistance surfaced at the height of the campaign, when an open letter calling for the re-election of Conservatives appeared in the *Daily Telegraph*. The letter was presented as a spontaneous initiative by the small business community, with apparently 5,000 signatories and a statement that implored voters to give the Conservatives a chance 'to finish what they have started'. The 'story' was duly picked up by the BBC and other television news providers and largely covered without critical scrutiny (Moore and Ramsay, 2015). Within hours, however, it emerged that the letter had in fact originated from the Conservative Party's campaign headquarters (Mason and Watt, 2015). This prompted a freelance journalist, Alex Andreou (2015a), to investigate further with the help of Twitter users and followers of his blog. It was not long before they identified several names on the letter that had been dupli-cated, as well as references to companies that no longer existed or claimed not to have signed. They even found Conservative Party candidates themselves among the signatories.

Most remarkable, however, was that this spontaneous collaborative investiga-tion was conducted and the results published on the same day that the original let-ter appeared in the *Telegraph* and the story ran on television news channels. It was an example of investigative reporting in real time, producing a counter-narrative that implicated the mainstream media as complicit in a Conservative Party public relations initiative. The euphoric sense of triumph was underlined when Andreou tweeted, "Twitter is making it—in some ways—more difficult to lie. We are talk-ing directly to each other, with no mediators. It's wonderful" (Andreou, 2015b).

Yet despite the timely and comprehensive way in which the story was unspun, this had very little impact in turn on the mainstream news agenda at large. Although some broadcasters did express a degree of scepticism over the letter, the BBC questioned its authenticity only in the *Daily Politics* show (Moore and Ramsay, 2015), a news programme with a relatively small audience. Elsewhere the letter was reported uncritically on a day when the Conservatives happened to have launched their small business manifesto and David Cameron gave a speech to an audience of small business leaders in London. For its part, the *Telegraph* offered no apology but instead, according to Andreou, quietly made corrections to the article based on the evidence garnered by him and his followers.

The significance of this episode should be considered within the wider context of the disproportionate attention given over to the economy by media across the board. It echoed the sentiments of another letter published a month earlier by the *Telegraph* and signed by 103 business 'leaders' (Dominiczak, 2015). On that occasion, the pick-up by television news was even more pronounced, with the story running as a lead headline on three bulletins and occupying 38 percent of election coverage on television that evening (Cushion and Sambrook, 2015). Yet on the same day, as the Cardiff researchers pointed out, nowhere near the same level of attention was given to a poll of leading economists who questioned the government's austerity measures, published in the *Independent* newspaper (Chu, 2015). Nor did the BBC or television in general pay much regard to a letter signed by more than 140 health professionals criticising the government's record on the NHS, and which was published by the *Guardian* a few days later (Boseley, 2015).

Of course, what *makes* the news on any given day is always at some level subject to random factors, not least the variable 'size' of news stories and competition for air time. But the systematic imbalance in the BBC's attention to campaign issues and press coverage raises profound questions over its independence and capacity to resist the definitional power of (predominantly) right-wing newspapers. The BBC's independence of both government and commercial influences has arguably always been compromised by its structural dependence on the license fee and charter renewal, which periodically gives the government of the day power to determine the BBC's fate (Schlesinger, 1987; Born, 2005). But these pressures have intensified with unprecedented levels of imposed austerity over recent years, an ever more belligerent press, and a government that has made clear its intent to privatise and commercialise much of what's left of the BBC and public service media more broadly.

It wasn't supposed to be like this. The days when newspapers like the *Sun* could have such a pivotal election influence as it claimed to have had in 1992 seem like a bygone era. The year 2015 in particular was ideally poised to mark a new chapter in election coverage, for better or for worse. The legacy of the phone hacking scandal coupled with the enduring crisis of funding faced by most newspapers seemed to both delegitimise and undermine their agenda influence. And whereas television—and the BBC in particular—remained the dominant source of news, social media platforms seemed to be having a growing reciprocal influence in determining the election issues under the spotlight. It is no doubt for these reasons—as well as the breakup of the two-party political system since 2010— that the media coverage of this election attracted such intense academic scrutiny.

But it would be an oversimplification to attribute the Conservatives' unexpected victory solely to the hidden machinations of press power. After all, the fact that the mainstream news agenda was to some extent out of step with the public agenda

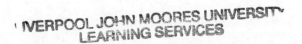

(as measured by monthly issue tracking polls) suggests very little in the way of agenda setting effects. Whether the media agenda had any influence on actual voting outcomes is a separate question altogether. But the important point for our purposes is that the evidence cited earlier casts doubt over assumptions that the BBC has a greater agenda influence than newspapers—much less that the national press offer a meaningful plurality counterweight to the BBC's dominance of news consumption. Ironically, the evidence from the 2015 election suggests that if anything, the BBC *amplified* an agenda that, if not set by the right-wing press, at least prioritised the issues favoured by Conservative communications strategists.

By the same token, we ought to be equally sceptical of arguments that the BBC provides a substantive check on the enduring gatekeeping role of the mainstream press. At a time when many public service broadcasters around the world—including the BBC—are facing varying degrees of existential crises, public debate is all too often reduced to a choice between preservation or market-based reforms, with the latter usually amounting to cutbacks or closures.

What's left off the agenda is the possibility of radical democratic reform aimed at reconstituting the independence, accountability and internal plurality of public service media. And this is an issue that is intimately tied to questions of media ownership. The idea that a substantive section of any democratic media system needs to be in public hands is one that retains a great deal of force (Aalberg and Curran, 2012; Cushion, 2012), in spite of the digital transition and corresponding end of channel scarcity (which underlined the original rationale for public service media). But the way in which public service broadcasters are structured, regulated and governed can have profound implications for independence in relation to both the state and market.

The Long Tail Reconsidered

It's worth emphasising that the bulk of scholarly attention to the long tail has focused on the entertainment industry and empirical studies largely grounded in the disciplines of economics and management science. As a consequence, there has been comparatively little attention to the civic and cultural implications of shifts in the pattern of content distribution, especially in the context of news and information markets. Nevertheless, we have seen that long tail theory provides a useful basis from which to re-examine narratives around the *redistribution* of gatekeeping and agenda power. In particular, the notion of coexistence at the heart of long tail theory (whether or not the prevailing trend favours one end of the curve or the other) reveals clues that help explain some of the conflicting narratives and arguments reviewed in previous chapters. But in spite of the seductive appeal of the long tail vision, its diversifying and democratising potential does not seem to have been realised, at least when it comes to the news.

In the following chapter, we will try to figure out why the long tail promise has not been fulfilled by addressing coexistence in a different sense, namely the interconnectedness of incumbent and emergent sources of agenda control. But first we ought to re-examine the normative claims and assumptions that underpin the long tail ideal and which were so vividly captured by Steve Albini's optimistic reflections on the state of the music industry, as discussed in the previous chapter. Much of the subsequent discussion has addressed the question of whether or to what degree the explosion of niche is tempering the pervasive reach of mainstream culture. What we haven't really addressed is whether tempering the reach of mainstream culture is actually a *good thing* from the perspective of plurality and democracy.

To get to the bottom of this question, we need to go back to the assumption underpinning long tail theory that users intrinsically prefer tailored content. As we have seen, it is a view implicitly shared by proponents of long tail theory and advocates of personalisation algorithms alike. We have also seen that some of the flaws in this assumption may be one reason why the playing field does not seem to be levelling out in the way that long tail optimists predicted, or at least nowhere near as consistently and unquestionably.

But there is another problem with this assumption that undermines the *normative* claims behind long tail theory, in that it overlooks the importance of collective sensibilities when it comes to the consumption of news, entertainment and culture. Part of what makes news *news* or entertainment *entertaining* or music and films and books *meaningful* is that they form part of a shared culture. Sometimes that collective experience is limited to a niche or fragmented audience. But sometimes it extends to the 'imaginary community' of society at large. I'm not much of a football fan myself, but every four years I watch and follow the World Cup finals fairly closely. Why? The only plausible explanation I can think of is that I am drawn to the sense of spectacle that goes along with such events. In other words, I am pulled by the fact that millions of other people are watching at the same time. It is an event that transcends the barriers of niche, fragmented and national audiences. That's what makes it somehow feel exciting and important, like a global news headline that fills screens and dinner table conversations everywhere at once.

Consider my toddler, whose favourite TV show is *Postman Pat*. He has learnt that whenever the television is on, his parents have the power to select episodes of the show on demand, and he has become accustomed to demanding that they do so. When he gets his way, he seems quietly satisfied but rarely remains focused for the duration of the episode. But here's the strange thing: every morning at 7.30 the show airs on the BBC's younger children's channel *CBeebies*. And whenever the television is on at that moment and the theme tune starts, he shrieks and quivers with excitement in a way that he never quite expresses when the show is 'selected'.

What accounts for this marked difference in reception? Clearly the excitement with which he greets the scheduled airing of the show has something to do with a sense of surprise and unexpectedness. If we think about it, this element of surprise is simply a by-product of the fact that the show was not selected *on demand*. Somewhere in the back of his mind, he knows that when the show airs at its scheduled time, it is not just playing for him and him alone.

What this suggests is that there is something transcendent in the collective imaginary of cultural consumption that is not quite realised when content is uniquely selected, either by individual users themselves or by algorithms on behalf of individual users. This collective imaginary is not necessarily in conflict with the personal and subjective dimension but, on the contrary, may serve to support and reinforce it. In a thought-provoking essay on the relationship between music and self-identity, David Hesmondhalgh argued that the individual emotions we may experience from listening to music are often intensified by the sense that they are shared, or potentially shared, by others:

> This [sense] can be especially strong at a live performance, but it is just as possible when experiencing music individually, when we might, however semi-consciously and fleetingly, imagine others—a particular person, or untold thousands—being able to share that response.
>
> (2008, p. 2)

It seems reasonable to assume that the more atomised our pattern of consumption, the more distant we become from that collective imaginary. This touches on the concern at the heart of public sphere critiques that have surfaced recurrently throughout this book, whether in the shape of cocoons, echo chambers or filter bubbles. They share a core conviction that the more individualised our consumption patterns become—particularly in respect of news and information—the more fragmented, polarised and exclusive the public sphere becomes.

But is the long tail theory and personalisation ideal really about the progressive atomisation of consumption in this sense? After all, personalisation metrics are not based purely on what we as individuals have consumed, shared or searched for in the past. If they were, we would be offered an extremely limited range of content indeed. As we have seen, one of the peculiar features of the cultural economy is that the value of products is contingent on a degree of novelty or newness (Garnham, 2000), even if it is bound up with the familiar. This is not the same for coffee. If I have a favourite brand and type of coffee, chances are I would actively seek to consume it again and again, perhaps from the same outlet, the same size, the same amount of sugar and so forth. But I'd be unlikely to purchase my favourite book more than once. I might not even read the one I purchased more than once, although I may well seek out other titles by the same or similar authors.

Of course, a favourite book will likely be more treasured than any given cup of coffee. But in the case of arts and media, the magnitude of impact or the degree of utility—to use the language of economics—does not translate into recurring demand. Personalising algorithms are wise to this reality. Their real power consists in their potential to make targeted recommendations or suggestions for *new* content based not only on my own prior choices but also on the prior choices of others who share similar characteristics to me. This is why social networking turned out to be such a valuable tool for targeted advertising—because it doesn't just target us in isolation but continually alerts us to the content choices of our friends. For long tail and personalisation optimists, this is what makes the likes of Facebook and Twitter essential platforms for the support of niche cultures and communities, along with something approximating an integrated public sphere.

Hesmondhalgh (2008), for his part, argues that both the individual and collective dimensions of cultural consumption are at least partly the products of capitalist appropriation. In other words, markets function in such a way as to (somewhat artificially) generate feelings of autonomy, authenticity and collectivity in the consumption of culture as a means of fuelling further consumption. But our primary concern for now is whether the *collective* dimension of personalisation is enough to avoid descent into the kind of solipsism associated with cocoons, echo chambers and filter bubbles. Anderson believed that rather than isolating us in our own private universe, algorithms enable us to congregate with people with whom we share a true and genuine affinity, as opposed to those we are lumped with as a result of "superficial mass cultural overlaps." He concluded that "mass culture may fade, but common culture will not. We will still share our culture with others, but not with everyone" (2009 [2006], p. 191).

Radical Containment

Niche culture and alternative media have always existed alongside the mainstream. But what defines the narrative of coexistence (in the sense we have considered it thus far) is a conviction that the former will *flourish* under digital conditions as the grip of mainstream culture on the public consciousness starts to loosen. As we have seen, this prediction is based partly on what is at best an incomplete and inadequate conception of the complex drivers behind cultural consumption. But let us assume for a moment that Anderson's vision was realised: mass culture still exists but it has ceded considerable ground to both a wide and long tail consisting of niche, alternative and radical interest communities. Let us also assume, as Anderson does, that most people do not remain rigidly within particular communities, or that they at least allow themselves to be exposed to perspectives and interests representing a broad cross section of society. Indeed, we don't have to stretch our imaginations too far in this respect because, as we saw in chapter 9, there is considerable evidence in support of such patterns in online news consumption.

But does this picture represent the ultimate democratisation of culture? Does it render critical questions of media ownership and agenda control finally obsolete? I'm not so sure. The issue here is not to do with the expanding world of niche, but with the opportunity cost of the receding world of mass. Whereas the critical literature has been preoccupied with the presumed fragmenting and polarising effects of this process on the public sphere, much less attention has been given to the precise implications for the exposure of radical or subversive ideas. If, as Steve Albini intimated, the long tail has special resonance for all things alternative, could its flourishing come at the expense of that corner of mass culture—however marginalised and peripheral—that was once occupied by *radical* alternatives?

Some have certainly questioned why, for instance, the anti-war movement during the 1960s and '70s penetrated both the box office and Billboard charts in ways that cannot be said of equally controversial wars post-2000 in Afghanistan and Iraq (Garofalo, 2013). In the 1970s, chart-topping songs reached millions of homes around the world. These included songs with radical political statements by recording artists including John Lennon ("War Is Over"), Pink Floyd ("We Don't Need No Education") and Sex Pistols ("Anarchy in the UK").

It's worth noting at this point that when a UK Facebook campaign in 2009 briefly interrupted the grip of music reality TV shows on the coveted Christmas number one spot, it seemed to epitomise the social network's capacity to mobilise widespread resistance to popular culture (Pidd, 2009). The song that the campaign propelled to the top of the charts (by US rock band Rage Against the Machine) captured the spirit of countercultural defiance in its repeated refrain "fuck you I won't do what you tell me." But it was a song that was originally released nearly two decades earlier and subsequent similar campaigns based around more contemporary songs failed to make much impact.

I'm not suggesting that protest music is a thing of the past. But its erosion within contemporary mainstream culture suggests we need to ask more questions of the long tail beyond simply whether or to what degree it is counterbalancing the head. In particular, we need to ask whether there are particular forms of discourse and expression that are becoming increasingly contained within niche communities and what impact this may have on the possibilities for ideological and cultural resistance. We have to at least consider the potential for the long tail to produce a rebalancing effect, but one that may hinder rather than nurture what Castells called 'counter-power'. In this scenario, as shown in Figure 13.3, the long tail does not look dissimilar to Anderson's vision, but it masks a potentially growing containment of voices 'from below' within the tail itself. In other words, along with the

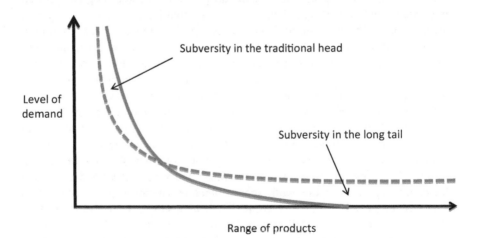

Figure 13.3 Ghettoisation

potential impact of fragmentation and polarisation on the public sphere, we should also consider the potential *ghettoisation* of radical ideas.

But whereas this seems plausible in respect of the music landscape, the effects of ghettoisation on news agendas is harder to gauge. In chapter 3 I suggested that, on the surface at least, scrutiny of state-corporate power is increasingly ubiquitous in mainstream news narratives. This is what underlines the view of McNair (2006) and others (e.g. Jenkins, 2006; Boydstun, 2013), that the news agenda is intrinsically resistant to control by powerful sources in any generalizable sense. A crucial premise here is that the threat of control is mitigated partly by the diversified channels through which news definitions are communicated, negotiated and contested. It is a conception that is therefore intimately connected to the long tail ideal.

But the central problem with this view—which we have encountered throughout the book so far—is that it relies on a fairly limited scope of analysis in relation to media coverage that outwardly invokes notions of agenda chaos and resistance. For instance, the documenting and exposure of the Abu Ghraib prisoner abuse scandal in 2004 was, as McNair points out, a function of "digital cameras and the rapid global dissemination of the photographs made possible by new media technologies" (McNair, 2006, p. 158). The professional news media were also clearly instrumental in bringing the prisoner abuse scandal at Abu Ghraib to the attention of mass global audiences. But they played an equally pivotal role in ensuring the story was largely confined to the actions of a few low-ranking soldiers, contrary to hard evidence available to journalists at the time of a top-down directed policy of torture (Bennett et al., 2006).

The Angry Buzz Goes Silent

In chapter 3, we examined a number of other examples of news crises and explosions that appear to have come under control at key moments and contexts, whether it was the 'end of story' framing in respect of BAe's plea bargain settlement with the Serious Fraud Office in 2010, the relative inattention given to certain stories that emerged during Cablegate, or the narrow framework of debate admitted in coverage of the bank bailout in 2008. We have also seen throughout the book how social media agendas—although at times relatively autonomous—do not on the whole wield much in the way of reciprocal influence over mainstream media platforms. We have seen this both in the general swathe of empirical research data and in case studies around election coverage of the Labour leadership victory of Jeremy Corbyn or the national security files leaked by Ed Snowden.

Part of the problem may have something to do with the particular pressures faced by long-form journalism in the information age. Amid the constant demands of a real-time news cycle, breaking and sound bite news tends to be privileged over in-depth analysis and investigation (Fenton, 2010). This imbalance has been exacerbated by perpetual newsroom cuts that target the most expensive and risky forms of journalism. In the world of current affairs, it has manifested in what seems to be a fading spotlight on hard-hitting original investigations that challenge dominant narratives and perspectives, especially around national security and the war on terror.

In 1988, the British current affairs series *This Week* broadcast its most notorious film, *Death on the Rock*, at peak time to 6.5 million viewers, questioning the official narrative surrounding state assassinations of three suspected terrorists (Holland, 2006). But within three years, the television company behind the series lost its franchise, marking the beginning of a decline in current affairs investigations across the board, but especially those broadcast on the main flagship terrestrial channels at peak time. In 1998, another flagship current affairs series specialising in investigative reports broadcast its last edition, with channel controllers citing the intensifying struggle for ratings in the multichannel era as the reason for its closure (Goddard et al., 2007). The decline in investigative and foreign affairs output continued during the 2000s (Hughes, 2013). This was in spite of increases in the quantity of current affairs output overall, with investigations focused on consumer and human interest topics. Between 2009 and 2014, viewing of current affairs covering political, social or economic issues declined by over 30 percent (Ofcom, 2015a).

As mainstream channels, stations and titles faced ever-greater competition for audiences from the lengthening tail of news provision, it was perhaps inevitable that investigative reporting—the costliest form of newsgathering—would face the razor edge of cuts. But it is not just the direct costs of investigative newsgathering (with little guarantee of a story, let alone a scoop) that makes it such a financially risky prospect. It is also the kind of reporting that tends to attract the highest rate of lawsuits and editorial controversies that can bring news organisations into disrepute. Amid a climate of caution hanging over from a string of such controversies at the BBC in recent years, coupled with unceasing austerity pressures, it is not surprising that some journalists have spoken off the record about a growing culture of conformity and repression within the newsroom (Schlosberg, 2013).

Conclusion

Over the last two chapters we have examined the intricacies of long tail theory against the backdrop of the dispersal narratives examined in part II. I have tried to show how the long tail—at least in its most recognised and celebrated conception—embodies many of the ideas at the heart of these narratives. But we have also seen how the long tail can help to explain the coexistence of conflicting theories and empirical data that suggest on the one hand widening opportunities for grassroots and participatory platforms to (re)shape the media agenda at large, and on the other preservation and consolidation of elite agenda power.

Ultimately, however, the limitation of the long tail consists in its assumed emancipatory potential. Its advocates tend not to confront the possibility that forces of agenda resistance have been both redirected to and *contained* within the lengthening tail. In any case, what seems certain is that there has not been a *radical* redistribution of voice in the information age, and that evolving gatekeeping practices and meaning making power remain the preserve of large-scale institutions, even if they have assumed somewhat diversified roles in originating and facilitating news flows. Little wonder then that Google's Eric Schmidt himself dismissed the significance of the long tail as early as 2008 when he remarked that "while the tail is very interesting, the vast majority of revenue remains in the head [. . .] when you get everybody together they still like to have one superstar" (Resnikoff, 2013).

In the following chapter, and against the backdrop of the transferral narratives we explored in part III, we will interrogate Google's own role in sustaining the superstar paradigm (at least when it comes to news consumption). This invokes the notion of coexistence not between head and tail, but between different branches of the head.

Notes

1. See National Readership Survey—Newsbrands: Print/PC. Available at http://www.nrs. co.uk/latest-results/nrs-padd-results/newspapers-nrspaddresults/ (last accessed 23 March 2016).
2. See General Election 2015 —Media analysis from Loughborough University Communication Research Centre. Available at http://blog.lboro.ac.uk/general-election/ (last accessed 28 March 2016).
3. See Ipsos MORI Research Archive—Issues facing Britain. Available at https://www. ipsos-mori.com/researchpublications/researcharchive.aspx?contenttype=Issues+ Facing+Britain+(Issues+Index)&page=2 (last accessed 28 March 2016).

Chapter 14

The Media-Technology-Military-Industrial Complex

This book began by tracing the invisible qualities of agenda power and the role of media ownership within that equation, drawing on the 'radical view' of power articulated by Stephen Lukes (2005 [1974]). His emphasis on the obscurity and profundity of 'non-decision-making' was built on the power elite theory developed by US sociologist C. Wright Mills (1959) more than a decade earlier. It also resonated with the concept of a military-industrial complex articulated by former Republican US President Dwight D. Eisenhower. In his farewell address in 1961, Eisenhower issued a famous warning to the American people:

> We must guard against the acquisition of unwarranted influence, whether sought or unsought, by the military-industrial complex. The potential for the disastrous rise of misplaced power exists and will persist.[1]

According to Mills, this kind of misplaced power in late capitalist democracies was not to be found in the observable decision-making and conflicts of day-to-day partisan politics. To understand its true configuration and form, we had to look to the growing interdependence and shared interests of transnational capital, political authority and the military establishment. Like Eisenhower, Mills reflected on the exponential growth and consolidation of corporations, the military establishment and government bureaucracy during the post-war period, along with the rapid development of communication technologies and infrastructures. These were not coincidental and autonomous processes, but were mutually constitutive of an ever more integrated elite power structure, and one that transcended the formal checks and balances of the political system.

But equally, the power elite was not reducible to a conspiratorial clique, or any crude conception of *secretive* authority. Indeed, Mills made it clear that

> the truth about the nature and the power of the elite is not some secret which men of affairs know but will not tell [. . .] Often they are uncertain about their roles, and even more often they allow their fears and their hopes to affect their assessment of their own power. No matter how great their actual power, they tend to be less acutely aware of it than of the resistances of others to its use.
>
> (1959, p. 4)

In part I we discussed the ways in which the subtleties of agenda power could make it imperceptible even from the vantage point of those who exercise it. This is essentially because control is never unequivocal and uninterrupted but subject to forces of resistance, both from below and from competing elite interests. The question that Mills posed was not simply whether this dimension of struggle is real or illusory, but whether it fully captured the extent and nature of elite power in post-industrial societies. For both Mills and his descendants, who took a similar radical view of power (e.g. Lukes, 2005 [1974]; Hall, 1982), this was the essential flaw in the pluralist vision of capitalist democracy. To use Hall's words, it took "the part for the whole" (1982, p. 85) and thus failed to explain the underlying and less visible elements of consensus, along with the exercise of control in the *absence* of conflict.

But for critics of Mills, the suggestion of any kind of definable club at the top echelons of state-corporate power lacked empirical foundation and flew in the face of what seemed to be an opposite and prevailing trend. This was characterised by growing *disunity* among elite factions as the political economy became evermore complex and fractured. As Daniel Bell observed in respect of corporate power in post-war America: "I can think of only one issue on which the top corporations would be united: tax policy. In almost all others, they divide" (1962, p. 63).

Related problems for Bell concerned where the boundaries of the power elite were drawn and how they could be identified, along with the degree of concentration and centralisation of decision-making power, and its precise configuration and operation. But the question of elite consensus or conflict was to become central to debates about media ownership and agenda power. According to Michael Schudson, the media in Western democracies are characterised by a "vital arena of acceptable controversy" in which disconnects between dominant political and economic groups inhibit the ability of any one group to set or control the media agenda (1995, p. 43).

For Bell, some of the fault lines that divided industrial interests in the post-war period included those between railroads, trucking and airlines; or between coal, oil and natural gas. In part III, we traced similar fault lines in the digital information economy, which have resulted in public squabbles and legal battles between content owners, intermediaries and network operators. Whether it be wars *of* words or wars *over* words, the media-technology complex hardly seems to reflect anything like an 'interlocking directorate' that Mills ascribed to the power elite.

But on closer examination, as we have already encountered in a number of contexts, the picture is much less fractious than the rhetoric suggests. In this chapter, we review the underlying and overall consonance of interests between different players in the information economy, as well as evidence of an intensifying alliance and collaboration that extends to the wider military-industrial complex. Although the composition of the power elite inevitably varies according to place and time, the essential characteristics of revolving doors, intimate social relations and strategic partnerships remain as pertinent today as they did in the 1950s.

But I want to emphasise at the outset that none of this detracts from the very real tensions between corporate interests that exist both within and across communications sectors and the resultant conflicts over a broad range of policy issues. Instead, I will try to persuade you that these tensions are not the whole story, and perhaps not even half the story. More crucially, they have little bearing on the processes and outcome of information and agenda filtering.

The Centrality of Ownership

At the heart of the power elite theory developed by Mills is the idea of concentrated ownership and control of critical resources. But it is worth considering whether ownership is still as central to debates about media plurality (and about the media's role more broadly in sustaining or undermining democratic life). Indeed, for some, contemporary media plurality issues have more to do with diversity of exposure, privacy and copyright than with critical questions about media ownership. For instance, Helberger et al. (2015) argue that in contrast to traditional gatekeeping, the scarcity upon which the new gatekeeping power depends is not to do with control of critical resources (like television studios, cable networks, printing presses, etc.). Nor is it, by extension, to do with access to information, given the ever-expanding horizon of news and information sources accessible through digital communications. Rather it is the scarcity of user attention that is said to be the key leverage of gatekeeping power, and the mechanisms through which it is wielded are "related to interaction with users, the amount of knowledge and control they have over the user base" (Helberger et al., 2015, p. 67). In other words, whereas traditional gatekeeping concerns revolved around the ownership and control of production and distribution resources, all that really matters now is control of *access to the user*.

But this argument is problematic partly because user access has always—in one form or another—been a critical scarce resource in the economics of journalism. Ever since the first press baron era, competition for copy sales, eyeballs and advertisers has been predicated on the reality that audiences can 'choose' from a range of different news providers as well as platforms, or redirect their attention away from news altogether in favour of other genres, especially entertainment. In some ways, personalisation is the logical extension of a process of intensifying audience targeting and segmentation that has been going on for decades (Turow, 1997; Born, 2005). The particular ways in which dominant players secure access to the user-audience may be evolving, but that in itself does not fundamentally resolve the problem of ownership in converged media industries. Nor does it ameliorate concerns regarding access to information, particularly given the *hidden* qualities of personalisation filters, as well as the enduring boundaries of an aggregate or common agenda. As we have seen, the digital media space is evolving in ways that are, if anything, creating a resurgence of 'superstar effects' as regards dominant voices in the public sphere.

Accumulation

With regard to intermediaries, a related argument suggests that their unprecedented market power has little to do with the kind of ownership and control practices synonymous with the 'closed' industry paradigm. As we saw in chapter 8, the distinguishing feature of intermediaries is precisely that they do *not* control in the way that network operators control infrastructure and content owners control copyright.

But it's worth emphasising that although the basis of their market power may be novel, the means of their expansion is more familiar and very much rooted in ownership and accumulation. Google, for instance, has always been a cash-rich company, which in recent years it has leveraged in gobbling up potential competitive threats and acquiring the rights associated with technological innovation in areas far beyond its core business.

Back in the dim and distant past of the early 2000s, however, Google trod a different path. When Steve Jobs famously launched the first iPhone in an event resembling more of a stadium rock concert than a corporate presentation, he was joined on stage by Eric Schmidt, who exclaimed that what he liked about "the new architecture of the internet" is that companies like Google and Apple could "merge without merging" (Wu, 2010, p. 255). It was a perfect pitch to both the new generation of dot-com investors and the openness movement—no more exclusive partnerships and corporate tie-ins synonymous with the command-and-control era.

But ever since then, Google has been acquiring companies at a jaw-dropping rate. Much of the services that now define the Google user experience—from YouTube to Google Maps—are the product of such acquisitions. Although search remains at the core of its business, Google is now many different things, permeating virtually every corner of the tech industrial landscape, from designing and manufacturing mobile handsets to operating its own wireless networks. In the first nine months of 2014 alone the company spent more than $9 billion on buying up tech businesses (Oreskovic, 2015). And although this activity slowed somewhat in 2015, its restructuring under a new umbrella group—Alphabet Inc.—may well clear the path for a further widening in scope of its takeover strategy (Hockenson, 2015). Facebook similarly has been deploying its huge cash reserves to buy up companies both close to and far removed from its core business (Luckerson, 2015).

The Blood, the Veins and the Heartbeat

To get to the heart of the ownership matter, we have to consider how concentration in news markets is intensifying under the shadow of digital monopolies like Google and Facebook. Indeed, what is truly unprecedented about the market power of Google and Facebook is not the extent of dominance within their own industries but the immense influence they wield over others. This is precisely *because* they occupy the hinterland between industries built on network and copyright control. In so doing, they have assumed control of something far more widely consequential: the means to connect these industries with end users. If 'referral traffic' is the blood that now sustains much of the cultural industries, and the pipes and networks through which that traffic flows are the veins, then intermediaries provide the heartbeat—and there is no industry now more dependent on that heartbeat than journalism. Facebook and Google together account for more than 70 percent of users directed to the websites of major news publishers (Beck, 2015). From any perspective this translates into a stunning degree of market influence, and it helps explain the farce and chaos that followed Germany's ancillary copyright law, as we saw in chapter 8.

To understand the impact in turn on concentration within news markets, we have to get to grips with how dependence on referral traffic has raised capital costs in the world of digital journalism and erected new barriers to market entry. Although newsgathering may be cheaper than ever before, this is cancelled out to some extent by the growing costs of competing on *volume*, while the ever-expanding sea of information noise means that prospective new entrants often need sky-high marketing budgets in order to compete (Curran et al., 2012). This has resulted not only in rising advertising costs, as major brands outbid smaller players in keyword auctions (Rampton, 2014), but also in the development of new marketing specialisms, namely strategies of search and social media optimisation that have particular resonance for the news industry (Poell and Van Dijck, 2014). These in turn have spawned a whole new professional class of skilled marketers and agencies that make competing with the big names a very expensive business.

Size Matters

In the previous chapter we saw how a number of blind spots can serve to obscure the extent of concentration in the news media both at the provider and content levels. Uncover these blind spots and what we are left with, by any measure, is a highly concentrated picture of news consumption and editorial voice. How has this happened? Given that so much of the traffic to news websites is 'referred' by intermediaries, the intricacies of Google's news algorithm is a good place to start. For some time now—and long before Facebook introduced its news quality metrics—Google has been weighting news providers according to a broad spectrum of what it considers reliable indicators of news quality. But it turns out machines are not much better at assessing quality than human beings. They may be free of subjective bias in one sense, but this means they rely (somewhat paradoxically) on metrics that systematically favour large scale and incumbent providers. One look at Google's most recent patent filing for its news algorithm reveals just how much size matters in the world of digital news: the size of the audience, the size of the newsroom, and the volume of output.[2]

In relation to audience, Google rewards providers that have an established record of click-throughs from its pages; those that feature prominently in user surveys and data collected by market research agencies; and those with a relatively global reach as detected by clicks, tweets, likes and links from users based in other countries. For newsroom capacity, Google imbeds metrics into its algorithm that guestimates numbers of journalistic staff (with reference to bylines) as well as the number of 'bureaus' operated by the news provider.

It's not hard to see how these metrics can disproportionately favour large-scale providers. But above all, Google's quality weighting hangs on volume. According to the patent filing:

> A first metric in determining the quality of a news source may include the number of articles produced by the news source during a given time period [. . .] [and] may be determined by counting the number of non-duplicate articles [. . .] [or] counting the number of original sentences produced.
>
> (Curtiss et al., 2014)

Some volume metrics favour long-form and original news, which are fairly uncontentious indicators of quality (even if they still favour news organisations with relative scale and resource advantage). But others are more problematic. For instance, Google rewards organisations that provide a breadth of news coverage, which penalises news organisations that are more specialist in their topical focus. Specialising in this sense is really the only way that potential new entrants, who lack the resources and scale of incumbent providers, can compete by offering a 'quality' news alternative.

Perhaps the most contentious metric is one that purports to measure what Google calls 'importance' by comparing the volume of a site's output on any given topic to the total output on that topic across the web. In a single measure, this promotes both concentration at the level of provider (by favouring organisations with volume and scale) as well as concentration at the level of output (by favouring organisations that produce more on topics that are widely covered elsewhere). In other words, it is a measure that single-handedly reinforces both an aggregate news agenda as well as the agenda setting power of a relatively small number of publishers.

Google engineers may well argue that the variety of volume metrics imbedded in the algorithm ensures that concentration effects are counterbalanced by pluralising effects, and that there is no more legitimate or authoritative way of measuring news quality than relying on a full spectrum of quantitative indicators. Rightly or wrongly, Google believes that 'real news' providers are those that can produce significant amounts of original, breaking and general news on a wide range of topics and on a consistent basis.

At face value, that doesn't sound like such a bad thing. In a world saturated with hype, rumour and gossip, it's not surprising that most people are attracted to news brands that signal a degree of professionalism. Part of Google's corporate and professed social mission is to match users to the content they value most, and if most people prefer major news brands, then that's where it should direct the traffic. As recent research suggests, mainstream news brands signal credibility and 'gatekeeping trust' in ways that would be risky and contentious for intermediaries to challenge (Carpentier, 2014).

But there is no getting around the fact that Google *pre-emptively* views these brands as more likely to produce what it considers quality news. The company made clear as much when it stated in its patent filing that "CNN and BBC are widely regarded as high quality sources of accuracy of reporting, professionalism in writing, etc., while local news sources, such as hometown news sources, may be of lower quality."

When the 'mainstream' is held as the ultimate benchmark of good quality news, we start to run into real problems from the perspective of media ownership and plurality. For one thing, Google's quality metrics give favoured news organisations a *prior* weighting, which means that the ranking of stories is not exclusively matched to the keywords of any given search. An article by a relatively unknown provider may thus find itself outranked by competitors with greater scale and brand presence, even if the article is more keyword relevant, in depth and original. This discriminates in particular against new entrants who face the uphill struggle of trying to get their voices heard and acquire a piece of the referral traffic pie. It also epitomises some of the problems of Google's increasingly interventionist approach to 'guiding' users in their search for content (see chapter 9).

Perhaps of greatest concern for our purposes, Google's news algorithm discriminates against those providers that focus on topics, issues and stories beyond or on the fringes of the mainstream agenda. Even its 'originality' metric, which purports to favour diverse perspectives in the news generally, is limited to measuring the number of 'original named entities' that appear in any given article in comparison with related coverage on the same story or issue.

Clearly (and perhaps for good reason) Google does not want to get involved actively in the business of deciding what issues and stories are more or less news-*worthy*. It prefers to leave that to editors and users. Indeed, this is the basis on which both Google and Facebook claim to play no editorial role in filtering the news, in spite of the breadth of filtering metrics that they apply to an individual's feed or search ranking. The problem, however, is that by favouring certain types of news organisations (i.e. those with scale and established brand presence), Google is to some extent endorsing and reinforcing a mainstream agenda consensus (and potentially one with a Western bias, given its stated preference for sources like the BBC and CNN). This also seems at odds with Google's posturing as a guardian of openness, diversity and technological disruption. Because the company makes no money directly from its news services (which do not carry sponsored listings), why would it be so concerned to amplify the voices of dominant and mostly incumbent or legacy news providers?

Answering this question requires us to revisit the problem of search interventionism. As we saw in chapter 9, Google's algorithm is becoming ever more adept in pre-empting and predicting our content choices. In doing so, it follows a certain probability logic in favouring those types of content that are more *likely* to be preferred and selected by particular users on the basis of its quality metrics. The ultimate goal is to reduce the user's search costs and increase the seamlessness of its service. Although its news services do not carry adverts, search competition is still 'only a click away', and challenging users by promoting smaller, newer or alternative providers poses inherent risks for the business of user retention. You will recall from chapter 9 that the business model of intermediaries rests on the central objective of maximising not only the volume of user traffic but also the depth and duration of engagement. Google's news services are an essential piece of that puzzle.

Amid all the concerns over fragmentation and legal confrontations over copyright, it's not hard to see how the potential symbiosis between Google News page ranks and the editorial agendas of mainstream news providers gets overlooked. In part III, we saw how both Twitter's algorithm code and instructions given to Facebook's news curating team can systematically favour news stories covered by mainstream providers in trending topics, which in turn may serve to reinforce a mainstream news agenda set largely by incumbent news organisations. It is equally clear from what we know of Google's algorithm that far from undermining dominant news institutions, it may be actively reinforcing them as the most credible and authoritative news sources. Ultimately, we should not expect intermediaries to be any less risk averse than mainstream news providers when it comes to the prospect of challenging users with alternative viewpoints and voices. Yet this is precisely what is needed if we want to redress the symptoms of concentrated media power.

The Interlock

On 18 February 2014, hundreds of privacy and civil liberty activists filled City Hall in Oakland, California, protesting against the local government's state of the art surveillance system known as the Domain Awareness Center (Levine, 2014a). The program was based on a centralised hub receiving real-time closed-circuit television (CCTV) and other audio, video and data feeds from around the city and integrating them with a range of surveillance applications including face recognition software. Funded by the federal government, it was hailed by officials as an innovative and comprehensive public safety initiative.

This was not, however, enough to convince concerned local citizens for whom the scope and reach of the programme posed, from the outset, unprecedented threats to privacy and civil liberties. But the protestors at this particular meeting had even bigger worries on their mind. After reams of internal email disclosures were enforced by the Public Records Office, it became clear that the programme was not just about protecting residents in the event of a natural disaster or terror attack, as officials proclaimed. It seemed to be targeted at least as much at political activists and civil disobedients in a way that touched a nerve for a city with a troubling history of police brutality. In the end, the protestors won a significant concession from the authorities, who agreed to limit the project to cover surveillance only at the city's port and airport rather than its entire metropolitan area as originally planned.

But there was a little-noticed sting in the tale. Among the thousands of emails disclosed was an exchange between a city official, Renee Domingo, and Scott Ciabattari, a 'strategic partnerships manager' at Google (Levine, 2014a). In one email in particular, Domingo solicited a presentation from Google of "demos and products" that could work with the Domain Awareness Center, as well as more general ideas of "how the city might partner with Google." The company appeared eager to participate in the very practices of blanket public surveillance programs that it had poured public scorn over in response to the Snowden revelations.

Indeed, arguably even testier than the relationship between Google and publishers in recent years, has been that between Google and the US and UK governments in the battle over surveillance and encryption. In 2013, classified documents leaked by Ed Snowden suggested that the National Security Agency (NSA) had surreptitiously tapped into the backbone infrastructure of a number of intermediaries, including Google, prompting a chorus of outrage over what appeared to be a hacking of their servers (Carroll, 2013). Intermediaries also responded with action by installing or upgrading encryption of their servers and software, prompting the US government to look to the courts in order to force open the 'back door' (Greenberg, 2016), and the UK government to enshrine similar measures in proposed new legislation (Baraniuk, 2016).

Yet the apparent collaboration between Google and Oakland city officials was by no means an isolated example, nor was the impetus on behalf of Google to develop its partnerships with the surveillance and military state. Consider Michelle Quaid, Google's Chief Technology Officer for the Public Sector between 2011 and 2015 and voted the number one most powerful woman by *Entrepreneur* magazine in 2014 (Levine, 2014b). Prior to joining Google, she had built a prodigious career in roles spanning the US Department of Defense and several intelligence agencies. At Google, she self-styled her job as that of a 'bridge builder' between big tech and big government, especially the world of military and intelligence. Other senior positions within Google's 'Federal' division exemplify the company's efforts to cash in on lucrative partnerships with the military and security establishment. The most senior is perhaps Shannon Sullivan, head of Google Federal, which is the company's government-facing division. Sullivan was a former defence director for BAe Systems, the world's largest arms manufacturer, as well as a senior military advisor to the US Air Force.

In fact, the close ties between Google and the intelligence community in the US have a long history, going back to the company's origins on the campus of Stamford University. In 2015, investigative journalist Nafeez Ahmed revealed that in developing the prototype software behind its search engine, Google's founders collaborated closely with a secret intelligence programme administered by the Central Intelligence Agency (CIA). According to Ahmed (2015), "Google continued to be nurtured by various government agencies, private sector conglomerates and global financiers, especially through a nebulous Pentagon think-tank known as the Highlands Forum, where such networks convene regularly to this day." Curiously, although the story was picked up in one German and one Hungarian newspaper, and covered by Forbes in its Czech-language edition, it received barely a mention in the US or any English-language media.

But it's not just the security state that has developed entrenched links with Google. Notwithstanding the temporary spat over surveillance revelations in 2013, the Obama administration had from the outset forged a long-term love-in with Google along with other intermediary giants (Kang and Eilperin, 2015). The regular exchange of senior staff between the top branches of government and the boards of big tech companies has produced not so much a revolving as a spinning door between Silicon Valley and the White House. Louisa Terrell, former legal counsel to Obama, joined Facebook as Head of Public Policy in 2011 before being appointed Advisor to the Chairman of the FCC in 2013, and in 2015, Facebook hired former FCC Chairman Kevin Martin to direct its mobile and global access policy.

Tech companies have also ratcheted up their political donations in recent years, establishing political action committees (PACs) to front their political lobbying efforts and campaign contributions during election cycles. Not surprisingly, Google's is the largest PAC and has grown exponentially since its inception in 2006 (Vara, 2014). In the 2014 midterm elections, it spent $1.6 million compared to a mere $40,000 in 2006. By comparison, Facebook spent nearly half a million dollars on the 2014 elections, whereas the overall contribution of tech companies exceeded $6 million. Surprisingly, given the long-standing personal support offered by tech CEOs and founders for the Democratic Party (and Obama in particular), both Google and Facebook—and tech companies as a whole—gave more money to Republicans in 2014 than Democrats. As if to rub salt in the Democrats' wound, that same year Google's Michelle Quaid joined the board of the campaign technology company Voter Gravity, which serves Republican candidates and provides technological support for a number of conservative groups (Vogel, 2014).

In Europe, Google had 10 employees in 2015 devoted to lobbying European politicians, an investment that appears to have borne some fruit, at least with the UK government (Boffey, 2016). According to an investigation by the *Observer* newspaper in 2015, "Britain has been privately lobbying the EU to remove from an official blacklist the tax haven through which Google funnels billions of pounds of profits" (Boffey, 2015). In 2014, towards the end of his stint as EU Competition Commissioner, Joaquín Alumnia complained bitterly of the pressure he had come under from member state governments to go easy on Google (Fairless, 2014). Alumnia spearheaded antitrust investigations into the company during his four-year tenure and, coincidentally perhaps, was also revealed to be one of the victims of GCHQ (Government Communications Headquarters) and NSA surveillance in a target list leaked by Ed Snowden (Ball and Hopkins, 2013).

There have also been a number of key cross-appointments between intermediaries and media organisations over recent years. In 2010 Google hired Madhav Chinnappa, former head of development and rights for BBC News, to lead its partnerships team for Europe, the Middle East and Africa, while in 2015, senior Google executive Michelle Guthrie was poached by Australia's leading broadcaster ABC. The following year, Facebook recruited the editor of Storyful—News Corp's social media news agency—to manage its journalism partnerships, while Google's vice president for communications and public affairs in Europe, the Middle East and Africa is (at the time of writing) Peter Barron, former editor of the BBC's *Newsnight*.

Communications and public relations (PR) roles have also provided a persistent bridge between newsroom and government employment over recent years. In Britain, the conviction and imprisonment of former *News of the World* editor Andy Coulson in 2015 was in more ways than one a PR disaster for Prime Minister David Cameron, who had hired Coulson to direct his communications after he quit the paper in 2010. But less prominent is the interlocking directorate between media, the state and the defence industry. William Kennard, for instance, has served on the boards of the *New York Times*, AT&T and a number of companies owned by the Carlyle Group, a major US defence contractor (Ahmed, 2015). His full-time roles have included chairman of the FCC from 1997 to 2001, managing director of the Carlyle Group from 2001 to 2009, and US ambassador to the EU from 2009 to 2013.

Perhaps more significant than the formal links between big tech, media and the government/military/security establishment are the various milieus and forums in which their representatives congregate, both socially and professionally (for a sweeping survey see Freedman, 2014, pp. 47–50). The annual Sun Valley conference in Idaho, for example, is credited with spawning major tech-media mergers such as Comcast's purchase of NBC in 2009 and the deal that put the *Washington Post* in the hands of Amazon founder Jeff Bezos in 2013.

As for social cliques, Britain's 'Chipping Norton Set' refers to a gang of media and political elites based in the upmarket Oxfordshire village of the same name. Its members include David Cameron, Elizabeth Murdoch (daughter of Rupert), Rebekah Brooks (now CEO of Murdoch's UK newspaper operations) and Rachel Whetstone (former Google director of communications and public policy). The resilience of such intimate ties in the aftermath of Leveson was demonstrated in December 2015, when the Murdochs hosted David Cameron among others for a Christmas drink (Martinson, 2015). This came off the back of ongoing and persistent meetings between Murdoch and senior government ministers in the year leading up to the 2015 general election (Media Reform Coalition, 2015).

Of course, there is nothing legally or perhaps even ethically wrong with politicians having meetings or developing close friendships with media executives. The problem concerns the degree to which this kind of interaction—which takes place beyond public scrutiny or participation—yields a trickle-down influence over both media and policy agendas and/or facilitates reciprocal influence between them. One of the most striking features of testimony given to the Leveson Inquiry by former prime ministers (including close friends of Rupert Murdoch) was the frank admission that their views were affected by, in the words of Tony Blair, "how we are treated by them" (Blair, 2012).

This kind of testimony resonates strongly with Thomas Meyer's account of 'media democracy' (2002), according to which political leaders and processes have become enslaved to a 'media logic' that ultimately puts unelected media proprietors in the driving seat of policymaking: "The leitmotif of effective spin-control is that you can only control the media by submitting to them" (2002, p. 52). But although some politicians openly concur with this view, it paints a potentially misleading picture of one-way influence in the power relationship between media and political elites. After all, the parties and meetings are just as much testament to the media courting political elites as the other way round. Political actors may need the media to secure "the primary resource of their political lives" (Meyer, 2002, p. 52) by shaping media and public agendas in their favour, but media and technology groups depend on political actors for policies that favour both their immediate and wider commercial interests. This mutual dependency and instinct towards collaboration is as clear in the exchanges between Google and Oakland city officials as it was in the discussion at Chequers between Margaret Thatcher and Rupert Murdoch in 1981, prior to the approval of Murdoch's purchase of the *Times* and *Sunday Times* newspapers (McSmith, 2012). It is this kind of interdependence—rather than power imbalance—which is fundamental to the phenomenon of regulatory capture.

Of course, there remains to a large degree a black box between evidence of an interlocking directorate and the kind of gatekeeping practices and agenda effects that have been the preoccupation of this book. Put simply, it is very difficult if not impossible to establish *causal* links between the integrated elite structure that we have sketched and the policy, media and public agendas that surface at any given time and in any given context. This is the reason that Leveson found no smoking gun of impropriety in policy deliberations over News Corp's proposed buyout of BskyB in 2010, in spite of the frequent backchannel communications between government officials and News Corp lobbyists throughout the bid process. There is also something perhaps inevitable about the kinds of intimate social ties that develop between powerful elites with mutually dependent interests (Chang, 2008).

But rather than absolving the need for regulation of media ownership and plurality, such uncertainties and inevitabilities are precisely why we need it. Just as the development of social ties around shared interests may seem inevitable, so does a degree of ideological and paradigmatic groupthink that goes along with it. Implicit in the interactions between Google's strategic partnership director and Oakland city officials was not only a mutual recognition of potentially shared interests, but also a nod to the legitimacy of the Domain Awareness Center as a public safety initiative. In other words, what was in the respective interests of Google and city officials was—according to them—*also* in the interests of Oakland's citizens. But as we saw, this assumption was highly contested—and contestable—both in terms of its definition of the problem (the nature and severity of threats to public safety) and its conception of the appropriate solution (blanket and intrusive surveillance).

Ultimately this kind of groupthink facilitates interest 'capture' and the kind of institutional corruption that involves neither criminality nor conscious intent, but which may nevertheless progressively erode public trust and legitimacy of authoritative power (Lessig, 2013). It is precisely the job of regulation to minimise the *risks* posed by this kind of corruption and capture that are intrinsic to concentrations of political and economic power. How this can be achieved amid all the complexities of the converged media environment is the subject of the following and final part of the book.

Conclusion

This chapter began by reflecting on the development of power elite theory by C. Wright Mills and the concept of a military-industrial complex invoked by outgoing US president Eisenhower in 1961. We went on to examine the enormous market power accumulated by intermediaries as well as their unparalleled cross-market influence over news industries. Far from disentangling media plurality from critical questions of media ownership (as some have suggested), the rise of intermediaries makes these questions even more urgent and central to plurality debates.

We then examined the intricacies of Google's news algorithm in an effort to reveal the myriad ways in which it favours news organisations with scale and resource advantage over smaller and newer providers, and mainstream players over those that concentrate on marginal issues and stories. I speculated that this may explain the evidence presented in chapter 8 of a growing concentration in news consumption around the head of the distribution curve. Although more research is needed into the effects of algorithmic filtering on media agendas (as well as their effects both at the individual and aggregate levels), the hidden biases in Google's quality metrics suggest a strong interdependency has developed between intermediaries and major news brands.

We went on to consider interdependencies with other centres of power. This was observed in evidence of strategic partnerships, collaborations and revolving doors between tech companies, media groups, government, and the military and security establishment. Although the examples pointed to were by no means exhaustive, they paint a picture of a complex network of institutional power with media, communications and technology players occupying key nodes and playing crucial enabling roles within it. This does not mean that the 'club' functions as an entirely exclusive, cohesive, centralised and coordinated vehicle of elite power. It does not even tell us much about how or to what degree power is mobilised, much less its ultimate effects on agendas in all the contexts considered in this book.

But these are all empirical questions that are *raised* by the emergent media-technology-military-industrial complex. And they are questions that are overlooked by the narratives of cultural chaos and convergence, which assert or imply that research into the manifest limits of agendas, as well as their potential ideological qualities, belongs to an outdated 'control paradigm' in media studies (McNair, 2006). This is in spite of the fact that established media brands still account for the vast majority of news consumption on all platforms—and in spite of heightened concerns around journalist autonomy against the background of austerity, technological disruption and, in Pentagon-speak, the 'long war' (Tisdall and MacAskill, 2006).

Notes

1. See https://www.eisenhower.archives.gov/research/online_documents/farewell_address.html (last accessed 28 March 2016).
2. See United States Patent Application Publication No. US 2014/0188859 A1. 3 July 2014. Available at https://docs.google.com/viewer?url=patentimages.storage.googleapis.com/pdfs/US20140188859.pdf (last accessed 28 March 2016).

Part V

Demanding the Impossible

Chapter 15

Sources of Control

Plurality Reconsidered

Plurality is not a contentious word. As Des Freedman notes, opposing it "would be like being against citizenship or apple pie or oxygen" (2014, p. 76). Nor is it one that has been in any way marginalised from media policy discourse. From the FCC's 'diversity index' to the UK's 'public interest test' regime for dealing with media mergers and acquisitions, the concept of plurality has long been embodied in legislative and regulatory frameworks, as well as debates over reform.

But one of the great ironies and challenges of media plurality and ownership policy is that the very practices of agenda control it is intended to check can play a profound role in shaping its outcomes. In general terms, the power to normalise certain assumptions, legitimise particular frameworks—and above all, exclude alternatives—is what makes policy and regulatory issues "in an important sense, ideological constructions" (Hancher and Moran, 1989, p. 297). But it is also intimately linked to the kind of agenda power considered in the wider context of the book: the gatekeeping, agenda setting and meaning making roles played by media institutions make the business of media policymaking acutely vulnerable to capture and corruptive influence. In these final chapters we examine the gaps, inconsistencies and, ultimately, impossibilities that frame contemporary plurality debates, with a focus on the UK, but with resonance for the challenges facing media reform activists and campaigners in many other countries around the world.[1]

Consider, for a start, the language in which these debates are couched and the very emphasis on the word 'plurality' (over terms like 'ownership' and 'concentration'). In the aftermath of the phone hacking scandal, reform of media ownership rules briefly rose to prominence on the media policy agenda, as senior political figures called for renewed caps or fixed limits on ownership after decades of liberalisation (Sabbagh et al., 2012). But questions of ownership policy quickly morphed into questions of plurality reform, as Ofcom set the agenda for a series of consultations and inquiries into the issue, culminating in its plurality measurement framework unveiled in 2015 (Ofcom, 2015b).

The emphasis on measuring media *plurality* says something about the way that Ofcom conceives of the current health of the UK media system. It might have been labelled a framework for measuring media *concentration,* but that would imply an altogether less optimistic outlook on the status quo. An emphasis on concentration suggests that there is a policy problem that needs to be solved. An emphasis on plurality suggests that there is a *potential* policy problem that needs to be guarded against.

Mapping the Gates

Throughout this book we have examined concentrated media power in various forms and contexts—from the inter-media agenda setting leverage of the press to the influence of algorithms over newsgathering priorities and personalised agendas; from the consolidation of online news consumption around the head of the news distribution curve; to the tightening interlock between major media, tech and state institutions.

At the heart of our analysis has been an emphasis on the 'closing-off' practices inherent in all forms of content discrimination. This is the glue that binds gatekeeping practices as diverse as internet service providers (ISPs) charging content providers for different traffic speeds, intermediaries employing news filters in their search and social media algorithms, network operators choosing which channels or stations to carry, aggregators selecting and prioritising articles from wholesale providers, and editors deciding what's news according to professional values or commercial logic. There is nothing illegitimate about these practices in and of themselves. Most are inevitable, many are necessary and some can have considerable civic benefits, especially in helping users navigate the ever-expanding news and information terrain. But each of these practices requires specific regulatory attention because of their potential to marginalise or exclude particular voices, issues or ideas from the public domain; each has the potential to both embody and support the act of 'non-decision-making'—the core ingredient of agenda power (Lukes, 2005 [1974]).

In chapter 8 I argued that in the converged media environment, we can think of three categories of gatekeepers that can impact on the flow of information and the range of voices heard in a media system more broadly. Borrowing terms from Wu (2010), these were defined as those who control content, those who control network infrastructure and those who control the 'switch' or 'access to the user' (Helberger et al., 2015).

But although useful in evaluating market structure and power, this categorisation is limiting when it comes to identifying and measuring the range of audible voices in a media system, as well as designing effective remedies to concentration. For instance, although aggregators may be considered intermediaries to the extent that they match content with users, their role in hosting, packaging and prioritising stories is closer to the kind of editorial gatekeeping practiced by conventional news providers.

On the other hand, the default categorisation of media owners by policymakers has long been based on a traditional medium or platform (i.e. print, television, radio and online). But this is even more limiting given the complexities of the converged media environment. It is of course still true that television remains the main platform for news in most parts of the world, and that very few news providers operate across broadcasting, print and online platforms. But we are rapidly moving into an age when *most* news providers are both multimedia and multiplatform, and thus the meaning of those distinctions—from an ownership and plurality perspective—is eroding.

The main source of confusion stems from categorising online news as a separate and comparable category alongside print and broadcasting. For a start, the internet is clearly not a single medium in the same sense as print, radio or television. If I stream the BBC News channel live through my laptop, am I consuming television or online news? Especially problematic is the risk that companies like MSN and Buzzfeed are deemed to share more similar characteristics with each other than they do with television, radio or print outlets. In fact, Buzzfeed is much closer to a broadcaster like CNN, to the extent that it produces and publishers its own news, than it is to an intermediary like MSN, which predominantly aggregates and filters news produced by others.

For its part, Ofcom (2015b) subdivides online news market players between content originators (those who produce original news), aggregators (those who host and compile news produced by others) and intermediaries (those who act primarily as *gateways* to news on other sites), and it further distinguishes between wholesale and retail news providers. More on that in a moment, but it's worth emphasising that Ofcom's primary categorisation is still based on a traditional conception of platform. As technologies and platforms continue to evolve, this is likely to create more conceptual difficulties than it solves.

To begin with, I want to suggest what I think is a more robust categorisation for the converged news market as a whole, and one that centres on the varied gatekeeping roles alluded to earlier. In particular, we can conceive of five categories of media ownership that reflect the spectrum from editorial to more structural forms of control: providers, aggregators, portals, gateways and facilitators.

At the editorial end of the spectrum are news *providers*, which exercise control over newsgathering resources. They may also mobilise brand power (or gatekeeping trust) in order to leverage their content to a critical mass user base, either via third parties and/or their own edited channels.[2] Where wholesale news providers *exclusively* serve particular retail outlets (as is often the case, for instance, with local commercial radio stations), it makes no sense to consider the retail outlet as a distinct source of news. Although such retailers may play a role in extending the reach of particular news providers, this does not really capture what we mean by gatekeeping. In the same way that we wouldn't consider different channels of the BBC as constituting different news sources, it follows that retailers acting as exclusive carriers of wholesale news providers should be considered as an extension of the wholesale provider's voice.

To be clear, a news provider may publish or broadcast on its own platforms (in print, broadcasting and/or online) *as well as* provide content for third-party aggregators or exclusive retailers. It may also itself carry news content supplied by others. But the defining characteristic of news providers is that their core business is based on copyright: the production and ownership of original news content.

It follows that a secondary form of gatekeeping is denoted by *aggregators*, which source the majority of their content from wholesale providers. Unlike retailers that carry the content of a single wholesale provider, aggregators exercise a degree of editorial control in the selection, arrangement and prioritisation of stories. In other words, their editorial function is implicit in packaging, layout and design, rather than production. But this can nevertheless have significant implications for the framing and promoting of particular issue agendas.

A third form of gatekeeping that is close to aggregators but one step further removed from editorial control may be considered *portals*. These are defined as platforms that predominantly carry *channels* supplied and operated by third parties. The most obvious examples here would be satellite and cable television providers, but we can also conceive of portals as online platforms that 'embed' third-party content. These gatekeepers exercise only a modicum of editorial influence in the selection of which channels to carry or embed, as well as their arrangement in menus or electronic programme guides.

In the fourth group, gatekeepers exercise a much weaker degree of editorial influence over news output. They may, however, still exercise a profound gatekeeping role in their power to *point* users towards particular types of content or particular types of content providers. They consist of news *gateways*, such as search and social networking sites, as well as open publishing and content sharing platforms. Their primary news activity resides in guiding news selection through recommendation, filtering and highlighting.

Of course, such services may also be used as end points of news consumption, particularly in catching up on headlines or breaking news. But this level of news engagement does not fully capture the impact of voice in the terms we have considered here and which embodies the essence of media ownership concerns. If I use Twitter to find out about the news on my mobile phone while at work or on the move, but then digest the stories and form my views by watching them on BBC Television, can we really say that my news consumption has significantly diversified beyond the BBC? On the other hand, gateways can also host news content in full, such as television news reports on YouTube. But if I tend to watch Sky News reports on YouTube, does that mean that the voice of Sky has been in any way diluted by my use of a separate platform to view its content?

Whether the content they host is limited to headlines, snippets or full articles and reports, the common defining feature of gateway sources is that they do not play a role in either producing or packaging news output. Rather, their gatekeeping function is to assist users in searching for, or encountering news content, and in doing so they necessarily engage in 'closing off', filtering and discriminating practices, as we examined at length in part III.

The final category of gatekeepers refers to those companies that *facilitate* access to a network, and includes internet service providers, browsers, mobile operators and app platforms. The distinguishing feature of these services is that they play neither a packaging nor a filtering role in news content and thus have no *direct* bearing on news consumption. However, they do have power to varying degrees over traffic management—that is, the power to admit, exclude, prioritise or otherwise determine the accessibility of particular content and services. This may impact on the relative prominence of different news services and thus, potentially at least, on the range of voices heard.

Tensions and Overlaps

As we have seen, conflicts abound between those who control different gates in the news ecosystem: whether between content owners and ISPs over net neutrality, between intermediaries and publishers over copyright or news quality, or between public service broadcasters and the commercial press, gatekeepers old and new rarely seem to act in concert or pull collective strings of agenda control. But we have also seen how this picture fundamentally obscures the growing alliances and mutual dependencies that exist between all large-scale gatekeeping institutions, from Google's interconnection arrangements with network operators to Facebook's deal with publishers over instant articles. What's more, it obscures the growing *consonance* in news agendas promoted by intermediaries, broadcasters and the press. As we saw in chapter 8, research on coverage of the 2015 UK election overwhelmingly showed that far from offering alternatives, the BBC, newspapers and even the most influential news and political voices on Twitter sang from the same hymn sheet when it came to the issue agenda, and it was one that did not fully comport with public priorities (as measured by monthly tracking polls).

The waters are further muddied by the growing institutional overlap between the gatekeeping categories. Google, for instance, plays significant roles as both a gateway (through its search services and YouTube platform) and facilitator (through its wireless and mobile ISP services, as well as app platform). Microsoft inhabits the roles of aggregator (msn.com), gateway (through its search and social media services) as well as facilitator (through its internet service provision).

Facebook primarily inhabits the world of gateways through its role in filtering and guiding news consumption. But it is also increasingly playing the role of aggregator through its deals with publishers to host articles in full. On the other hand, 21st Century Fox—the holding company for film and broadcasting assets siphoned off from Murdoch's News Corporation in 2013 — is centred on content ownership but also has a controlling stake in Sky, which monopolises the satellite TV platform in the UK. As such, it can be said to exercise news gatekeeping roles as both provider (e.g. Fox News and Sky News) as well as portal (Sky plc).

Nevertheless, in spite of these difficulties, the five conceptual gatekeeping categories outlined in Table 15.1 offer a useful starting point in the measurement of media concentration and plurality. In focusing on gatekeeping roles, they capture the agenda setting power and volume of voice that is central to media ownership

Table 15.1 Gatekeeping Roles

Company	Provider	Aggregator	Portal	Gateway	Facilitator
BBC	X				
Microsoft		X		X	X
Google				X	X
21st Century Fox	X		X		
Facebook		X		X	

concerns in the post-digital age. But perhaps more importantly, they avoid the confusion that sets in when policymakers rely on the default categorisation of news market players by platform. The challenge for policymakers is to recognise both the interconnectedness of institutional gatekeepers and the relatively distinct roles that they continue to play overall in the new information paradigm.

Notes

1. For a summary of these challenges, see Freedman et al. (2016).
2. It's worth noting that the traditional distinction between wire agencies and news organisations has significantly blurred in the new news landscape. Organisations that were once dedicated to wholesale newsgathering on behalf of publishers or broadcasters now have established 'retail' brands of their own, as well as providing content to others. Likewise, established news brands are increasingly 'disaggregating' their content and licensing stories to third parties, especially aggregators.

Chapter 16

The Politics of Measurement

By any yardstick, determining the degree of concentration or pluralism in con-verged media systems is a messy business. A number of scholars in recent years have highlighted the limitations of purely economic approaches to measuring media concentration, pluralism or diversity, especially those based on market share analysis (e.g. Just, 2009; Iosifidis, 2010; Crauford Smith and Tambini, 2012; Freedman, 2014). The common thrust of these arguments is that econometrics alone fail to capture the power of *voice,* and that what we need is at least a com-bination of economic with more cultural-oriented and even qualitative indicators.

But for Eli Noam (2009), whose extensive work on media concentration in the US and globally has become something of an empirical gold standard, economet-rics provide the only value-free basis on which to determine levels of concentra-tion. The risk of combining economic with more cultural-oriented measures, he argues, is that the waters become irrevocably muddied and we fail to get a true picture of market power. The kind of inconsistencies, for instance, endemic in the way that the FCC's Diversity Index or Germany's KEK system weighted differ-ent media according to their presumed impact, are precisely what made them so ineffectual (Just, 2009).

On the other hand, Italy's Integrated Communications System (SIC), intro-duced under none other than Silvio Berlusconi during his second period in office, was on the face of it a simple and transparent economic indicator, as well as one that seemed appropriate to the converging media landscape. Based on a definition of the total media market, it set a cap on any media group that controlled more than 20 percent of revenues. But the total media market encompassed everything from book publishing to gaming, with the effect that even Berlusconi's media empire could never come close to breaching the threshold, allowing plenty of room for further expansion. As Natascha Just observed, "The SIC is ostensibly about adjusting to technological change (convergence), but in effect is more of a (political) cover to allow already dominant media to expand even further" (2009, p. 112).

In recognition of the need to incorporate more than just economic indicators, Ofcom has proposed a 'basket of metrics' that it intends to use as the basis for plurality reviews. But this too suffers from a number of conceptual flaws and, ultimately, reflects the politics and power relations that drive media policymaking in Britain and elsewhere. Its origins date back to 2010 amid News Corporation's controversial bid to buy out the remaining shareholders of what was then BskyB. At the time, Ofcom was asked by the government to conduct a 'market impact assessment' of the bid as part of the public interest test procedures for dealing with major media mergers.[1] Although its subsequent recommendations fell far short of prohibiting the deal, it did suggest the need for certain 'undertakings' by News Corporation in respect of Sky News (the flagship broadcaster over which the deal would grant Murdoch consolidated control).

But in conducting its assessment, Ofcom looked at the wider state of news plurality and made another recommendation that went beyond the immediate context of the proposed merger. Specifically, it called for regular 'plurality reviews', arguing that the current regime was no longer sufficient for addressing dynamic and rapidly changing media markets. With its scope limited to dealing only with proposed mergers and acquisitions, the public interest test procedures did not take account of 'organic' market changes that could impact on the degree of plurality or concentration.

This proved to be something of a Pandora's box. Amid the fallout from the phone hacking scandal and the subsequent Leveson hearings, the need for some kind of reform of the present system became a point of unlikely political consensus. In particular, Ofcom's recommendation for regular plurality reviews was endorsed by Lord Justice Leveson (2012), a separate and concurrent parliamentary inquiry into media plurality (House of Lords, 2014), as well as the government itself (DCMS, 2014). But after five years and five related public inquiries, Ofcom has only gotten as far as publishing its definitive measurement framework. The crucial corollary questions of what actually counts as plurality *sufficiency*, as well as what kind of remedies could be used to redress concentration remain, at the time of writing, *off the agenda*.

As for the framework itself, apart from the conceptual vagaries that stem from categorising market players by platform (as discussed in the previous chapter), we will now address four other methodological problem areas. These concern the *range* of metrics adopted; the way in which 'sources' are qualified; inattention to content (especially in the context of news agendas); and an absence of any clear bright lines.

An Overflowing Basket

The first problem can be simply stated as this: the broader the array of measures and indicators adopted, the greater the element of interpretation afforded to any decision-making body as regards plurality 'sufficiency'. Just as plurality can be thought of in many different ways, so it can be measured in many different ways. But that does not mean that all indicators are of equal value when it comes to assessing concentrated media power. No matter what happens to the media landscape over the coming years, some indicators will paint a more or less plural picture than others, effectively making it extremely difficult for policymakers to intervene on plurality grounds, even when there is a strong case for doing so. The more diluted the system of plurality measurement, the more it ultimately favours precisely those interests whose power it is intended to check.

A prime example of this can be found in Ofcom's qualitative narrative, which includes consideration of what it calls 'contextual factors'. These refer to existing plurality safeguards including adherence to the broadcasting code, internal plurality measures and the adoption of certain governance frameworks (e.g. editorial boards or trust ownership) that may mitigate the risks of a media institution serving as a megaphone for vested interests.

So far so good. But things start to become cloudy when Ofcom refers to another set of indicators that will inform its qualitative narrative, this time to do with *impact*. Here, the importance attached to certain news sources by audiences, including levels of trust, seems to add a certain weight to their reach and consumption. This creates something of a logical contradiction at the heart of Ofcom's approach. The contradiction arises because impact indicators are likely to be causally *related* to contextual factors. It is precisely the adoption of impartiality rules or adherence to other public service commitments, for instance, that may generate relatively high levels of audience trust. Ofcom's framework may thus consider a news provider to pose less of a concentration risk because of its adoption of such rules or commitments, but *more* of a risk because they engender what it conceives as 'impact'.

The Problem with Multi-sourcing

Another area of conceptual murkiness concerns what Ofcom refers to as multi-sourcing: the practice of consuming news from more than one source. This has become a buzzword for industry lobbyists and policymakers alike, and on the surface it seems to be an increasingly apparent phenomenon in the online news sphere. But in reality, the prevailing trend is in the exact opposite direction. To illustrate the confusion that abounds here, consider this statement made by the UK government, responding to a Parliamentary inquiry into media plurality:

> Consumers actively multisource—such that the large majority of individuals consume a range of different news sources.
>
> (DCMS, 2014)

Although no source for the claim was provided, the report did reference Ofcom's standard definition of news multi-sourcing. Yet for the very same year, Ofcom (2015c) reported that the majority of people—55 percent—get their news from only one or two sources across all platforms, a figure that *rose* to 59 percent in the following year. But even these figures may well be overstating the degree of diversity in news consumption, especially when we consider what counts as a 'source' in this sense.

In the previous chapter we mentioned Ofcom's distinction between content originators, aggregators and intermediaries in the online news sphere. But when it comes to survey questionnaires that interrogate the number of sources used 'for news nowadays', this distinction is not applied. For instance, in a news omnibus survey commissioned by Ofcom (2015c), respondents were asked which online sources they use and were presented with a list of options that included content originators alongside aggregators and intermediaries. In effect, then, the survey question framed them all as equivalent news sources.

To illustrate how this can distort the picture, let's consider a hypothetical example. Imagine that respondents A and B are both avid online news consumers and have both been following recent headline stories on tax evasion, terrorism and the environment. They also share a tendency to gravitate towards the editorial style and slant offered by both the *Daily Telegraph* and the *Daily Mail* online. Respondent A is conscious of her preference for these outlets and tends to visit their websites directly. She recalls reading recent articles on each of the headline stories: two on the *Telegraph* website and one on the *Mail* website. She therefore selects these two outlets from the list appended to the question "which of the following do you use for news nowadays?"

Respondent B is relatively less brand conscious but no less inclined towards the same stories by the same providers. He read a recent story on tax evasion (produced by the *Telegraph*) on Yahoo and another one on terrorism (produced by the *Mail*) on Facebook. He also read a third story on the environment—another from the *Telegraph*—which he recalls finding on Google News but ended up clicking on the link and reading the article in full on the *Telegraph* website. In his survey response, he therefore selects all four of these outlets—Yahoo, Facebook, Google News and the *Telegraph*—as sources he uses for news.

The data then reveal that between them, these respondents consume five different news sources. But it fails to capture the fact that not only have they based their answers on consumption of the same news agenda, but also the same selection of stories produced by the same two providers. So their answers suggest a picture of news diversity that simply does not reflect the reality of their consumption. From this perspective, multi-sourcing is an inherently problematic concept and one that does little to advance our understanding of media concentration or plurality. By considering the likes of Google, Yahoo and the BBC as equivalent news sources, we are both comparing apples with oranges and potentially double counting sources at the same time. But this has done little to detract from a baseline mainstream consensus around multi-sourcing, along with an equally flawed assumption that its rise has come at the *expense* of legacy media influence.

Risk and Harm

Although in some ways overflowing, there is one significant gap in Ofcom's basket: analysis of content. This is critical because concentration at the level of provider can only ever be a rather vague and unreliable proxy for concentration at the level of content—and it is the latter that we are really concerned about in debates over media ownership. We have also seen that the size of a media outlet—as measured in audience reach or share—is not necessarily proportionate to its agenda influence. The *Daily Telegraph*'s audience is only a small fraction of the size of the BBC's, yet its choice of stories and headlines had a disproportionate influence over the BBC's agenda during coverage of the UK general election in 2015 (Cushion and Sambrook, 2015).

In focusing on prior indicators such as consumption and reach metrics, Ofcom is effectively relying on evidence of 'risk' but obviating the question of 'harm'. While evidencing harmful effects of media concentration has always been a tricky endeavour, the least contentious and potentially most fruitful approach is to focus on agendas—specifically, the range of issues or frames that are adopted by news outlets that reach critical mass audiences (on any platform or across multiple platforms). This approach minimises the scope for subjective interpretation compared to making judgements of editorial bias. At the very least, we have seen how monitoring election or referendum campaign coverage can provide compelling insights into the diversity and prominence of particular issues during crystallising periods of democratic cycles. In an ideal world, policymakers would also draw on agenda case studies that zero in on major public interest stories—such as the phone hacking scandal or the intelligence files leaked by Ed Snowden—in order to examine both the availability and accessibility of alternative narratives, frames or 'attributes' (McCombs, 2004).

Clear Bright Lines

As we have seen, Ofcom's 'basket'—with its range of metrics and indicators—places considerable interpretive power in its own hands when it comes to reviewing and assessing the overall plurality picture. What's more, this meta-assessment is intrinsically opaque. This leads us to the final and overarching problem with Ofcom's framework in its explicit rejection of clear bright lines that can trigger specific remedies and solutions and minimise the risk of capture. It's worth remembering that in media policy terms, the risk of corruptive pressures is especially acute because they can flow in both directions. We can think of this as either commercial capture (politicians may be induced to take certain decisions under pressure from media groups) or politicisation (certain media groups may be induced to adopt particular editorial lines under pressure from political elites).

But one way of minimising the risk of capture or politicisation (and perhaps the only way) is to maximise clear bright lines in regulation. For its part, Ofcom has rejected proposals for fixed caps on media ownership, arguing that they are too rigid to account for the complexities and uncertainties in rapidly evolving news markets. But clear bright lines are not necessarily synonymous with hard limits or any one-size-fits-all approach to remedies, as we will see in the following chapter. What they do necessitate is that the precise triggers for regulatory intervention, along with a range of prescribed remedies, are explicitly set out in law rather than left to the discretionary judgement of government ministers or regulators. And although the nature of intervention (i.e. remedies) may warrant wider room for decision-making on a case-by-case basis, there is no reason why the particular contextual factors that any decision-making body could draw on, as well as how they could be used to inform decisions, should not be spelt out in statute. That would not only ensure greater transparency in the decision-making process, but would also provide a benchmark against which the designated authority can be held to account.

In fact, Ofcom did not initially ask for discretionary power to conduct plurality assessments on its own. In a response to questions by the Secretary of State in June 2012, it made clear its preference for Parliament to debate and legislate on the thorny issue of plurality sufficiency:

> It will be for Parliament to consider whether it can provide any further guidance on how sufficiency should be defined, and possibly, in so doing, the extent to which the current level of plurality delivers against this. Absent such guidance, this may have to be left to the discretion of the appropriate body empowered by Parliament to undertake any plurality reviews.
>
> (Ofcom, 2012a)

Ofcom also acknowledges the flaws and limitations of any approach to measuring plurality, arguing that its full spectrum of measures will provide the basis for a meaningful plurality 'assessment'. But the power to assess is really the heart of the matter when it comes to the politics of measurement—not so much the particular methodologies used, but the basis upon which judgements and recommendations are made. Without explicit guidelines enshrined in law, and amid intimate ties between media and political elites, the door will remain wide open to policy capture.

Note

1. These provisions were enshrined in the Communications Act 2003 and replaced a number of more formalistic media ownership limits.

Chapter 17

Safeguards and Remedies

How do you regulate concentrations of media power in a post-digital age? This is a question that has confounded recent media policy debates in many parts of the world, and it is one that remains deeply unresolved. The challenge facing policymakers has been underlined by the impact of new technologies on the public sphere and the emergence of new forms of gatekeeping and monopoly power wielded by digital intermediaries. At the same time, as we have seen throughout this book, 'old media' bottlenecks have not gone away and are in fact resurgent in the online news context.

One area of broad political consensus is that legacy frameworks for regulating media ownership are outdated and not fit for purpose. But in spite of this consensus, and for all the inquiries and consultations, we still haven't got round to discussing what to actually do about media concentration, even if it was to become apparent through Ofcom's measuring framework. It is a political stalemate that exemplifies the power of inaction in media policy, and in ownership regulation especially (Freedman, 2014). This chapter is an attempt to at least make a start in filling that void. Above all, I want to convince you that effective remedies are *possible*, notwithstanding the complexities of converged media power.

In chapter 10, I outlined five categories of gatekeeping in an effort to capture media ownership concerns and provide policymakers with a 'future-proof' framework for analysing that power. These categories can also point the way to concentration remedies and regulatory tools that are appropriate, proportionate and effective for each gatekeeping role. Although there is a broad range of tools that can have a bearing on news plurality, including public service regulation, antitrust regimes, or must-carry rules, the focus here is on five key areas that address the complexities of the evolving news market landscape: net neutrality rules, algorithm governance, behavioural and structural remedies, cross-subsidisation, and transparency measures in respect of interactions between senior media and political figures.

To be clear, the first two of these do not fall under media ownership or plurality-specific regulation but are related to broader frameworks for facilitating access to networks and nurturing competitive markets. But the principle of openness synonymous with the internet commons and the free flow of information are foundational to conceptions of media plurality and diversity in the digital environment.

Neutralising Networks

Let's start with the last of our aforementioned gatekeeping categories: the facilitators. You will recall from chapter 15 that this category refers to companies that enable access to the network and who—by virtue of the power of admission, exclusion and prioritisation—effectively manage content distribution. We saw in chapter 8 how concerns regarding this kind of gatekeeping power are expressed by proponents of net neutrality. In particular, net neutrality debates in the US and Europe have focused on the problem of ISPs charging content providers for access, a system that inevitably privileges those providers who are willing and able to pay for preferential treatment.

We have also seen how the lobbying power of Google in the US helped to shape the recent landmark net neutrality rules implemented by the FCC. From a plurality perspective, what matters above all in the context of net neutrality is the principle of access *equality*, and this is where the FCC rules—in bowing to pressure from Google—fell short. In particular, we saw in chapter 8 how Google was able to persuade the FCC in the eleventh hour to abandon its commitment to addressing unfair practice in *negotiated* access deals.

Although the EU has thus far implemented even weaker net neutrality rules (Hern, 2015), it has spearheaded antitrust investigations into Google regarding alleged discriminatory practices of its own. These investigations hinge on the very same concerns around access equality that underline net neutrality debates. The relative lobbying power of network operators, content owners and intermediaries may well explain the divergent paths followed in the US and Europe. But the often unspoken reality in net neutrality debates—even among the open rights movement—is that both network operators *and* intermediaries engage in discriminatory practices, often in collaboration, and in ways that can ultimately impact on the range of voices heard. In that sense, the struggle for net neutrality is far from over, and it is a struggle that is integral to the wider movement for progressive media reform. What is needed is a more robust approach focused on access equality that addresses the full range of discriminatory practices, in different contexts and on different types of networks.

In practice, it would be difficult if not impossible for such a framework to be wholly enshrined in net neutrality rules, not least because they will be chasing a moving target as technological changes bring new platforms and new bottlenecks. Nevertheless, at the very least, net neutrality rules should prohibit tiered pricing *and* enable regulators to intervene in response to complaints from providers of unfair treatment in negotiated access deals, in allocated traffic speeds, or as a result of exclusion from the network.

Such rules are inevitably limited in their scope to those that facilitate access to the open internet (i.e. internet service providers). In contrast, mobile app platforms like Apple's App Store and Google Play are controlled platforms, and as such fall under the broader framework of antitrust regulation. Norms of competition law dictate that authorities need only intervene in such cases—and should only intervene—where a company has significant market power to the degree that content discrimination could be considered anti-competitive practice. But it is important for plurality objectives that antitrust authorities remain sensitive and responsive to complaints relating to any and all 'gateway' services (including search, social media and content sharing platforms) as well as 'portals' (such as cable and satellite television providers, digital radio multiplexes, etc.), which wield monopoly-like power over networks and thus, gate control.

Algorithm Governance

A number of scholars in recent years have called for measures aimed at increasing the transparency and accountability of major news algorithms (e.g. Goodman, 2014; Napoli, 2014). In this book, we have addressed three potential ways in which these algorithms can threaten news plurality. First, generic weightings for news quality—especially those embedded in Google's news algorithm—can favour dominant and large-scale news providers over smaller players, new entrants and, crucially, those that promote alternative issue agendas. Second, personalisation filters can limit individual exposure to alternative perspectives or diverse expressions, catalysing polarisation, fragmentation and atomisation of the digital public sphere. Third, algorithms have the capacity to 'ghettoize' ideas and restrict the potential for subversive, radical or dissenting viewpoints to reach a critical mass audience. From the perspective of powerful interests that have control or influence over *editorial* news institutions, this amounts to a new and significant structural advantage, especially in their ability to contain crises or redirect attention in the midst of agenda 'explosions' (Boydstun, 2013).

Although we don't yet know the prevalence or extent of these trends, the risks are endemic in the growing interventionism that has shaped news algorithm development over recent years (Pariser, 2011). There is certainly a strong case to be made that the potential civic benefits of algorithm governance should override protections for commercial sensitivity. In any case, because Google has made clear that it makes no money from its news services, why not subject its algorithm to some form of public oversight that seeks to maintain the principles of openness, equality and neutrality synonymous with the internet commons?

That said, it would be neither practical nor desirable to eliminate personalised content filters in news algorithms altogether. These filters can play an important role in minimising search costs and making it easier for us to find the news content we are looking for. There is also an obvious risk that regulation in this area could merely result in a transfer of filtering powers from intermediaries to the state. Even if this produced relatively benign forms of must-carry status applied to particular types of news content, it is not clear whether it would challenge or merely reinforce existing quality metrics designed by intermediaries.

Given the inherent tension between personalisation filters and both privacy and speech rights, a policy emphasis on algorithm transparency would seem the most appropriate course for policymakers to chart—all the more so because of the hidden qualities of algorithm filters that can make news agendas appear natural and spontaneous rather than the work of complex code. Transparency enforcement also reflects the added value of the internet commons as a space within the wider news ecology where, in principle, the flow of content is not directed either by corporations or authorities.

This does not mean that more interventionist approaches such as must-carry rules no longer have a place on cable and satellite, and potentially in the world of aggregators like Yahoo or 'over-the-top' providers like Netflix. But there is important civic value in maintaining a diverse ecology of platforms, such that users and audiences can encounter news in different ways. The power of selection vested in users that news algorithms promise (but do not necessarily deliver) is a principle that public policy should seek to protect and advance. To that end, major news algorithms could be subject to periodic audits by independent experts to ensure that they are consistent with this principle, as well as baseline plurality objectives. However, given the relative complexity and infancy of this issue, there is a need for further research and deliberation—ideally at the supranational level—in order to chart the most effective course and develop robust frameworks for implementing algorithm governance.

Behavioural and Structural Remedies

In the case of news providers—and to a lesser extent aggregators—gatekeeping powers are more explicitly editorial and should therefore occupy the focus of ownership and plurality regulation. The associated risk here is that certain perspectives become dominant on the media, policy or public agenda at large by virtue of owner influence. This calls for a distinct approach to governance, one that is oriented towards maximising journalist autonomy and maintaining an arm's-length distance between proprietors and editorial output. There are a number of remedies that have been proposed and adopted in this regard, including editorial boards (consisting of a rotating panel of staff journalists) with veto powers over the appointment or dismissal of editors, or the redistribution of a proportion of shareholder voting rights among staff journalists.

Of course, the mere existence of an editorial board may do little to change the political leaning or content of a given outlet. But that is not, and *should* not be, the purpose of ownership regulation. Rather, the goal should be to ensure that editorial output is not exclusively tied to and shaped by the perspectives and interests of owners, and to at least create the *conditions* in which journalists can inflect a wider array of voices and perspectives onto the news agenda. It makes sense that a regulatory authority should have at its disposal a range of such remedies to apply in different circumstances and to different types of news institutions.

There may also be circumstances—relatively acute—in which media concentration reaches levels where the very *possibility* of achieving plurality goals through behavioural remedies seems remote. In these circumstances, structural remedies may be appropriate, including enforced divestment. But even here, legislation could be drafted with inbuilt flexibility to accommodate a range of circumstances where different forms of structural remedies could be applied. For instance, if it is determined that a given market is insufficient to support several providers, then an appropriate structural remedy might be based on the prescribed sale of shareholdings in order to eliminate a controlling interest in a given outlet, or the creation of trust or cooperative ownership structures that make news organisations more accountable to their audience-publics.

Of course, all this begs the question of when such remedies could and should be applied. In the previous chapter I argued that maximising 'clear bright line' guidance is the only way to ensure that the risk of capture or politicisation of media policymaking is minimised. In respect of identifiable triggers for intervention, this could amount to flexible caps or 'indicative thresholds', which Ofcom itself has suggested on the basis of consumption metrics (Ofcom, 2012b).

Cross-Subsidisation

Although some top-down plurality remedies are needed (as described earlier), there is arguably more potential and less difficulty for policy to deliver on plurality goals by following a more bottom-up approach, and supporting those forms of journalism that are clearly in the public interest but are nevertheless struggling to survive under market conditions.

The good news is that in many countries, the existential crisis faced by both newspapers and public service broadcasters has helped to ferment an emergent 'third sector' of not-for-profit news providers outside of both state and market frames that specialise in long-form or local news provision. Some have managed to capitalise on the cost efficiencies offered by digital platforms of newsgathering and publishing, as well as networked forms of collaborative journalism. The Center for Public Integrity in the US, the Bureau of Investigative Journalism in the UK, Netzwerke Recherche in Germany, and Chiaralettere in Italy are all examples of independent not-for-profit news organisations for whom holding power to account is a core part of their mission, along with broadening and challenging mainstream news agendas. Examples are even more common in local and hyperlocal journalism, where a number of charity- and trust-supported local news outlets are surviving—and some thriving—in an otherwise crisis-ridden sector, often subsisting on a hybrid mix of funding from advertising, donations and subscriptions (Levy and Picard, 2011).

Notwithstanding such success stories, the overall picture and future prospects for long-form and local journalism looks grim. Newspapers remain the primary vehicles for investigative reporting, but many are facing radical restructuring of their cost base in order to manage the digital transition, and long-form reporting is inevitably facing the thin end of the wedge. In 2016, the *Guardian* announced 250 job losses in the UK—many of them editorial—in an effort to stem its £60 million loss the previous year, while the *Independent* announced the closure of its print title altogether. Television has fared little better, with a sustained long-term decline in current affairs spending well documented (Hughes, 2013), and since 2010 there has also been a consistent year-on-year decline in news and current affairs investment by all public service broadcasters (Ofcom, 2015a).

At the local level, the crisis is even more pronounced. Local newspaper industries are facing acute levels of market concentration. According to a recent report by Kings College, University of London, just four companies account for over 70 percent of the local newspaper market across the UK, while their analysis of provision in local authority districts suggested that "monopoly coverage or dominance of a single provider is often not reduced by the availability of online content" (Ramsay and Moore, 2016).

Although recent years have seen the emergence of new online entrants such as Buzzfeed and Huffington Post, it remains to be seen whether they will be able to make a meaningful contribution to long-form and investigative news. At the same time, smaller players and newer entrants face an uphill struggle in trying to gain a piece of the referral traffic pie. As we saw in chapter 14, Google's news algorithm systematically favours large-scale and incumbent news brands based on metrics that reward volume of coverage and pre-existing traffic above all.

Some countries have attempted to address digital disruption to news publishing businesses by enforcing so-called ancillary copyrights. But as we saw in chapter 8, this approach has produced farcical results, with publishers in Germany waiving their right to be paid after Google blocked them from its listings, and Google shutting down its news service altogether in Spain (where a much tougher version of the law was passed).

But even if ancillary copyright laws were to prove workable, they would be unlikely to deliver on plurality goals. This is because the principal concern with news sustainability rests neither with particular providers nor with particular types of content, but rather with particular *forms* of journalism. A viable democracy depends as much on the circulation of diverse viewpoints as it does on particular news services that promote civic accountability and subject all levels of public authority—as well as both state and corporate centres of power—to meaningful journalistic scrutiny. Local and long-form journalism are both the most civic-oriented and financially endangered journalism practices throughout the democratic world.

Rather than relying on ancillary copyrights, a much more effective way of cross-subsidising professional news is therefore to target those forms of public interest journalism—namely local and long-form—that are most under pressure in the new media ecosystem. In doing so, it makes sense for any kind of subsidy to be open to a range of outlets to bid for—large and small, commercial and non-profit, local and national—and across all platforms of delivery. Supporting a diverse ecology of vehicles for these endangered forms of journalism speaks to wider plurality goals and offers the best prospect of pluralising the mainstream news agenda. The other benefit of this approach is that it incentivises *both* legacy news publishers as well as smaller and newer entrants to invest in local and long-form news, with potential positive knock-on effects for journalism jobs, especially at the local level.

There is now an equally strong case for such funds to be raised by a small levy on the revenues of digital intermediaries that wield monopoly market power in the search and social networking markets. These companies, as we have seen, have a critical bearing on news and information flows and derive significant underlying value from news content. Although Google does not profit directly from journalism, news forms an integral part of its user experience and volume base, and thus contributes substantially to the company's bottom line. In the UK alone, Google generated over £7 billion of revenues in 2015 with a search market share of over 90 percent. Facebook registered £105 million of UK revenues in 2014 and commands more than 80 percent of the social networking market.

Much of these revenues stem from advertisers that once supported news publishers. Notwithstanding debates over ancillary copyrights, this further underlines the moral and economic case for a levy. And given the demonstrable capacity for intermediaries to avoid corporation tax by redirecting profits away from the jurisdictions in which they are generated, a small levy on advertising revenues would be a practical and logical basis for the cross-subsidy. It would ensure that such corporations not only make a more meaningful contribution to the public purse (proportionate to the scale of their revenue), but also that the cross-subsidy supports those forms of public interest journalism most under threat.

Transparency of Contacts

There is one final aspect of reform that does not necessarily require the force of law but has critical implications for democratic societies, and it concerns the transparency of contacts between senior political and media figures. Throughout this book, we have encountered the endemic risks posed by intimate relations that span the media-political divide. In chapter 14, we surveyed some of the interdependencies and mutual interests that have developed within and across the media, political and security establishment, in both the US and UK.

In chapter 2, however, we encountered the intrinsic difficulties in evidencing harm that may result from these relationships. This is partly because crucial decisions may be taken or deals agreed beyond the reach of official records or public scrutiny. But even here, actual decisions or deals may not even materialise. The closer and more personal the relationship between powerful actors, the more likely a mutual understanding of reciprocal interests will develop and the less need there will be for things to be said and done. It is a theme that recalls the fundamental characteristics of Lukes's 'third dimension of power' (2005 [1974]), which we explored in part I.

There is a certain inevitability, as Leveson (2012) recognised, that the professional proximity of senior political and media actors will result in the development of close social relationships that can undermine accountability and transparency in media policymaking. However unhealthy these relationships may be from the perspective of democracy and the public interest, it is very difficult to prevent them or regulate them, precisely because they cross over into the personal and private sphere.

But a starting point—and one that Leveson himself strongly urged—is to enhance the transparency of media policymaking (and in particular, meetings between senior government ministers and officials) on the one hand, and senior media executives and proprietors on the other. Since 2010, the UK government has been proactively publishing details of all its meetings with external stakeholders. But these are published separately by each government department at different times, on disparate web pages, with varying titles and in different file formats. The result is a fog of transparency, especially when it comes to meetings with media proprietors for which the detail provided tends to be limited to blanket phrases like 'general discussion'.

Given the particular concerns attached to contacts with media executives and proprietors, details of these meetings should be published on a central register, made available in spreadsheet format, and updated at regular and defined intervals. Leveson himself also called for the quarterly disclosure of "the simple fact of long term relationships with media proprietors, newspapers editors or senior executives"; "details of all meetings and the fact and general nature of any discussion of media policy issues"; and "a fair and reasonably complete picture . . . of the frequency or density of other interactions (including correspondence, phone, text and email)." He also emphasised the urgency of such measures, stating that "the suggestions that I have made in the direction of greater transparency about meetings and contacts should be considered not just as a future project but as an immediate need" (2012, pp. 1457–1459).

Chapter 18

Conclusion

Historians have often interpreted major social and political change as reflective of fundamental shifts in the balance of power within societies. According to the Whig interpretation of history, for instance, the development of a commercial press in Britain during the eighteenth and nineteenth centuries was reflective of an emancipatory power shift, a liberation from the tyranny of state repression and control (Curran and Seaton, 2003). In contrast, progressive historians of a similar period tended to interpret epochal changes in the political and social structure of American society as reflective of a *changing guard*, from a slave-owning aristocratic elite to a new business and enterprise elite.

This book has examined similar conflicting trajectories in the narratives of change that foreground questions of media ownership in the twenty-first century. In part II, we looked at the emancipatory versions of the story that invoke a new consumer and citizen sovereignty in the practices of news selection. And we found that there is anecdotal evidence to support some of the claims, at least in respect of a rising 'fifth estate' culture based on participatory platforms, capable of both scrutinising and subverting mainstream news narratives. But on the whole, these arguments tend to overstate the reach and reciprocal agenda influence of participatory platforms, and underestimate the enduring pull of established news brands. They also overlook the limitations of the click-driven news paradigm in explaining the complexities of digital consumption and user preferences.

In part III, we turned our attention to arguments that invoke the 'changing guard' thesis of progressive historians, emphasising the transferral and transformation of gatekeeping and agenda setting power. According to this narrative, the primary threats to media plurality and diversity are now to be found in the world of online intermediaries and the concentrated power they wield over information flows and personal data collection. Again, there is some basis to these arguments, especially as regards the capacity of news algorithms to 'close off' particular types of news for particular types of users. But critical approaches that focus exclusively on intermediaries neglect the complex ways in which they are amplifying the voices of incumbent news providers, as well as the distinctions in the nature of gatekeeping power relating to personalised filtering and generalised editorial control.

Part IV attempted to explain and reconcile these narrativess through the conceptual prism of coexistence. First, against the backdrop of dispersal arguments we embarked on an extensive critical examination of long tail theory. In doing so, we unravelled the model's analytical power in explaining both the pluralisation of niches, represented by the tail, alongside the endurance of mainstream culture, represented by the head. But we also revealed its limitations insofar as the civic benefits of pluralisation depend on a widening as well as lengthening of the tail, a pattern that is not substantiated by the bulk of empirical research.

Referring back to the narratives of transferral, we then considered coexistence in a different sense, namely between traditional and new forms of gatekeeping power. In doing so, we traced the myriad ways in which the interests of conventional news providers and intermediaries are intersecting and coalescing. This set the scene for a re-examination of power elite theory with a focus on the webs of interconnections that make up the media-technology-military-industrial complex.

We can make three final observations. First, media ownership concerns have always been a proxy for concerns about the influence of dominant voices over public conversation as well as policy decision-making. To that extent, the potential ideological force of media ownership resides in its capacity to influence the range and ordering of issues and perspectives that surface in public and policy debate. More importantly, it is what gets left out—the crucial act of non-decision-making over the agenda—that captures the notion of control attached to media ownership. This does not mean that such control is necessarily located in the hands of media owners themselves, but rather that the particular ways in which media institutions are structured and media systems organised can affect their vulnerability to definitional power—whether that power is wielded autonomously by individual media owners, outside vested interests, or by a power elite acting in concert.

Second, in spite of channel proliferation and the explosion of niches, there remains at the meta levels of society (national and global), at any given time, a set of issues and perspectives that reach across fragmented and niche audiences, cultures and interests. In other words, there is still such a thing as a communicative space in which citizens and consumers convene en masse, and which forms the basis of shared meanings, interpretive schema and worldviews: the basis of a dominant culture (Williams, 2005 [1980]). For all the promise of participatory platforms of communication, of cultural chaos and convergence, and networked forms of resistance, empirical evidence overwhelmingly points to the enduring dominance of this space by a small number of institutional megaphones. In designing meaningful remedies to concentrated media power, policymakers need to address three burning questions that this raises: *Who* are the institutional megaphones? *How* are their voices amplified? *What* is the extent and nature of their influence over public and policy agendas?

The final observation is that answers to these questions are intrinsically difficult to arrive at. And this takes us back to the beginning of the book where, in the opening chapter, we reflected on the invisible qualities of gatekeeping and agenda setting power, both in historic and contemporary contexts; it is a theme that we have returned to on a number of occasions. For instance, in regard to the aforementioned *who* and *how* questions, there are potential methodological blind spots in the way that questions are framed or data interpreted in consumer market surveys; and there are discursive blind spots in the ways that both intermediaries and conventional news providers negate their own gatekeeping and agenda setting roles, especially the role that intermediaries play in amplifying or extending the reach of conventional news providers. And in regard to the *what* question—the most difficult of all—we encountered from the start the inherent difficulties in observing and exposing gatekeeping power in the 'third dimension' (Lukes, 2005 [1974]). In particular, there are potential blind spots in recurrent agenda crises where elites appear to lose all sense of control over the selection and framing of issues in any given controversy, but are also able to regain control in subtle ways and at pivotal moments. Above all, and underlying all three questions, is the obscurity generated by the frequent hostile rhetoric and legal battles between intermediaries, network controllers, news providers and governments, all of which veil the fundamental synergies and mutual interests that bind them.

However, none of these obstacles are insurmountable and *things could be different*. Although there is no entirely flawless approach to measuring the precise causes, extent and effects of concentrated media power, an approach centred on voice—especially in the context of agenda impact—captures the essence of media ownership concerns. Far from justifying inaction or inattention to media ownership, the very uncertainties inherent in measuring media plurality or concentration make critical research and progressive policymaking *more* necessary and *more* urgent. The rise of the fifth estate and participatory modes of resistance may have provided a cogent check on dominant voices emanating from mainstream press and broadcasters and exposed both the endurance and limits of the mainstream news agenda, but it is not enough to level the playing field. On the whole, mainstream press and broadcasters still have a much wider reach across fragmented audiences and a far deeper reach into the corridors of power. And elites—including media owners—still provide most if not all of the agenda 'cues' that determine the issues of salience in public conversation, even if the narrative does not always evolve in their favour.

The challenge for both policymakers and activists is to recognise that radical and progressive reform is both necessary and *possible*. We may not yet be in an age of a social media democracy (for better or for worse), but the power of grassroots channels of mobilisation and political communication has been well established and demonstrated. This limited sea change is not a reason to refrain from tackling concentrated media power but rather a basis for doing so. The need for reform of media plurality rules has been a much talked about issue for some time now, and in many parts of the world. But as digital news markets reach maturity and the political long grass continues to grow, we need a groundswell of pressure from below, along with politicians that have the courage to champion and act on policies that will promote a genuine redistribution of voice and communicative power.

And that, to borrow a term from the late Stuart Hall, would be a truly *redefining* moment.

References

Aalberg, T., & Curran, J. (2012). *How Media Inform Democracy: A Comparative Approach*. London: Routledge.

Abell, J. C. (2011, 2 February). Traditional media dominates the Twitter news agenda: Study. *Wired.com*. Retrieved from http://www.wired.com/2011/02/traditional-media-twitter/

Adler, M. (1985). Stardom and talent. *American Economic Review, 75*(1), 208–212.

Adorno, T. W., & Horkheimer, M. (1997 [1944]). *Dialectic of Enlightenment* (Vol. 15). London: Verso.

Ahmed, N. (2015, 3 December). How the mainstream media became a neo-Stalinist propaganda regime for wealthy neocons. *Media Reform Coalition*. Retrieved from http://www.mediareform.org.uk/media-ownership/how-the-mainstream-media-became-a-neo-stalinist-propaganda-regime-for-wealthy-neocons

Albini, S. (2014, 17 November). Steve Albini on the surprisingly sturdy state of the music industry—in full. *Guardian*. Retrieved from http://www.theguardian.com/music/2014/nov/17/steve-albinis-keynote-address-at-face-the-music-in-full

Anderle, A. (2015, 15 October). How Facebook and Google's algorithms are affecting our political viewpoints. *HuffingtonPost.com*. Retrieved from http://www.huffingtonpost.com/megan-anderle/how-facebook-and-googles-_b_8282612.html

Anderson, C. (2008, 27 June). Debating the long tail. *Harvard Business Review*. Retrieved from https://hbr.org/2008/06/debating-the-long-tail

Anderson, C. (2009 [2006]). *The Longer Long Tail: How Endless Choice Is Creating Unlimited Demand*. London: Random House Business Books.

Anderson, C. W. (2011). Deliberative, agonistic, and algorithmic audiences: Journalism's vision of its public in an age of audience transparency. *International Journal of Communication, 5*(March), 529–547.

Anderson, D. (2015, June). *A question of trust: Report of the investigatory powers review*. Retrieved from https://terrorismlegislationreviewer.independent.gov.uk/wp-content/uploads/2015/06/IPR-Report-Print-Version.pdf

Andreou, A. (2015a, 27 April). Small business letter to the *Telegraph*; an attempt to defraud the electorate? *Sturdyblog*. Retrieved from https://sturdyblog.wordpress.com/2015/04/27/small-business-letter-to-the-telegraph-an-attempt-to-defraud-the-electorate/

Andreou, A. (2015b, 27 April). *Twitter is making it—in some ways—more difficult to lie: We are talking directly to each other, with no mediators: It's wonderful [Tweet]*. Retrieved from https://twitter.com/sturdyAlex/status/592774168720121856

Asur, S., Huberman, B. A., Szabo, G., & Wang, C. (2011). Trends in social media: Persistence and decay. *SSRN*. Retrieved from http://papers.ssrn.com/sol3/papers.cfm?abstract_id=1755748

Axel Springer (2014, 5 November). *Axel Springer concludes its data documentation: Major losses resulting from downgraded search notices on Google.* Retrieved from http://www.axelspringer.de/en/presse/Axel-Springer-concludes-its-data-documentation-Major-losses-resulting-from-downgraded-search-notices-on-Google_22070687.html

Axford, B. (2011). Talk about a revolution: Social media and the MENA uprisings. *Globalizations, 8*(5), 681–686.

Bagdikian, B. (2000 [1983]). *The Media Monopoly.* Boston: Beacon Press.

Baker, E. C. (1997). Giving the audience what it wants. *Ohio State Law Journal, 58*(2), 311–418.

Baker, E. C. (2007). *Media Concentration and Democracy: Why Ownership Matters.* New York: Cambridge University Press.

Ball, J., & Hopkins, N. (2013, 20 December). GCHQ and NSA targeted charities, Germans, Israeli PM and EU Chief. *Guardian.* Retrieved from http://www.theguardian.com/uk-news/2013/dec/20/gchq-targeted-aid-agencies-german-government-eu-commissioner

Baraniuk, C. (2016, 8 January). Tech giants raise concerns over UK draft surveillance bill. *BBC News.* Retrieved from http://www.bbc.co.uk/news/technology-35263503

Bardoel, J., & Deuze, M. (2001). Network journalism: Converging competencies of old and new media professionals. *Australian Journalism Review, 23*(3), 91–103.

Barnett, S. (1998). Dumbing down or reaching out: Is it tabloidisation wot done it? *Political Quarterly, 69*(B), 75–90.

Barnett, S. (2015). Four reasons why a partisan press helped win it for the Tories. *UK Election Analysis 2015: Media, Voters and the Campaign.* Retrieved from http://www.electionanalysis.uk/uk-election-analysis-2015/section-8-media-influence-and-interventions/four-reasons-why-a-partisan-press-helped-win-it-for-the-tories/

Barzilai-Nahon, K. (2008). Toward a theory of network gatekeeping: A framework for exploring information control. *Journal of the American Information Science and Technology, 59*(9), 1–20.

Baudrillard, J. (1995). *The Gulf War Did Not Take Place.* Bloomington: Indiana University Press.

Baughan, N. (2015, 15 September). Do Facebook, Twitter and Google offer news publishers salvation? *Guardian.* Retrieved from http://www.theguardian.com/media-network/2015/sep/15/facebook-twitter-google-apple-news-publishers-instant-articles

BBC News (2012, 4 November). Brooks told Cameron she 'cried twice' during his speech. Retrieved from http://www.bbc.co.uk/news/uk-politics-20189595

BBC News (2014, 19 February). In full: Rebekah Brooks' email to James Murdoch on Tony Blair. Retrieved from http://www.bbc.co.uk/news/uk-26260790

BBC News (2015, 2 September). Brooks to return as Murdoch's UK boss. Retrieved from http://www.bbc.co.uk/news/business-34131605

Beck, M. (2015, 17 August). For major publishers, Facebook referral traffic passes Google again. *Marketing Land.* Retrieved from http://marketingland.com/for-major-publishers-facebook-referral-traffic-passes-google-again-138969

Bell, D. (1962). *The End of Ideology: On the Exhaustion of Political Ideas in the 1950s.* Cambridge, MA: Harvard University Press.

Benkler, Y. (2006). *The Wealth of Networks: How Social Production Transforms Markets and Freedom.* New Haven: Yale University Press.

Benkler, Y. (2011). A free irresponsible press: WikiLeaks and the battle over the soul of the networked fourth estate. *Harvard Civil Rights-Civil Liberties Law Review, 46,* 311–395.

Bennett, W. L., Gressett, L. A., & Halton, W. (1985). Repairing the news: A case study of the news paradigm. *Journal of Communication, 35*(2), 50–68.

Bennett, W. L., & Iyengar, S. (2008). A new era of minimal effects? The changing foundations of political communication. *Journal of Communication, 58*(4), 707–731.

Bennett, W. L., Lawrence, R. G., & Livingston, S. (2006). None dare call it torture: Indexing and the limits of press independence in the Abu Ghraib scandal. *Journal of Communication, 56*(3), 467–485.

Bermejo, F. (2009). Audience manufacture in historical perspective: From broadcasting to Google. *New Media & Society, 11*(1–2), 133–154.

Berry, M. (2013). The Today programme and the banking crisis. *Journalism, 14*(2), 253–270.

Blackden, R. (2011, 23 October). Rupert Murdoch urged to sell off newspapers by top News Corp shareholder. *Daily Telegraph*. Retrieved from http://www.telegraph.co.uk/finance/newsbysector/mediatechnologyandtelecoms/8843215/Rupert-Murdoch-urged-to-sell-off-newspapers-by-top-News-Corp-shareholder.html

Blair, T. (2012). *The Leveson inquiry: Witness statement by the RT Hon Tony Blair*. Retrieved from http://webarchive.nationalarchives.gov.uk/20140122145147/http:/www.levesoninquiry.org.uk/wp-content/uploads/2012/05/Witness-Statement-of-Tony-Blair1.pdf

Boczkowski, P. J. (2010). *News at Work: Imitation in an Age of Information Abundance*. Chicago: University of Chicago Press.

Boczkowski, P. J., & Mitchelstein, E. (2013). *The News Gap: When the Information Preferences of the Media and the Public Diverge*. Cambridge, MA: MIT Press.

Boffey, D. (2016, 30 January). Tories lobbying to protect Google's £30bn island tax haven. *Guardian*. Retrieved from http://www.theguardian.com/technology/2016/jan/30/google-tory-battle-protect-30bn-tax-haven-bermuda

Born, G. (2003). Strategy, positioning and projection in digital television: Channel Four and the commercialization of public service broadcasting in the UK. *Media, Culture & Society, 25*(6), 774–799.

Born, G. (2005). *Uncertain Vision: Birt, Dyke and the Reinvention of the BBC*. London: Vintage.

Boseley, S. (2015, 7 April). More than 140 top doctors attack government's record on NHS. *Guardian*. Retrieved from http://www.theguardian.com/society/2015/apr/07/more-than-100-top-doctors-attack-government-record-on-nhs

Bourdieu, P. (1998). *On Television and Journalism*. London: Pluto.

Boydstun, A. E. (2013). *Making the News: Politics, the Media and Agenda Setting*. Chicago: University of Chicago Press.

Brodkin, J. (2015, 23 February). Google warns FCC plan could help ISPs charge senders of web traffic. *Ars Technica*. Retrieved from http://arstechnica.com/business/2015/02/google-warns-fcc-plan-could-help-isps-charge-senders-of-web-traffic/

Bruns, A. (2011). Gatekeeping, gatewatching, real-time feedback: New challenges for journalism. *Brazilian Journalism Research Journal, 7*(2), 117–136.

Brynjolfsson, E., Hu, Y., & Simester, D. (2011). Goodbye pareto principle, hello long tail: The effect of search costs on the concentration of product sales. *Management Science, 57*(8), 1373–1386.

Brynjolfsson, E., Hu, Y., & Smith, M. D. (2010). Research commentary-long tails vs. superstars: The effect of information technology on product variety and sales concentration patterns. *Information Systems Research, 21*(4), 736–747.

Bundeskartellamt (2015, 9 September). *Bundeskartellamt takes decision in ancillary copyright dispute*. Retrieved from http://www.bundeskartellamt.de/SharedDocs/Meldung/EN/Pressemitteilungen/2015/09_09_2015_VG_Media_Google.html

Callinicos, A. (2012). Contradictions of austerity. *Cambridge Journal of Economics*, *36*(1), 65–77.

Cameron, D. (2015, 13 September). *The Labour Party is now a threat to our national security, our economic security and your family's security [Tweet]*. Retrieved from https://twitter.com/david_cameron/status/642984909980725248?lang=en-gb

Carpentier, F.R.D. (2014). Agenda setting and priming effects based on information presentation: Revisiting accessibility as a mechanism explaining agenda setting and priming. *Mass Communication and Society*, *17*(4), 531–552.

Carroll, R. (2013, 4 November). Google chairman: NSA spying on our data centres 'outrageous'. *Guardian*. Retrieved from http://www.theguardian.com/technology/2013/nov/04/eric-schmidt-nsa-spying-data-centres-outrageous

Castells, M. (2007). Communication, power and counter-power in the network society. *International Journal of Communication*, *1*(1), 29.

Castells, M. (2009). *Communication Power*. Oxford: Oxford University Press.

Chang, H. (2008). *Institutional Change and Economic Development*. Tokyo: United Nations University Press.

Chibnall, S. (2001 [1977]). *Law-and-Order News: An Analysis of Crime Reporting in the British Press* (Vol. 2). Abingdon: Routledge.

Christensen, C. (2011). Discourses of technology and liberation: State aid to net activists in an era of 'Twitter Revolutions'. *Communication Review*, *14*(3), 233–253.

Chu, B. (2015, 1 April). Two thirds of economists say coalition austerity harmed the economy. *Independent*. Retrieved from http://www.independent.co.uk/news/business/news/two-thirds-of-economists-say-coalition-austerity-harmed-the-economy-10149410.html

Clemons, E. K., Gao, G. G., & Hitt, L. M. (2006). When online reviews meet hyperdifferentiation: A study of the craft beer industry. *Journal of Management Information Systems*, *23*(2), 149–171.

Cohen, B. (1963). *The Press and Foreign Policy*. Princeton: Princeton University Press.

Compaine, B. M. (2005). The media monopoly myth: How new competition is expanding our sources of information and entertainment. *New Millennium Research Council*. Retrieved from http://cloudfront-assets.techliberation.com/wp-content/uploads/2008/02/Final_Compaine_Paper_050205.pdf

Conolly, L. W. (2009). *George Bernard Shaw and the BBC*. Toronto: University of Toronto Press.

Cooper, S. D. (2006). *Watching the Watchdog: Bloggers as the Fifth Estate*. Spokane, WA: Marquette Books.

Couldry, N. (2013). Why media ethics still matters. In S. J. Ward (ed.), *Global Media Ethics: Problems and Perspectives*. Chichester: Wiley-Blackwell.

Crauford Smith, R., & Stolte, Y. (2014). *The transparency of media ownership in the European Union and Neighbouring States* (Access-Info Research Report). Retrieved from http://www.access-info.org/wp-content/uploads/Transparency_of_Media_Ownership_in_the_EU-09-26-2014.pdf

Crauford Smith, R., & Tambini, D. (2012). Measuring media plurality in the United Kingdom: Policy choices and regulatory challenges. *Journal of Media Law*, *4*(1), 35–63.

Crawford, K. (2013). The hidden biases in big data. *Harvard Business Review*. Retrieved from https://hbr.org/2013/04/the-hidden-biases-in-big-data

Crenson, M. A. (1971). *The Un-Politics of Air Pollution: A Study of Non-Decision Making in the Cities*. London: Johns Hopkins Press.

Curran, J. (2002). *Media and Power*. London: Routledge.

Curran, J. (2011). *Media and Democracy*. London: Routledge.

Curran, J., Fenton, N., & Freedman, D. (2012). *Misunderstanding the internet*. London: Routledge.

Curran, J., & Seaton, J. (2003). *Power without Responsibility: The Press, Broadcasting and New Media in Britain*. London: Routledge.

Curtis, S. (2015, 13 May). EU 'right to be forgotten': One year on. *Daily Telegraph*. Retrieved from http://www.telegraph.co.uk/technology/google/11599909/EU-right-to-be-forgotten-one-year-on.html

Curtiss, M., Bharat, K.A., & Schmitt, M. (2014). *Patent identifier no. US 2014/0188859 A1*. United States: Google.com

Cushion, S. (2012). *The Democratic Value of News: Why Public Service Media Matter*. Basingstoke: Palgrave Macmillan.

Cushion, S., & Sambrook, R. (2015, 15 May). How TV news let the Tories fight the election on their own terms. *Guardian*. Retrieved from http://www.theguardian.com/media/2015/may/15/tv-news-let-the-tories-fight-the-election-coalition-economy-taxation

Daily Telegraph (2011, 19 July). Rupert Murdoch: This is the most humble day of my life [Video]. Retrieved from http://www.telegraph.co.uk/news/uknews/phone-hacking/8647807/Rupert-Murdoch-this-is-the-most-humble-day-of-my-life.html

Davies, H. (2015, 17 December). How Google's antitrust siege began not far from Windsor Castle's ramparts. *Guardian*. Retrieved from http://www.theguardian.com/technology/2015/dec/17/how-googles-antitrust-siege-began-eu

Davis, A. (2003). Whither mass media and power? Evidence for a critical elite theory alternative. *Media, Culture & Society, 25*(5), 669–690.

DCMS (2014). *Media ownership and plurality consultation report: Government response to the house of lords select committee on communications report in media plurality*. Department for Culture Media and Sport. Retrieved from http://www.parliament.uk/documents/lords-committees/communications/Mediaplurality/Governmentresponse.pdf

Deacon, D., & Golding, P. (1994). *Taxation and Representation: The Media, Political Communication and the Poll Tax*. London: J. Libbey.

Dencik, L. (2014). Why Facebook censorship matters. *JOMEC Blog, 13*.

De Nora, T. (2000). *Music in Everyday Life*. Cambridge: Cambridge University Press.

Diakopoulos, N. (2015). Algorithmic accountability: Journalistic investigation of computational power structures. *Digital Journalism, 3*(3), 398–415.

Di Cola, P. (2006). *False Premises, False Promises: A Quantitative History of Ownership Consolidation in the Radio Industry*. Washington, DC: Future of Music Coalition.

Djerf-Pierre, M. (2007). The gender of journalism. *Nordicom Review, 28*, 81–104.

Dominiczak, P. (2015, 1 April). 100 business chiefs: Labour threatens Britain's recovery. *Daily Telegraph*. Retrieved from http://www.telegraph.co.uk/news/politics/labour/11507586/General-Election-2015-Labour-threatens-Britains-recovery-say-100-business-chiefs.html

Dowell, B. (2012, 25 April). Rupert Murdoch: 'Sun wot won it' headline tasteless and wrong. *Guardian*. Retrieved from http://www.theguardian.com/media/2012/apr/25/rupert-murdoch-sun-wot-won-it-tasteless

Downing, J., Titley, G., & Toynbee, J. (2014). Ideology critique: The challenge for media studies. *Media, Culture & Society, 36*, 878–887.

Downing, J. D. (2000). *Radical Media: Rebellious Communication and Social Movements*. Thousand Oaks: Sage.

Doyle, G. (2002). *Media Ownership: Concentration, Convergence and Public Policy*. London: Sage.

Dragomir, M., & Thompson, M. (2015, 15 February). Who owns the media? Sometimes no one knows. *Open Society Foundations*. Retrieved from https://www.opensocietyfoundations.org/voices/who-owns-media-sometimes-no-one-knows

Duch-Brown, N., & Martens, B. (2014). *Search Costs, Information Exchange and Sales Concentration in the Digital Music Industry* (No. 2014–09). Brussels: Institute of Prospective Technological Studies, Joint Research Centre.

Dunn, H. S. (2013). Something old, something new . . .: Wikileaks and the collaborating newspapers—exploring the limits of conjoint approaches to political exposure. In B. Brevini, A. Hintz & P. McCurdy (eds.), *Beyond Wikileaks: Implications for the Future of Communications, Journalism and Society*. New York: Palgrave MacMillan.

Dutton, W. H. (2009). The fifth estate emerging through the network of networks. *Prometheus, 27*(1), 1–15.

Dwyer, C. (2011). Privacy in the age of Google and Facebook. *Technology and Society Magazine, IEEE, 30*(3), 58–63.

Dylko, I. B., Beam, M. A., Landreville, K. D., & Geidner, N. (2012). Filtering 2008 US presidential election news on YouTube by elites and nonelites: An examination of the democratizing potential of the internet. *New Media & Society, 14*(5), 832–849.

Dymond, J. (2015, 8 May). Election result: How David Cameron's Conservatives won it. *BBC.co.uk*. Retrieved from http://www.bbc.co.uk/news/election-2015-32661502

Eisenhower, D. D. (1961). *Farewell address*. Retrieved from https://www.eisenhower.archives.gov/research/online_documents/farewell_address.html

Elberse, A. (2008). Should you invest in the long tail? *Harvard Business Review, 86*(7/8), 88.

Elberse, A., & Oberholzer-Gee, F. (2006). *Superstars and Underdogs: An Examination of the Long Tail Phenomenon in Video Sales* (p. 43). Cambridge, MA: Division of Research, Harvard Business School.

Elstein, D. (2015, 20 May). Reflections on the election: Lessons to be learned. *Open Democracy UK*. Retrieved from https://www.opendemocracy.net/ourkingdom/david-elstein/reflections-on-election-lessons-to-be-learned

EMI Music [Producer]. (2009, 27 February). *Gang Starr—Mass Appeal [Video file]*. Retrieved from https://www.youtube.com/watch?v=y9lNbNGbo24

Entman, R. M. (2004). *Projections of Power: Framing News, Public Opinion, and U.S. Foreign Policy*. Chicago: University of Chicago Press.

Ericson, R. V., Baranek, P. M., & Chan, J.B.L. (1989). *Negotiating Control: A Study of News Sources*. Milton Keynes: Open University Press.

Eslami, M., Rickman, A., Vaccaro, K., Aleyasen, A., Vuong, A., Karahalios, K., . . . & Sandvig, C. (2015, April). I always assumed that I wasn't really that close to [her]: Reasoning about invisible algorithms in the news feed. In *Proceedings of the 33rd annual SIGCHI conference on human factors in computing systems* (pp. 153–162).

Fairless, T. (2014, 15 October). EU anti-trust chief decries political pressure in Google case. *Wall Street Journal*. Retrieved from http://www.wsj.com/articles/eus-antitrust-chief-defends-probe-into-google-1413395066

Fenton, N. (2010). Drowning or waving? New media, journalism and democracy. In N. Fenton (ed.), *New Media, Old News: Journalism and Democracy in the Digital Age*. London: Sage.

Fiske, J. (1996). *Media Matters: Race and Gender in US Politics*. Minneapolis: University of Minnesota Press.

Fiske, J. (2010). *Understanding Popular Culture*. London: Routledge.

Fleder, D., & Hosanagar, K. (2009). Blockbuster culture's next rise or fall: The impact of recommender systems on sales diversity. *Management Science*, *55*(5), 697–712.

Fowler, M. S., & Brenner, D. L. (1982). A marketplace approach to broadcast regulation. *Texas Law Review*, *60*, 207–210.

Frank, R. H., & Cook, P. J. (1995). *The Winner-Take-All Society: How More and More Americans Compete for Fewer and Bigger Prizes, Encouraging Economic Waste, Income Inequality, and an Impoverished Cultural Life*. New York: Free Press.

Franklin, B. (1997). *Newszak and News Media*. London: Arnold.

Fraser, M. (2009). Five reasons for crash blindness. *British Journalism Review*, *20*(4), 78–83.

Freedman, D. (2008). *The Politics of Media Policy*. Cambridge: Polity Press.

Freedman, D. (2009). Smooth operator? The propaganda model and moments of crisis. *Westminster Papers in Communication and Culture*, *6*(2), 59–72.

Freedman, D. (2014). *The Contradictions of Media Power*. London: Bloomsbury.

Freedman, D., Obar, J., Martens, C., & McChesney, R. W. (Eds.) (2016). *Strategies for Media Reform: International Perspectives*. New York: Fordham University Press.

Freedom House (2013). *One Step Forward, One Step Back: An Assessment of Freedom of Expression in Ukraine During Its OSCE Membership*. Retrieved from https://www.freedomhouse.org/sites/default/files/FREEDOM%20HOUSE%20One%20Step%20Forward,%20One%20Step%20Back%20-%20Assessment%20of%20FOE%20in%20Ukraine%20ENG_0.pdf

Frith, S. (1996). Music and identity. In S. Hall & P. du Gay (eds.), *Questions of Cultural Identity*. London: Sage.

Fukuyama, F. (1989). The end of history? *National Interest*, Summer, 3–18.

Galtung, J., & Ruge, M. H. (1965). The structure of foreign news: The presentation of the Congo, Cuba and Cyprus Crises in four Norwegian newspapers. *Journal of Peace Research*, *2*(1), 64–90.

Gans, H. J. (1979). *Deciding What's News: A Study of CBS Evening News, NBC Nightly News, Newsweek, and Time*. New York: Pantheon Books.

Gans, H. J. (2004). *Democracy and the News*. Oxford: Oxford University Press.

Garnham, N. (2000). *Emancipation, the Media and Modernity: Arguments about the Media and Social Theory*. Oxford: Oxford University Press.

Garofalo, R. (2013). Pop goes to war, 2001–2004: US popular music after 9/11. In J. Ritter & J. M. Daughtry (eds.), *Music in the Post-9/11 World*. New York: Routledge.

Gellman, B., & Poitras, L. (2013, 7 June). US, British intelligence mining data from nine US internet companies in broad secret programme. *Washington Post*. Retrieved from https://www.washingtonpost.com/investigations/us-intelligence-mining-data-from-nine-us-internet-companies-in-broad-secret-program/2013/06/06/3a0c0da8-cebf-11e2–8845-d970ccb04497_story.html

Gentzkow, M., & Shapiro, J. M. (2010). *Ideological Segregation Online and Offline* (No. w15916). Cambridge, MA: National Bureau of Economic Research.

Glasser, T. L. (1984). Competition and diversity among radio formats: Legal and structural issues. *Journal of Broadcasting*, *28*, 122–142.

Goddard, P., Corner, J., & Richardson, K. (2007). *Public Issue Television: World in Action 1963–98*. Manchester: Manchester University Press.

Goel, V. (2014, 29 June). Facebook tinkers with users emotions in news feed experiment, stirring outcry. *New York Times*. Retrieved from http://www.nytimes.com/2014/06/30/technology/facebook-tinkers-with-users-emotions-in-news-feed-experiment-stirring-outcry.html?_r=0

Goodman, E. (2014). Informational justice as the new media pluralism. *LSE Media Policy Project.* Retrieved from http://blogs.lse.ac.uk/mediapolicyproject/2014/11/19/informational-justice-as-the-new-media-pluralism/

Google (2014, 11 December). *An Update on Google News in Spain.* Retrieved from http://googlepolicyeurope.blogspot.be/2014/12/an-update-on-google-news-in-spain.html

Greenberg, J. (2016, 25 March). To fight the FBI, Apple ditched secrecy for openness. *Wired.com.* Retrieved from http://www.wired.com/2016/03/fight-fbi-apple-ditched-secrecy-openness/

Greenwald, G. (2015, 14 June). The Sunday Times' Snowden story is journalism at its worst—and filled with falsehoods. *TheIntercept.com.* Retrieved from https://theintercept.com/2015/06/14/sunday-times-report-snowden-files-journalism-worst-also-filled-falsehoods/

Gunter, J. (2015, 13 September). Tory theme of Corbyn's 'threat to national security' draws criticism. *Guardian.* Retrieved from http://www.theguardian.com/politics/2015/sep/13/tory-theme-corbyn-threat-national-security-criticised

Habermas, J. (1962 transl. 1989). *The Structural Transformation of the Public Sphere: An Inquiry into a Category of Bourgeois Society.* Cambridge: Polity Press.

Hall, S. (1982). The rediscovery of ideology: Return of the repressed in media studies. In M. Gurevitch, T. Bennet, J. Curran & J. Woollacott (eds.), *Culture, Society and the Media.* London: Methuen.

Hall, S., Critcher, T., Jefferson, T., Clarke, J., & Roberts, B. (1978). *Policing the Crisis: Mugging, the State, and Law and Order.* Basingstoke: Macmillan.

Hancher, L., & Moran, M. (1989). *Capitalism, Culture and Economic Regulation.* Oxford: Clarendon Press.

Hansen, E. (2002, 22 April). Google pulls anti-scientology links. *CNet.* Retrieved from http://www.cnet.com/uk/news/google-pulls-anti-scientology-links/

Harper, T., Kerbaj, R., & Shipman, T. (2015, 14 June). British spies betrayed to Russian and Chinese. *Times.* Retrieved from http://www.thesundaytimes.co.uk/sto/news/uk_news/National/article1568673.ece

Hebdige, D. (1979). *Subculture: The Meaning of Style.* London: Routledge.

Helberger, N., Kleinen-von Königslöw, K., & van der Noll, R. (2015). Regulating the new information intermediaries as gatekeepers of information diversity. *Info, 17*(6), 50–71.

Herman, E. S., & Chomsky, N. (2002 [1988]). *Manufacturing Consent: The Political Economy of the Mass Media.* New York: Pantheon Books.

Hermida, A., Lewis, S. C., & Zamith, R. (2014). Sourcing the Arab Spring: A case study of Andy Carvin's sources on Twitter during the Tunisian and Egyptian revolutions. *Journal of Computer-Mediated Communication, 19*(3), 479–499.

Hern, A. (2014, 6 August). Wikipedia swears to fight 'censorship' of 'right to be forgotten' ruling. *Guardian.* Retrieved from http://www.theguardian.com/technology/2014/aug/06/wikipedia-censorship-right-to-be-forgotten-ruling

Hern, A. (2015, 27 October). EU net neutrality laws fatally undermined by loop holes, critics say. *Guardian.* Retrieved from http://www.theguardian.com/technology/2015/oct/27/eu-net-neutrality-laws-fatally-undermined-by-loopholes-critics-say

Herrera, T. (2014, 18 August). What Facebook doesn't show you. *Washington Post.* Retrieved from https://www.washingtonpost.com/news/the-intersect/wp/2014/08/18/what-facebook-doesnt-show-you/

Hervas-Drane, A. (2007). Word of Mouth and Recommender Systems: A Theory of the Long Tail. NET Institute Working Paper No. 07–41.

Hesmondhalgh, D. (2008). Towards a critical understanding of music, emotion and self-identity. *Consumption, Markets and Culture, 11*(4), 329–343.

Hickman, M. (2015, 29 October). Did Murdoch win? *Open Democracy UK*. Retrieved from https://www.opendemocracy.net/uk/martin-hickman/did-murdoch-win

Hindman, M. (2008). *The Myth of Digital Democracy*. Princeton: Princeton University Press.

Hintz, A. (2014). Outsourcing surveillance-privatising policy: Communications regulation by commercial intermediaries. *Birkbeck Law Review, 2*, 349–368.

Hockenson, A. (2015, 11 August). Away from Google, Alphabet can acquire whatever it wants. *TNW*. Retrieved from http://thenextweb.com/opinion/2015/08/11/away-from-google-alphabet-can-acquire-whatever-it-wants/

Holland, P. (2006). *The Angry Buzz: This Week and Current Affairs Television*. London: IB Tauris.

Holmes, D. (2015, 8 May). Facebook thinks you're too dumb to realize its scientific papers are really just pr. *Pando Daily*. Retrieved from https://pando.com/2015/05/08/facebook-thinks-youre-too-dumb-to-realize-its-scientific-papers-are-really-just-pr/

House of Lords (2014). *Media plurality*. Select Committee on Communications. Retrieved from http://www.publications.parliament.uk/pa/ld201314/ldselect/ldcomm/120/120.pdf

Hudack, M. (2014, 22 May). Please allow me to rant for a moment about the state of the media. *Facebook.com*. Retrieved from https://www.facebook.com/mhudack/posts/10152148792566194

Hughes, J. (2013). An uncertain future: The threat to current affairs. *International Broadcasting Trust*. Retrieved from http://ibt.org.uk/documents/reports/An-Uncertain-Future-the-threat-to-current-affairs.pdf

Human Rights Watch (2006). *Race to the Bottom: Corporate Complicity in Chinese Internet Censorship*. Retrieved from https://www.hrw.org/reports/2006/china0806/

Human Rights Watch (2011). *Bangladesh: Broken Promises from Government to Halt RAB Killings*. Retrieved from http://www.hrw.org/news/2011/05/10/bangladesh-broken-promises-government-halt-rab-killings

Ingram, M. (2014, 22 May). Facebook's product guy is right, the media sucks—but journalists are also right: Facebook has to share the blame. *Gigaom.com*. Retrieved from https://gigaom.com/2014/05/22/facebooks-product-guy-is-right-the-media-sucks-but-journalists-are-also-right-facebook-has-to-share-the-blame/

Iosifidis, P. (2010). Pluralism and concentration of media ownership: Measurement issues. *Javnost—The Public, 17*(3), 5–21.

Ipsos MORI (2015). *. . . would you generally trust them to tell the truth, or not?* Retrieved from https://www.ipsos-mori.com/Assets/Docs/Polls/Veracity%202014%20trend.pdf

Jaffe, M. (n.d.). *Harassment and Karen Klein: A Case study*. Civic Media Project, MIT Press. Retrieved from http://civicmediaproject.org/works/civic-media-project/karenkleinharassment

Jarvis, J. (2009). *What Would Google Do?* New York: Harper Collins.

Jenkins, H. (2006). *Convergence Culture: Where Old and New Media Collide*. New York: NYU Press.

Jenkins, H. (2010, 14 August). Google and the search for the future. *Wall Street Journal*. Retrieved from http://www.wsj.com/articles/SB10001424052748704901104575423294099527212

Jones, O. (2015, 13 September). *The sort of rhetoric you'd expect from a tinpot dictatorship: How utterly embarrassingly pathetic [Tweet]*. Retrieved from https://twitter.com/owenjones84/status/642996631596609536?lang=en-gb

Jopson, B., & Waters, R. (2015, 25 February). Google makes late pitch to modify internet rules. *Financial Times*. Retrieved from http://www.ft.com/cms/s/0/84e15b44-bd10-11e4-9902-00144feab7de.html#axzz3vvZUpBwO

Just, N. (2009). Measuring media concentration and diversity: New approaches and instruments in Europe and the US. *Media Culture and Society, 31*, 97–117.

Kacholia, V. (2013, 23 August). News feed FYI: Showing more high quality content. *Facebook.com*. Retrieved from https://www.facebook.com/business/news/News-Feed-FYI-Showing-More-High-Quality-Content

Kafka, P. (2015, 11 September). Google and Twitter team up to offer their own instant articles—with a twist. *Recode.net*. Retrieved from http://recode.net/2015/09/11/google-tries-its-own-version-of-instant-articles-with-a-twist/

Kang, C., & Eilperin, J. (2015, 28 February). Why Silicon Valley is the new revolving door for Obama staffers. *Washington Post*. Retrieved from https://www.washingtonpost.com/business/economy/as-obama-nears-close-of-his-tenure-commitment-to-silicon-valley-is-clear/2015/02/27/3bee8088-bc8e-11e4-bdfa-b8e8f594e6ee_story.html

Karppinen, K. (2013). *Rethinking Media Pluralism*. New York: Fordham University Press.

Kawashima, N. (2011). Are the global media and entertainment conglomerates having an impact on cultural diversity? A critical assessment of the argument in the case of the film industry. *International Journal of Cultural Policy, 17*(5), 475–489.

Kay, J. (1992, 11 April). It's the Sun wot won it. *Sun*, 1.

Kelly, J. W., Fisher, D., & Smith, M. (2006, May). Friends, foes, and fringe: Norms and structure in political discussion networks. In *Proceedings of the 2006 international conference on digital government research* (pp. 412–417). Los Angeles, CA: Digital Government Society of North America.

Kepplinger, H. M. (2007). Reciprocal effects: Toward a theory of mass media effects on decision makers. *Harvard International Journal of Press/Politics, 12*(2), 3–23.

Kim, N. S., & Telman, D. A. (2015). Internet giants as quasi-governmental actors and the limits of contractual consent. *Missouri Law Review, 80*(3), 723–770.

Kim, S. H., Scheufele, D. A., & Shanahan, J. (2002). Think about it this way: Attribute agenda-setting function of the press and the public's evaluation of a local issue. *Journalism & Mass Communication Quarterly, 79*(1), 7–25.

Klein, E. (2013, 2 December). Being a viral genius is going viral. *Washington Post*. Retrieved from https://www.washingtonpost.com/news/wonk/wp/2013/12/02/being-a-viral-genius-is-going-viral/

Kucharczyk, J. (2013, 1 July). Ancillary copyright in Germany: From opt-out to opt-in on Google news. *Disco (Disruptive Competition Project)*. Retrieved from http://www.project-disco.org/intellectual-property/070113-ancillary-copyright-in-germany-from-opt-out-to-opt-in-on-google-news/#.Vobi5fmLSM_

Lafrance, A. (2015, 29 April). Facebook is eating the internet. *TheAtlantic.com*. Retrieved from http://www.theatlantic.com/technology/archive/2015/04/facebook-is-eating-the-internet/391766/

Lardinois, F. (2013, 6 June). Google, Facebook, Dropbox, Yahoo, Microsoft, Paltalk, AOL and Apple deny participation in NSA Prism surveillance program. *TechCrunch.com*. Retrieved from http://techcrunch.com/2013/06/06/google-facebook-apple-deny-participation-in-nsa-prism-program/

Lee, A. M., Lewis, S. C., & Powers, M. (2014). Audience clicks and news placement: A study of time-lagged influence in online journalism. *Communication Research, 41*(4), 505–530.

Lessig, L. (2001). *The Future of Ideas*. New York: Random House.

Lessig, L. (2013). Institutional corruption defined. *Journal of Law, Medicine & Ethics*, *41*(3), 553.

Leveson, B. (2012). *An Inquiry into the Culture, Practices and Ethics of the Press: Executive Summary*. Retrieved from http://webarchive.nationalarchives.gov.uk/20140122145147/http://www.official-documents.gov.uk/document/hc1213/hc07/0779/0779.pdf

Levine, Y. (2014a, 7 March). Oakland emails give another glimpse into the Google-Military-Surveillance complex. *Pando.com*. Retrieved from https://pando.com/2014/03/07/the-google-military-surveillance-complex/

Levine, Y. (2014b, 23 April). The revolving door between Google and the Department of Defence. *Pando.com*. Retrieved from https://pando.com/2014/04/23/the-revolving-door-between-google-and-the-department-of-defense/

Levy, D., & Newman, N. (2013). Digital news report 2013. *Reuters Institute for the Study of Journalism*. Retrieved from http://reutersinstitute.politics.ox.ac.uk

Levy, D., & Newman, N. (2014). Digital news report 2014. *Reuters Institute for the Study of Journalism*. Retrieved from http://reutersinstitute.politics.ox.ac.uk

Levy, D.A., & Picard, R. (Eds.) (2011). *Is There a Better Structure for News Providers? The Potential in Charitable and Trust Ownership*. Oxford: Reuters Institute for the Study of Journalism.

Lewis, J. (2006). *Shoot First and Ask Questions Later: Media Coverage of the 2003 Iraq War*. New York: Peter Lang.

Lotan, G. (2011, 12 October). Data reveals that 'occupying' Twitter trending topics is harder than it looks. *Giladlotan.com*. Retrieved from http://giladlotan.com/2011/10/data-reveals-that-occupying-twitter-trending-topics-is-harder-than-it-looks/

Luckerson, V. (2015, 15 April). *How Google perfected the Silicon Valley acquisition*. Retrieved from http://time.com/3815612/silicon-valley-acquisition/

Lukes, S. (2005 [1974]). *Power: A Radical View*. Basingstoke: Palgrave MacMillan.

Lunden, I. (2015, 2 June). Disconnect.me files antitrust case against Google in Europe over banned anti malware android app. *TechCrunch.com*. Retrieved from http://techcrunch.com/2015/06/02/disconnect-me-files-antitrust-case-against-google-in-europe-over-banned-anti-malware-android-app/

MacAskill, E., & Rushe, D. (2013, 1 November). Snowden document reveals key role of companies in NSA data collection. *Guardian*. Retrieved from http://www.theguardian.com/world/2013/nov/01/nsa-data-collection-tech-firms

Malik, S. (2011, 29 April). Activists claim purge of Facebook pages. *Guardian*. Retrieved from http://www.theguardian.com/uk/2011/apr/29/facebook-activist-pages-purged

Manning, P. (2001). *News and News Sources: A Critical Introduction*. London: Sage.

Mansell, R. (2014). Governing the gatekeepers: Is formal regulation needed? *LSE Media Policy Project*. Retrieved from http://eprints.lse.ac.uk/62538/1/__lse.ac.uk_storage_LIBRARY_Secondary_libfile_shared_repository_Content_Mansell,R_Mansell_Governing%20gatekeepers_2014.pdf

Marcuse, H. (2002 [1964]). *One-Dimensional Man: Studies in the Ideology of Advanced Industrial Society*. London: Routledge.

Marsden, C. (2014). Europe can learn from US how not to do net neutrality. *LSE Media Policy Project*. Retrieved from http://blogs.lse.ac.uk/mediapolicyproject/2014/01/21/europe-can-learn-from-us-how-not-to-do-net-neutrality/

Martinson, J. (2015, 21 December). Murdoch at the centre of power again as Cameron drops round for drinks. *Guardian*. Retrieved from http://www.theguardian.com/media/2015/dec/21/rupert-murdoch-david-cameron-christmas-party

Mason, R., & Watt, N. (2015, 27 April). Small business owners' letter in *Telegraph* was orchestrated by Tories. *Guardian*. Retrieved from http://www.theguardian.com/politics/2015/apr/27/small-business-owners-letter-telegraph-conservative-party

McCarthy, K. (2015, 13 March). This isn't net neutrality. This is Net Google. This is Net Netflix—the FCC's new masters. *Register*. Retrieved from http://www.theregister.co.uk/2015/03/13/net_neutrality_rules/

McChesney, R. (2004). *The Problem of the Media: US Communication Politics in the Twenty-First Century*. New York: Monthly Review Press.

McCombs, M. E. (2004). *Setting the Agenda: The Mass Media and Public Opinion*. Oxford: Polity.

McCombs, M. E., & Shaw, D. L. (1972). The agenda-setting function of mass media. *Public Opinion Quarterly, 36*(2), 176–187.

McGee, J. (2013). Online gatekeepers and the future of gatekeeping theory: The case of Karen Klein. *Aichi Shukutoku Knowledge Archive*. Retrieved from http://aska-r.aasa.ac.jp/dspace/handle/10638/5306

McLaughlin, A. (2006, 7 June). The debate over net neutrality. *Google Official Blog*. Retrieved from https://googleblog.blogspot.co.uk/2006/06/debate-over-net-neutrality.html

McLuhan, M., Gordon, W. T., Lamberti, E., & Scheffel-Dunand, D. (2011). *The Gutenberg Galaxy: The Making of Typographic Man*. Toronto: University of Toronto Press.

McMillan, R. (2014, 23 June). What everyone gets wrong in the debate over net neutrality. *Wired.com*. Retrieved from http://www.wired.com/2014/06/net_neutrality_missing/

McMillan, R. (2015, 26 February). How Google's silence helped net neutrality win. *Wired.com*. Retrieved from http://www.wired.com/2015/02/google-net-neutrality/

McNair, B. (2006). *Cultural Chaos: Journalism, News and Power in a Globalised World*. London: Routledge.

McNair, B. (2012). WikiLeaks, journalism and the consequences of chaos. *Media International Australia, 144*(1), 77–86.

McSmith, A. (2012, 17 March). Revealed: Murdoch's secret meeting with Mrs Thatcher before he bought the *Times*. *Independent*. Retrieved from http://www.independent.co.uk/news/media/press/revealed-murdochs-secret-meeting-with-mrs-thatcher-before-he-bought-the-times-7575910.html

Media Reform Coalition (2015, 14 December). *Behind closed doors: News Corp bosses met with the government 10 times during the year to March 2015*. Retrieved from http://www.mediareform.org.uk/blog/meeting-murdoch-news-corp-bosses-still-have-keys-to-the-back-door-of-government

Meraz, S. (2009). Is there an elite hold? Traditional media to social media agenda setting influence in blog networks. *Journal of Computer-Mediated Communication, 14*(3), 682–707.

Meraz, S., & Papacharissi, Z. (2013). Networked gatekeeping and networked framing on Egypt. *International Journal of Press/Politics, 18*(2), 138–166.

Mercille, J. (2013). The role of the media in fiscal consolidation programmes: The case of Ireland. *Cambridge Journal of Economics, 38*, 281–300.

Meyer, T. (2002). *Media Democracy: How the Media Colonise Politics*. Cambridge: Polity Press.

Miliband, R. (1973). *The State in Capitalist Society*. London: Quartet Books.

Miller, C. C. (2013, 7 June). Tech companies concede to surveillance program. *New York Times*. Retrieved from http://www.nytimes.com/2013/06/08/technology/tech-companies-bristling-concede-to-government-surveillance-efforts.html

Mills, C. W. (1959). *The Power Elite*. New York: Oxford University Press.

Moore, M., & Ramsay, G. (2015, October). UK election 2015: Setting the agenda. *Media standards trust*. Centre for the Study of Media, Communication and Power, Kings College London. Retrieved from https://www.kcl.ac.uk/sspp/policy-institute/publications/MST-Election-2015-FINAL.pdf

Mortimer, C. (2015, 20 September). British army 'could stage mutiny under Corbyn', says senior serving general. *Independent*. Retrieved from http://www.independent.co.uk/news/uk/politics/british-army-could-stage-mutiny-under-corbyn-says-senior-serving-general-10509742.html

Mosco, V. (2004). Capitalism's Chernobyl? From ground zero to cyberspace and back again. In A. Calabrese & C. Sparks (eds.), *Toward a Political Economy of Culture—Capitalism and Communication in the Twenty-First Century*. Oxford: Rowman and Littlefield.

Murdock, G. (1982). Large corporations and control of the communications industries. In T. Bennett, J. Curran & J. Woollacott (eds.), *Culture, Media and Society*. London: Routledge.

Mylonas, Y. (2014). Crisis, austerity and opposition in mainstream media discourses of Greece. *Critical Discourse Studies*, *11*(3), 305–321.

Napoli, P.M. (2010). *Audience evolution: New technologies and the transformation of media audiences*. New York: Columbia University Press.

Napoli, P.M. (2011a). Diminished, enduring, and emergent diversity policy concerns in an evolving media environment. *International Journal of Communication*, *5*, 1182–1196.

Napoli, P.M. (2011b). Exposure diversity reconsidered. *Journal of Information Policy*, *1*, 246–259.

Napoli, P.M. (2014). Digital intermediaries and the public interest in standard in algorithm governance. *LSE Media Policy Project*. Retrieved from http://blogs.lse.ac.uk/mediapolicyproject/2014/11/07/digital-intermediaries-and-the-public-interest-standard-in-algorithm-governance/

Newman, N. (2011). Mainstream media and the distribution of news in the age of social discovery. *Reuters Institute for the Study of Journalism*. Retrieved from http://reutersinstitute.politics.ox.ac.uk/

Newman, N., Levy, D.A., & Nielsen, R.K. (2015). Reuters institute digital news report 2015. *Reuters Institute for the Study of Journalism*. Retrieved from http://www.digitalnewsreport.org/

News Corporation (2011). *Response to Ofcom Invitation to Comment on Measuring Plurality Across Media*. Retrieved from http://stakeholders.ofcom.org.uk/binaries/consultations/measuring-plurality/responses/news-corporation.pdf

Noam, E. (2009). *Media Concentration in America*. New York: Oxford University Press.

Norris, P. (2000). *A Virtuous Circle: Political Communications in Postindustrial Societies*. Cambridge: Cambridge University Press.

Nunez, M. (2016, 3 May). Want to know what Facebook really thinks about journalists? Here's what happened when it hired some. *Gizmodo*. Retrieved from http://gizmodo.com/want-to-know-what-facebook-really-thinks-of-journalists-1773916117

Oborne, P. (2015, 17 February). Why I have resigned from the *Telegraph*. *Open Democracy*. Retrieved from https://www.opendemocracy.net/ourkingdom/peter-oborne/why-i-have-resigned-from-telegraph

O'Carroll, L. (2015, 28 August). Phone hacking: CPS may bring corporate charges against Murdoch publisher. *Guardian*. Retrieved from http://www.theguardian.com/uk-news/2015/aug/28/phone-hacking-cps-may-bring-corporate-charges-rupert-murdoch-publisher

Ofcom (2006, 27 April). *Ofcom guidance on the definition of control of media companies.* Retrieved from http://stakeholders.ofcom.org.uk/binaries/consultations/media2/statement/media_statement.pdf

Ofcom (2012a, 19 June). *Measuring media plurality.* Retrieved from http://stakeholders.ofcom.org.uk/binaries/consultations/measuring-plurality/statement/statement.pdf

Ofcom (2012b, 5 October). *Measuring media plurality.* Retrieved from http://stakeholders.ofcom.org.uk/binaries/consultations/measuring-plurality/letters/advice.pdf

Ofcom (2015a). *Public service broadcasting: Annual report 2015 annex.* Retrieved from http://stakeholders.ofcom.org.uk/binaries/broadcast/reviews-investigations/psb-review/psb2015/PSB_Annual_Report_2015_Background_and__methodology.pdf

Ofcom (2015b). *Measurement framework for media plurality.* Retrieved from http://stakeholders.ofcom.org.uk/binaries/consultations/media-plurality-framework/summary/Media_plurality_measurement_framework.pdf

Ofcom (2015c). *News consumption in the UK: Research report.* Retrieved from http://stakeholders.ofcom.org.uk/binaries/research/tv-research/news/2015/News_consumption_in_the_UK_2015_report.pdf

Open Society Foundations (2014). *Digital journalism: Making news, breaking news.* Retrieved from https://www.opensocietyfoundations.org/sites/default/files/mapping-digital-media-overviews-20140828.pdf

Oreskovic, A. (2015, 30 October). Google slammed the brakes on its acquisition machine, with the lowest deal-making since 2009. *Tech Insider.* Retrieved from http://www.techinsider.io/google-has-slowed-acquisition-spending-2015-10

Pariser, E. (2011). *The Filter Bubble: What the Internet Is Hiding from You.* London: Penguin UK.

PBS (n.d.). *The battle over Citizen Kane: About the programme.* Retrieved from http://www.pbs.org/wgbh/amex/kane2/

Peltier, S., & Moreau, F. (2012). Internet and the 'Long Tail versus superstar effect' debate: Evidence from the French book market. *Applied Economics Letters, 19*(8), 711–715.

Peters, J. W. (2010, September 5). Some newspapers shift coverage after tracking readers online. *New York Times.* Retrieved from http://www.nytimes.com/2010/09/06/business/media/06track.html

Pew Research (2013). *The role of news on Facebook: Common yet incidental.* Retrieved from http://www.journalism.org/2013/10/24/the-role-of-news-on-facebook/

Pfanner, E. (2012, 11 March). Germany trying to cut publishers in on web profits. *New York Times.* Retrieved from http://www.nytimes.com/2012/03/12/business/global/germany-trying-to-cut-publishers-in-on-web-profits.html?_r=3

Pidd, H. (2009, 20 December). Rage against the machine beats X factor's Joe to Christmas no. 1. *Guardian.* Retrieved from http://www.guardian.co.uk/music/2009/dec/20/rage-against-machine-christmas-number-1

Pilger, J. (2014, 5 December). War by media and the triumph of propaganda. *JohnPilger.com.* Retrieved from http://johnpilger.com/articles/war-by-media-and-the-triumph-of-propaganda

Pingree, R. J., Quenette, A. M., Tchernev, J. M., & Dickinson, T. (2013). Effects of media criticism on gatekeeping trust and implications for agenda setting. *Journal of Communication, 63*(2), 351–372.

Plunkett, J., & Sedghi, A. (2015, 6 May). Sun has torn into Ed Miliband even more viciously than it hit Kinnock. *Guardian.* Retrieved from http://www.theguardian.com/media/2015/may/06/sun-ed-miliband-neil-kinnock-murdoch-labour

Poell, T., & Van Dijck, J. (2014). Social media and journalistic independence. In J. Bennett & N. Strange (eds.), *Media Independence: Working with Freedom or Working for Free?* London: Routledge.

Ponsford, D. (2015, 16 June). Hold the front page (and pages two and three of the Daily Express)—businessman writes book. *Press Gazette*. Retrieved from http://www.pressgazette.co.uk/hold-front-page-and-pages-two-and-three-daily-express-businessman-writes-book

Rampton, J. (2014, 7 July). 5 reasons you shouldn't use AdWords. *Forbes.com*. Retrieved from http://www.forbes.com/sites/johnrampton/2014/07/07/5-reasons-you-shouldnt-use-adwords/#3f324e937dbb

Ramsay, G., & Moore, M. (2016). *Monopolising Local News: Is There an Emerging Local Democratic Deficit in the UK Due to the Decline of Local Newspapers?* Centre for the Study of Media, Communication and Power, Kings College London.

Resnikoff, P. (2013, 22 July). Google chairman: The future is the exact opposite of the long tail. *Digital Music News*. Retrieved from http://www.digitalmusicnews.com/2013/07/22/longtail/

Ridley, L. (2015, 26 November). Jeremy Corbyn 'systematically' attacked by British press the moment he became leader, research claims. *Huffington Post UK*. Retrieved from http://www.huffingtonpost.co.uk/2015/11/26/jeremy-corbyn-media-coverage_n_8653886.html

Rieder, R. (2015, 16 June). Rieder: Buzzfeed a burgeoning journalistic force. *USA Today*. Retrieved from http://www.usatoday.com/story/money/columnist/rieder/2015/06/15/buzzfeed-expands-as-journalism-force/71250444/

Robinson, N. (2013, 7 March). Economy: There is no alternative (TINA) is back. *BBC News*. Retrieved from http://www.bbc.co.uk/news/uk-politics-21703018

Rosen, S. (1981). The economics of superstars. *American Economic Review*, *71*(5), 845–858.

Rosenblatt, J., & Satariano, A. (2016, 22 January). Google paid Apple $1 billion to keep search bar on iPhone. *Bloomberg*. Retrieved from http://www.bloomberg.com/news/articles/2016-01-22/google-paid-apple-1-billion-to-keep-search-bar-on-iphone

Ross, T. (2015). *Why the Tories Won: The Inside Story of the 2015 Election*. London: Biteback.

Rusbridger, A. (2013, 19 August). David Miranda, schedule 7 and the danger that all reporters now face. *Guardian*. Retrieved from http://www.theguardian.com/commentisfree/2013/aug/19/david-miranda-schedule7-danger-reporters

Sabbagh, D., O'Carroll, L., & Plunkett, J. (2012, 12 June). Murdoch's share of newspaper market is too big, says Miliband. *Guardian*. Retrieved from http://www.theguardian.com/media/2012/jun/12/murdoch-share-newspaper-miliband

Saeed, S. (2015). Phantom journalism: Governing India's proxy media owners. *Journalism Studies*, *16*(5), 663–679.

Scannell, P. (1996). *Radio, Television and Modern Life*. Oxford: Blackwell.

Schechter, D. (2009). Credit crisis: How did we miss it? *British Journalism Review*, *20*(1), 19–26.

Schlesinger, P. (1987). *Putting 'Reality' Together: BBC News*. London: Methuen.

Schlesinger, P., & Tumber, H. (1994). *Reporting Crime: The Media Politics of Criminal Justice*. Oxford: Clarendon Press.

Schlosberg, J. (2013). *Power Beyond Scrutiny: Media, Justice and Accountability*. London: Pluto.

Schmerer, K. (2012, 17 September). Google protests German copyright proposal. *TechWeek-Europe.co.uk*. Retrieved from http://www.techweekeurope.co.uk/workspace/german-copyright-google-news-92748

Schmidt, E. (2011, 21 September). *Testimony of Eric Schmidt, Executive Chairman, Google Inc. before the senate committee on the judiciary subcommittee on antitrust, competition policy, and consumer rights.* Retrieved from http://searchengineland.com/figz/wp-content/seloads/2011/09/Eric-Schmidt-Testimony.pdf

Schudson, M. (1995). *The Power of News.* Cambridge, MA: Harvard University Press.

Schumpeter (2014, 20 December). Sailing through a scandal. *Economist.* Retrieved from http://www.economist.com/news/business/21636753-why-phone-hacking-affair-has-left-rupert-murdoch-better-sailing-through-scandal

Schwarz, J. (2016, 8 February). Top UK media publishers and publications—ranked for 2015. *SimilarWeb.* Retrieved from https://www.similarweb.com/blog/index-top-u-k-media-publishers-and-publications-of-2015

Sevignani, S. (2015). *Privacy and Capitalism in the Age of Social Media.* London: Routledge.

Shehata, A., & Strömbäck, J. (2013). Not (Yet) a new era of minimal effects a study of agenda setting at the aggregate and individual levels. *International Journal of Press/Politics, 18*(2), 234–255.

Shirky, C. (2011, 4 February). WikiLeaks has created a new media landscape. *Guardian.* Retrieved from http://www.theguardian.com/commentisfree/2011/feb/04/wikileaks-created-new-media-landscape

Shoemaker, P. J., & Reese, S. D. (1996). *Mediating the Message: Theories of Influences on Mass Media Content.* White Plains, NY: Longman.

Shoemaker, P. J., & Vos, T. (2009). *Gatekeeping Theory.* New York: Routledge.

Sigal, L. V. (1973). *Reporters and Officials: The Organization and Politics of Newsmaking.* Lexington, MA: D. C. Heath.

Silver, L. (2015, 13 September). David Cameron warned Corbyn is a threat to families and people told him to piss off. *Buzzfeed.* Retrieved from http://www.buzzfeed.com/laurasilver/u-ok-dave#.kbXgQD0rE

Singer, J. B. (2014). User-generated visibility: Secondary gatekeeping in a shared media space. *New Media & Society, 16*(1), 55–73.

Smyrnaios, N., Marty, E., & Rebillard, F. (2010). Does the long tail apply to online news? A quantitative study of French-speaking news websites. *New Media & Society, 12*(8), 1244–1261.

Snow, J. (2015, 16 June). Edward Snowden: Publishing the position of the government? *Channel 4 News.* Retrieved from http://blogs.channel4.com/snowblog/edward-snowden-publishing-position-government/25520

Somaiya, R. (2014, 26 October). How Facebook is changing the way its users consume journalism. *New York Times.* Retrieved from http://www.nytimes.com/2014/10/27/business/media/how-facebook-is-changing-the-way-its-users-consume-journalism.html?_r=1

Sousa, H., & Santos, L. A. (2014). Portugal at the eye of the storm: Crisis, austerity and the media. *Javnost-the Public, 21*(4), 47–61.

Srull, T. K., & Wyer, R. S. (1980). Category accessibility and social perception: Some implications for the study of person memory and interpersonal judgments. *Journal of Personality and Social Psychology, 38*, 841–856.

Stern, J. (2013, 7 June). Dissecting big tech's denial of involvement in NSA's Prism spying program. *ABC News.* Retrieved from http://abcnews.go.com/Technology/nsa-prism-dissecting-technology-companies-adamant-denial-involvement/story?id=19350095

Stupp, C. (2014, 2 December). The fight to get Google to pay for news continues in Europe. *Nieman Lab.* Retrieved from http://www.niemanlab.org/2014/12/the-fight-to-get-google-to-pay-for-news-continues-in-europe/

Sunstein, C.R. (2000). Television and the public interest. *California Law Review, 88,* 499–564.

Sunstein, C.R. (2001). *Republic.com.* Princeton: Princeton University Press.

Sunstein, C.R. (2009). *Republic.com 2.0.* Princeton: Princeton University Press.

Tambini, D. (2008). *What is financial journalism for? Ethics and responsibility in a time of crisis and change.* Retrieved from http://eprints.lse.ac.uk/21663/1/What_is_financial_journalism_for_(author).pdf

Tambini, D., Leonardi, D., & Marsden, C. (2008). The privatisation of censorship: Self regulation and freedom of expression. In D. Tambini, D. Leonardi & C. Marsden (eds.), *Codifying Cyberspace: Communications Self-Regulation in the Age of Internet Convergence.* Abingdon: Routledge.

Tan, T.F., & Netessine, S. (2009). *Is Tom Cruise Threatened? Using Netflix Prize Data to Examine the Long Tail of Electronic Commerce.* Philadelphia: Wharton Business School, University of Pennsylvania.

Temple, M. (2008). *The British Press.* Maidenhead: Open University Press.

Thompson, J.B. (1990). *Ideology and Modern Culture: Critical Social Theory in the Era of Mass Communication.* Cambridge: Polity.

Thurman, N. (2011). Making 'The Daily Me': Technology, economics and habit in the mainstream assimilation of personalized news. *Journalism, 12*(4), 395–415.

Tisdall, S., & MacAskill, E. (2006, 15 February). America's long war. *Guardian.* Retrieved from http://www.theguardian.com/world/2006/feb/15/politics.usa1

Trepte, S., & Reinecke, L. (2011). *Privacy Online: Perspectives on Privacy and Self-Disclosure in the Social Web.* Berlin: Springer.

Tuchman, G. (1978). *Making News: A Study in the Construction of Reality.* New York: Free Press.

Tufekci, Z. (2014). Engineering the public: Big data, surveillance and computational politics. *First Monday, 19*(7).

Tunç, A. (2015). Media ownership and finances in Turkey. *Media Observatory.* Retrieved from http://mediaobservatory.net/radar/media-integrity-report-media-ownership-and-financing-turkey

Turow, J. (1997). *Breaking up America: Advertisers and the New Media World.* Chicago, London: University of Chicago Press.

Turow, J. (2012). *The Daily You: How the New Advertising Industry Is Defining Your Identity and Your Worth.* New Haven: Yale University Press.

Usher, N. (2015, 11 June). Who's afraid of a big bad algorithm? *Columbia Journalism Review.* Retrieved from http://www.cjr.org/analysis/whos_afraid_of_a_big_bad_algorithm.php

Van Aelst, P., & Walgrave, S. (2011). Minimal or massive? The political agenda–setting power of the mass media according to different methods. *International Journal of Press/Politics,* doi:10.1177/1940161211406727.

van der Westhuizen, C. (2013, 23 September). South Africa's ruling ANC gunning for 'censorship lite'. *Index on Censorship.* Retrieved from https://www.indexoncensorship.org/2013/09/south-africas-ruling-anc-gunning-censorship-lite/

Vara, V. (2014, 3 November). Why Silicon Valley PACs are supporting Republicans. *New Yorker.* Retrieved from http://www.newyorker.com/business/currency/silicon-valley-pacs-supporting-republicans

Vartanova, E. (2011). The Russian media model in the context of post-Soviet dynamics. In D.C. Hallin & P. Mancini (eds.), *Comparing Media Systems Beyond the Western World.* Cambridge: Cambridge University Press.

Vogel, K. P. (2014, 27 January). Google exec boosts GOP data effort. *Politico.com*. Retrieved from http://www.politico.com/story/2014/01/google-michele-weslander-quaid-gop-data-102631

Vu, H. T. (2014). The online audience as gatekeeper: The influence of reader metrics on news editorial selection. *Journalism, 15*(8), 1094–1110.

Waugh, P. (2015, 8 November). Jeremy Corbyn's nuclear weapons vow would be a 'worry' if he got into power UK defence chief Sir Nick Houghton warns. *Huffington Post*. Retrieved from http://www.huffingtonpost.co.uk/2015/11/08/jeremy-corbyns-nuclear-we_n_8502836.html

Webster, J. G., & Ksiazek, T. B. (2012). The dynamics of audience fragmentation: Public attention in an age of digital media. *Journal of Communication, 62*(1), 39–56.

White, D. M. (1950). The 'gate keeper': A case study in the selection of news. *Journalism Quarterly, 27*, 383–390.

Williams, R. (2005 [1980]). *Culture and Materialism: Selected Essays*. London: Verso.

Wu, T. (2003). Network neutrality, broadband discrimination. *Journal of Telecommunications and Technology Law, 2*, 141–179.

Wu, T. (2010). *The Master Switch: The Rise and Fall of Information Empires*. New York: Random House.

Yglesias, M. (2014, 22 May). Facebook product director furious at Facebook's effect on news. *Vox.com*. Retrieved from http://www.vox.com/2014/5/22/5742148/facebook-product-director-furious-at-facebook-s-effect-on-news

Zaller, J. (2003). A new standard of news quality: Burglar alarms for the monitorial citizen. *Political Communication, 20*(2), 109–130.

Index

Note: figures and tables are denoted with italicized page numbers; end note information is denoted with an n and note number following the page number.